# CBMS

Conference Board of the Mathematical Sciences

## Issues in Mathematics Education

Volume 15

# U.S. Doctorates in Mathematics Education

## Developing Stewards of the Discipline

Robert E. Reys
John A. Dossey
Editors

**American Mathematical Society**
in cooperation with
**Mathematical Association of America**

# U.S. Doctorates in Mathematics Education

Developing Stewards of the Discipline

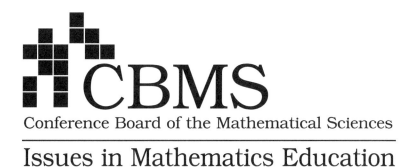

# CBMS

Conference Board of the Mathematical Sciences

## Issues in Mathematics Education

Volume 15

# U.S. Doctorates in Mathematics Education

## Developing Stewards of the Discipline

Robert E. Reys

John A. Dossey

Editors

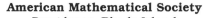

**American Mathematical Society**
Providence, Rhode Island
in cooperation with
**Mathematical Association of America**
Washington, D. C.

2000 *Mathematics Subject Classification.* Primary 97–XX, 00–XX.

---

**Library of Congress Cataloging-in-Publication Data**

U.S. doctorates in mathematics education : developing stewards of the discipline / Robert E. Reys, John A. Dossey, editors.

    p. cm. — (Conference Board of the Mathematical Sciences issues in mathematics education ; v. 15)

    Includes bibliographical references.

    ISBN 978-0-8218-4584-4 (alk. paper)

    1. Mathematics—Study and teaching—United States. 2. Doctor of mathematics degree—United States 3. Doctor of Education degree—United States. I. Reys, Robert E. II. Dossey, John A. III. Title: U.S. doctorates in mathematics education.

QA13.U74 2008

510.71′173—dc22

    2008017013

---

# Table of Contents

# Preface

Public concern over the readiness of United States' students to compete in an ever globalized market is often linked to their preparation in mathematics. Other concerns voice questions about teachers' knowledge and the overall capability of schools to motivate and educate our youth. Underlying these conversations and questions about the state of mathematics education in the United States is the quality of mathematics curricula available and the quality of teacher education programs in mathematics. Both of these concerns are directly related to the experiences these teachers have and what they learned about students' acquisition of mathematical knowledge as a result of their experience and university programs. In the end, the structure and content of university programs in mathematics education will be influenced in most cases by individuals with doctorates in mathematics education. To what degree are these professionals prepared to design and provide both knowledge of mathematics education and mathematics content to pre- and in-service teachers? To what extent are these professionals able to work with mathematicians in shaping high quality programs for pre- and in-service teachers of mathematics? To what degree are these professionals prepared to guide students in designing, delivering, and evaluating learning experiences? To what degree are these professionals prepared to conjecture about and conduct research focused on answering questions arising from the learning and teaching of mathematics? To what extent are these professionals prepared to communicate relevant research in mathematics education to teachers, parents and politicians? To what extent are these professionals prepared to become active players in shaping policy that impacts students and teachers? To what extent are these professionals prepared to work in careers beyond higher education, including district and state mathematics supervisors, commercial publishers, and test developers?

It was to answer such questions that the Second National Conference on Doctoral Programs in Mathematics Education was held in Kansas City, MO in September 2007. A copy of the program is included in Appendix A. Over 150 participants (See Appendix B) representing 90 different institutions from over 40 states in the USA, as well as Japan, Norway and Spain attended. The institutions represented produced more than 70 percent of all doctoral graduates in mathematics education from institutions of higher education in the USA from 2000 to 2005. Participants represented mathematics, mathematics education, and curriculum and instruction departments from the participating universities.

The present program followed up on a Conference on Doctoral Programs in Mathematics Education held in 1999. That Conference revealed a wide variety of doctoral programs as well as a growing shortage of doctorates in mathematics education. Keynote presentations, along with issues raised and plans for action were captured in the publication of *One Field, Many Paths: U. S. Doctoral Programs in Mathematics Education* (Reys & Kilpatrick, 2001). Since the 1999 Conference a number of events have occurred, some related to the Conference and others independent. However, all have influenced the trajectory of change in doctoral programs in mathematics education. These events include:

- The Conference stimulated the Association of Mathematics Teacher Educators (AMTE) to include in their website (www.amte.net) information about doctoral programs in mathematics education. This website posts information about doctoral programs in mathematics education from more than 60 different institutions. The site is dynamic to allow institutions to update information, and for new institutions to provide information about their doctoral program in mathematics education.
- The Conference also stimulated the AMTE to appoint a Task Force to consider the formulation of common core elements for doctorates in mathematics education. A document entitled *Principles to Guide the Design and Implementation of Doctoral Programs in Mathematics Education* was developed and later published by the AMTE. This document remains available at the AMTE website.
- The AMTE and the National Council of Teachers of Mathematics issued a joint statement related to the *Principles to Guide the Design and Implementation of Doctoral Programs in Mathematics Education*. This statement remains available at www.amte.net and www.nctm.org
- In 2000, the National Science Foundation, partially in response to the growing shortage of doctorates in mathematics education, began to establish Centers for the Learning and Teaching that were designed to help develop the infrastructure and strengthen the capacity of doctoral preparation in mathematics and science education. The following centers were established with a specific focus on mathematics education:
  - Appalachian Collaborative Center for Learning, Assessment and Instruction in Mathematics (ACCLAIM)-University of Tennessee, University of Louisville, University of Kentucky, Ohio University, University of West Virginia
  - Center for the Mathematics Education of Latinos (CEMELA)-University of Arizona, University of New Mexico, University of California-Santa Cruz, University of Illinois-Chicago
  - Center for Teaching and Learning in the West (CLT-West)-Montana State University, University of Montana, Colorado State University, University of Northern Colorado, Portland State University
  - Center for Proficiency in Teaching Mathematics (CPTM)-University of Georgia, University of Michigan
  - Center for the Study of Mathematics Curriculum (CSMC)-University of Missouri, Michigan State University, University of Western Michigan, University of Chicago
  - Diversity in Mathematics Education (DIME)-University of Wisconsin, University of California-Berkeley, University of California-Los Angeles, Vanderbilt University

- Mid-Atlantic Center for Mathematics Teaching and Learning (MAC-MTL)-University of Maryland, University of Delaware, Penn State University
  - Center for Mathematics in America's Cities (Metro Math)-Rutgers, University of Pennsylvania, City University of New York
- In 2000 the Carnegie Initiative on the Doctorate (CID) was started and included a careful examination of doctoral preparation in various disciplines. Among other products of the CID was the publication of *Envisioning the Future of Doctoral Education: Preparing Stewards of the Discipline* (Golde & Walker, 2006) and *The Formation of Scholars: Rethinking Doctoral Education for the Twenty-first Century* (Walker, Golde, Jones, Bueschel & Hutchings, 2008).
- In 2007 the American Statistical Association published *Using Statistics in Mathematics Education Research* and the Education School Project published *Educating Researchers* by Arthur Levine. These documents are a reminder that multiple groups are focusing on doctoral preparation, and offering ideas and resources of interest to faculty engaged in doctoral programs in mathematics education.
- In 2000 the National Council of Teachers of Mathematics released *Principles and Standards for School Mathematics* and further elaborated on its contents with their 2006 publication *Curriculum Focal Points for Prekindergarten through Grade 8 Mathematics: A Quest for Coherence*. These publications, in combination with a number of national and international studies on the state of the mathematics curriculum for example, *The Intended Mathematics Curriculum as Represented in State-Level Curriculum Standards: Consensus or Confusion* (B. Reys, 2006), brought a national focus on the mathematical education of teachers of mathematics and those that provide university experiences for them.

The work of the CLTs and their resulting products, together with a flurry of activity focusing on doctoral programs, provided an excellent backdrop for this Second National Conference on Doctoral Programs in Mathematics Education.

An Advisory Panel composed of John Dossey, Department of Mathematics, Illinois State University (emeritus); Jim Fey, Departments of Mathematics and Mathematics Education, University of Maryland; W. James Lewis, Department of Mathematics and Statistics, University of Nebraska; Vena Long, Professor of Mathematics Education, University of Tennessee; Sid Rachlin, Professor of Mathematics Education, East Carolina University, Barbara and Robert Reys, Professors of Mathematics Education, University of Missouri, and James Wilson, Professor of Mathematics Education, University of Georgia; and doctoral students, Nevels Nevels, University of Missouri; Dawn Teuscher, University of Missouri; and Catherine Ulrich, University of Georgia was established. Robert Glasgow, Southwest Baptist University, served as an external evaluator. Members of the Advisory Panel met in September 2006 to formulate plans for the conference themes and possible speakers.

The Conference was organized around several major questions:

> What constitutes core knowledge for doctoral students in mathematics education?
>
> What are some issues and challenges in delivering doctoral programs in mathematics education?

What can we learn about doctoral preparation from other countries?

Would accreditation of doctoral programs in mathematics education strengthen our profession?

What next steps need to be addressed in doctoral preparation?

The Conference program was organized to address these issues in large group sessions. Smaller Breakout Sessions provided opportunities to address some selected issues in more depth. The Conference program (Appendix A) identifies the themes and leaders in mathematics education that provided either keynote addresses or led the Breakout Sessions.

This book *U. S. Doctorates in Mathematics Education: Developing Stewards of the Discipline* contains papers prepared prior to and presented during the Conference. Three background papers developed prior to the Conference provide a backdrop for the conference. The first paper provides a glimpse of the history of doctoral programs in mathematics education since 1960, reporting information about the number of graduates and the institutions that prepared them. A survey was made of doctoral programs and students currently in doctoral programs in mathematics education, and results from those surveys are reported in the other two papers. All participants had an opportunity to read these papers prior to the Conference.

The Conference included several keynote addresses, smaller Breakout Sessions and two panel discussions. The keynote addresses provided a broad view of the landscape, and were followed by discussions in organized Breakout Sessions that focused on some specific aspects of doctoral programs. Given the interest in international comparisons taking place within public education and building on a similar session in the first Doctoral Conference in 1999, a panel discussion reflecting an international glimpse of doctoral preparation provided an opportunity to examine how doctoral programs function in other countries and cultures. Another discussion section focused on different perspectives regarding whether accreditation of doctoral programs would provide guidance to the development of doctoral programs or potentially stifle innovation in doctoral programs in mathematics education.

The next-to-last section contains three unsolicited papers. One provides a perspective from several doctoral students that participated in the Conference. Another is from a young faculty member reflecting on his doctoral preparation in light of his new position as an assistant professor in a research extensive university. The third paper is from two faculty members addressing the specific challenge of designing a doctoral program in mathematics education for students without a strong mathematics background.

The final section contains a commissioned paper providing a reflection on the Conference. It offers possible next steps in the continuing process of improving doctoral programs in mathematics education.

To all conference participants, we express our thanks for your contributions. (Appendix B provides a list of all Conference participants.) To all contributors of papers, we say thanks for taking the time and care to record your thoughts so that issues, ideas, and suggestions offered during the Conference have an opportunity to reach a broader audience. A special thanks to all of the Advisory Panel for their behind the scenes work that contributed to the success of the conference.

Finally we thank the National Science Foundation for providing the financial support for the project, including John (Spud) Bradley, our project officer. This Conference was funded by the National Science Foundation but the positions taken and opinions expressed in this volume do not reflect any endorsement by the National Science Foundation.

We also thank the Conference Board of the Mathematical Sciences for reviewing the manuscript and offering suggestions for improving the papers. A special thanks to Oscar Chávez and Dan Ross for their technical help, and to Kristin Judd for her work in preparing this book for publication. We hope *U. S. Doctorates in Mathematics Education: Developing Stewards of the Discipline* will both inform and stimulate the continuing dialogue that will assist institutions in their continuing efforts to improve and strengthen their doctoral programs in mathematics education.

*Robert Reys*
*University of Missouri*
*Columbia, MO 65211*
*reysr@missouri.edu*

*John Dossey*
*Illinois State University*
*Eureka, IL 61530*
*jdossey@ilstu.edu*

# Part 1

# Background

CBMS Issues in Mathematics Education
Volume 15, 2008

# Doctoral Production in Mathematics Education in the United States: 1960-2005

Robert Reys, Robert Glasgow, Dawn Teuscher, and Nevels Nevels

Prior to the 1999 *Conference on Doctoral Programs in Mathematics Education* a survey was conducted to provide information on issues and trends with regard to programs in the U.S. (Reys, Glasgow, Ragan, & Simms, 2001). This paper reports a more comprehensive summary of doctoral graduate production in mathematics education from 1960 to 2005.

## Production of Doctorates in Mathematics Education: NORC Data

Identifying current doctoral programs in mathematics education is not an easy task, and the reasons are varied (Glasgow, 2000). Institutional priorities are constantly changing and, as a result, new programs are added and other programs are discontinued. For example, since 2000 new doctoral programs were established at Montclair State University and Texas State University, while doctoral programs in mathematics education at American University and the University of Chicago were discontinued.

Another deterrent to having accurate information about programs is that individuals receiving doctorates with an emphasis in mathematics education are difficult to track. The most complete and reliable data on doctoral graduates are summarized annually in a report titled *Doctoral Recipients from United States Universities* published by the National Opinion Research Center (NORC, 2006). This effort to monitor earned doctorates in United States universities is supported by the National Science Foundation (NSF). The annual reports provide the number of doctorates in various academic areas, including mathematics education, along with some demographic information on the graduates.

The NORC reports are based on self-reported data provided by graduate students upon completion of their doctorate. Every Graduate School in the United States requires their students to complete the doctoral survey prior to graduation. Students must identify their 'primary field of dissertation research', and there is a unique code for mathematics education (♯874). However, there are also codes for Mathematics, Education, Curriculum and Instruction, Elementary Education, and Secondary Education. Some graduates who pursued the study of mathematics education report that they did not mark "mathematics education" as their major field (Glasgow, 2000). Instead, they indicated the department within which the mathematics education program resided (e.g., Curriculum and Instruction). In

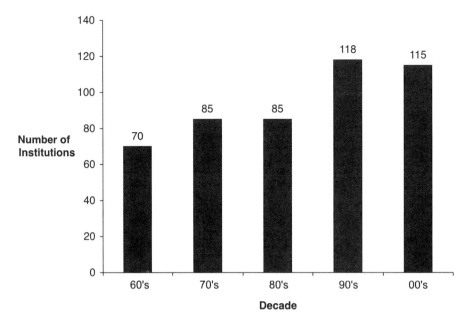

FIGURE 1. Number of Institutions Graduating Doctorates in Mathematics Education by Decade (Source: NSF/NIH/USED/ NEH/USDA/NASA, 1960-2005 Surveys of Earned Doctorates.)

other cases, a graduate may mark mathematics education because it is the primary focus of their dissertation although their program of study is in another area (e.g., Educational Psychology). Despite these issues, the data summarized in this report are based on graduates who coded "mathematics education" as their major area of emphasis on the NORC survey.

A special request was made to NORC for a summary of the production of doctorates in mathematics education from 1960 (the earliest data available) to 2005 (most recent data available). Since 1960, 167 different institutions have produced doctoral graduates with mathematics education as their designated major area of emphasis. Figure 1 summarizes the number of institutions graduating doctorates in mathematics education by decade over the past 45 years.

Figure 2 reports the number of graduates listing mathematics education as their emphasis area by decade. The 863 graduates is a projection based on 518 graduates actually reported from 2000-2005. Figure 2 shows an upward trend since the 1960s with the annual graduations fairly stable over the last two decades. The era with the largest production was the 1970s (1095 students). While many reasons may account for this significant bump in graduates during the 1970s, it is likely that the NSF institutes (both summer and year-long) played a significant role in encouraging more people to pursue doctorates in the sciences, including mathematics education.

The data suggest that the 70's were the boom era for producing doctorates in mathematics education. Mathematics education doctoral degrees were awarded by 85 different institutions during this decade. Although more institutions began

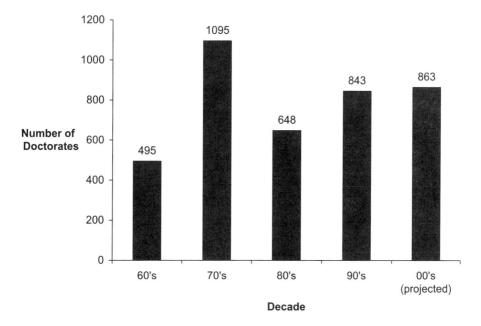

FIGURE 2. Number of Doctorates in Mathematics Education
Granted by Decade (Source: NSF/NIH/USED/NEH/USDA/NASA,
1960-2005 Survey of Earned Doctorates.)

to graduate doctorates in mathematics education after the 1980s, the number of
graduates did not rise significantly. Figure 3 shows the average number of doctorates
produced per institution per decade.

Mathematics has often been characterized as a male dominated domain. Indeed,
an examination of the annual production of doctorates in mathematics provides
evidence of the dominance of degrees awarded to males. Over the last decade the
ratio of males to females receiving PhDs in mathematics is between 2 to 1 and 4
to 1. However a look at gender differences of doctorates in mathematics education
provides a very different picture, and one that has changed dramatically over the
years.

Figure 4 reports the number of males and females receiving doctorates in mathematics education over a 45-year period. In the 1960s, the ratio of male to female
doctorates graduating in mathematics education was 5 to 1, and in the 1970s about
3 to 1. The ratio of male to female has shrunk in recent years and currently is about
2 to 3, or two males graduating with a doctorate in mathematics education for every
three females.

Minorities are also greatly underrepresented in mathematics education at both
the undergraduate and graduate levels. While Figures 1–4 report NORC data from
1960, the collection of data on the ethnicity/racial background of mathematics
education degree recipients (Asian, Hispanic, Black, and Native American) began
in 1973. Figure 5 reports frequencies of Caucasian and underrepresented group

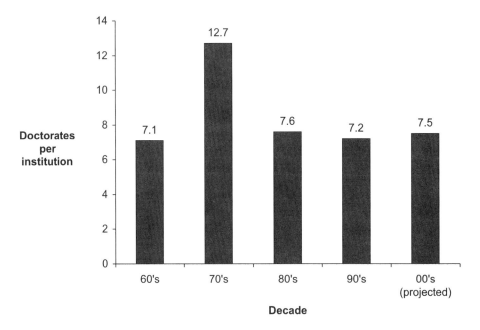

FIGURE 3. Number of Mathematics Doctorates produced per institution by decade. (Source: NSF/NIH/USED/NEH/USDA/NASA, 1960-2005 Survey of Earned Doctorates.)

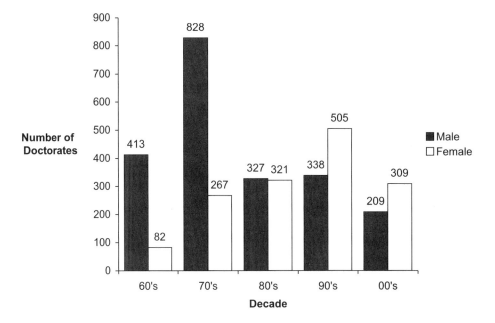

FIGURE 4. Number of doctorates (by gender) in mathematics education awarded from 1960 to 2005. (Source: NSF/NIH/USED/NEH/USDA/NASA, 1960-2005 Survey of Earned Doctorates.)

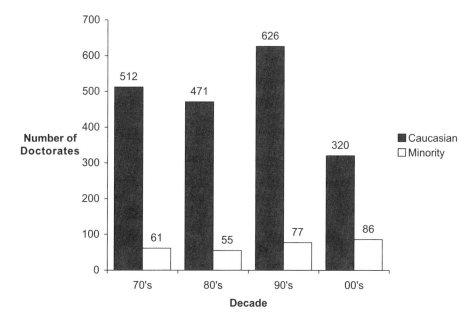

FIGURE 5. Total frequency of Caucasian and minorities receiving doctorates in mathematics education. (Source: NSF/NIH/USED/ NEH/USDA/NASA, 1960-2005 Survey of Earned Doctorates.)

degree recipients from 1973 to the present. In 1973, six graduates representing various minority populations and 78 Caucasian graduates received doctorates in mathematics education. Figure 5 shows a steady increase in total graduates from underrepresented groups since the 1980s.

Figures 1–5 provide an overall summary of the number of doctorates awarded in mathematics education over the last 45 years. Next, we describe the role different institutions have played in producing doctorates in mathematics education.

## Production of Doctorates in Mathematics Education by Institutions

Figure 1 shows the number of institutions awarding doctorates in mathematics education grew from 70 in the 1960s to 115 in 2000s. These programs vary greatly in the number of graduates produced. An examination of the number of doctorates awarded over time by institutions is constantly changing. Table 1 shows the largest producers of doctorates during the last fifteen years and Table 2 reports institutions that have awarded the most doctorates in mathematics education from 1960 to 2005. Examining these tables reveals that seven of the institutions in Table 1 were not in Table 2, yet they are now the institutions awarding the largest number of doctorates in mathematics education. This is a reminder that programs are constantly evolving, and these changes impact their production of the number of doctorates in mathematics education awarded. While these changes impact many programs, an examination of the largest producers of each decade shown in Table 3 reveals stability in the top five producers over the 4.5 decades.

TABLE 1. Top 30 Institutions in Production of Mathematics Education Doctorates, 1990-2005. (Source: NSF/NIH/USED/NEH/USDA/NASA, 1960-2005 Survey of Earned Doctorates.)

| Rank | Institution | Number of Graduates in 90's | Number of Graduates in 00's | Total |
|---|---|---|---|---|
| 1 | Teachers College-Columbia University | 77 | 41 | 118 |
| 2 | University of Georgia | 56 | 33 | 89 |
| 3 | University of Texas | 49 | 17 | 66 |
| 4 | The Ohio State University | 38 | 13 | 51 |
| 5 | Georgia State University | 33 | 7 | 40 |
| 6 | Florida State University | 26 | 13 | 39 |
| 6 | Illinois State University | 11 | 28 | 39 |
| 8 | North Carolina State University | 16 | 20 | 36 |
| 9 | Rutgers University | 21 | 14 | 35 |
| 10 | University of Oklahoma | 18 | 13 | 31 |
| 10 | American University | 19 | 12 | 31 |
| 11 | University of Maryland | 17 | 11 | 28 |
| 12 | State University of New York-Buffalo | 17 | 7 | 24 |
| 13 | Indiana University | 16 | 6 | 22 |
| 13 | University of Wisconsin | 18 | 4 | 22 |
| 13 | Temple University | 13 | 9 | 22 |
| 16 | University of Northern Colorado | 12 | 9 | 21 |
| 16 | Oregon State University | 10 | 11 | 21 |
| 18 | University of Iowa | 14 | 5 | 19 |
| 19 | Syracuse University | 11 | 7 | 18 |
| 20 | New York University | 13 | 4 | 17 |
| 20 | Vanderbilt University | 13 | 4 | 17 |
| 20 | University of Missouri | 6 | 11 | 17 |
| 23 | University of Minnesota | 10 | 5 | 15 |
| 23 | University of Pittsburgh | 12 | 3 | 15 |
| 23 | University of California-Berkeley | 8 | 7 | 15 |
| 23 | University of South Carolina | 12 | 3 | 15 |
| 27 | University of Illinois | 6 | 8 | 14 |
| 27 | University of Virginia | 6 | 8 | 14 |

*Continued on next page*

| Rank | Institution | Number of Graduates in 90's | Number of Graduates in 00's | Total |
|------|-------------|------|------|-------|
| 27 | University of Tennessee | 9 | 5 | 14 |
| 27 | University of South Florida | 9 | 5 | 14 |

TABLE 2. Top 30 Institutions in Production of Mathematics Education Doctorates, 1960-2005. (Source: NSF/NIH/USED/NEH/USDA/NASA, 1960-2005 Survey of Earned Doctorates.)

| Rank | Institution | Number of Doctorates Granted | Average Doctorates Per Year |
|------|-------------|------|------|
| 1 | Teachers College-Columbia University | 309 | 7.02 |
| 2 | University of Georgia | 179 | 4.07 |
| 3 | Ohio State University | 165 | 3.75 |
| 4 | University of Texas | 158 | 3.59 |
| 5 | Florida State University | 130 | 2.95 |
| 6 | New York University | 124 | 2.82 |
| 7 | Indiana University | 98 | 2.23 |
| 8 | Rutgers University | 95 | 2.16 |
| 9 | University of Maryland | 94 | 2.14 |
| 10 | University of Illinois | 89 | 2.02 |
| 11 | University of Northern Colorado | 88 | 2.00 |
| 12 | Oklahoma State University | 83 | 1.89 |
| 13 | Georgia State University | 79 | 1.80 |
| 14 | University of Wisconsin | 77 | 1.75 |
| 15 | University of Michigan | 73 | 1.66 |
| 16 | Temple University | 68 | 1.55 |
| 17 | State University of New York-Buffalo | 62 | 1.41 |
| 18 | University of Oklahoma | 57 | 1.30 |
| 19 | Vanderbilt University | 56 | 1.27 |
| 20 | Michigan State University | 53 | 1.20 |
| 21 | University of Minnesota | 51 | 1.16 |
| 22 | North Carolina State University | 47 | 1.07 |

*Continued on next page*

| Rank | Institution | Number of Doctorates Granted | Average Doctorates Per Year |
|------|-------------|------------------------------|------------------------------|
| 22 | University of Virginia | 47 | 1.07 |
| 24 | The Pennsylvania State University | 45 | 1.02 |
| 25 | Purdue University | 43 | 0.98 |
| 25 | University of Iowa | 43 | 0.98 |
| 27 | American University | 42 | 0.95 |
| 28 | Boston University | 41 | 0.93 |
| 28 | Illinois State University | 41 | 0.93 |
| 28 | University of Missouri | 41 | 0.93 |

Teachers College, Columbia University has consistently been the largest producer of doctorates in mathematics education since 1960. The top 5 overall producers also ranked among the top 20 for each decade. Three of the overall top 5 producers (Teachers College, Ohio State University and Florida State University) were among the top 10 producers for each decade, with the other two institutions (University of Georgia and University of Texas) among the top 10 for all but one decade (1960's). Seven of the top 10 producers were among the top 20 for all 5 decades.

A total of thirty-nine institutions graduated doctorates in each of the five decades from 1960 to 2005. While many institutions produce graduates, the majority of institutions produce only a few graduates each decade. On the other hand, Table 3 shows the five institutions that produced the most graduates from 1960-2005 contributed about a fourth of all graduates during this 45 year period. Furthermore, the top 30 producers contributed about three-fourths of the doctorates in mathematics education over this time period.

The percentages reported in Table 3 are fairly stable across decades. It appears that the percentage of doctorates produced by the top producers may be decreasing slightly. If so, this is probably related to the increase in the number of different institutions offering a doctoral program in mathematics education in later decades.

Table 4 provides a summary of each of the 167 institutions that NORC reported graduating at least one doctoral student with an emphasis in mathematics education. It reports the number of doctorates in mathematics education awarded each decade by institution. Among other things Table 4 shows that since 1960 only 24 institutions have averaged awarding one or more doctorates a year with an emphasis in mathematics education.

TABLE 3. Percent of doctoral graduates in mathematics education produced by the largest producing institutions for each decade. (Source: NSF/NIH/USED/NEH/USDA/NASA, 1960-2005 Survey of Earned Doctorates.)

|  | 1960's | 1970's | 1980's | 1990's | 2000's | 1960-2005 |
|---|---|---|---|---|---|---|
| % of doctorates from top 5 producers | 36% | 26% | 34% | 30% | 27% | 26% |
| % of doctorates from top 10 producers | 55% | 47% | 52% | 42% | 39% | 40% |
| % of doctorates from top 20 producers | 73% | 70% | 70% | 60% | 61% | 59% |
| % of doctorates from top 30 producers | 86% | 82% | 83% | 74% | 71% | 72% |

TABLE 4. Institution and number of doctorates in mathematics education awarded per decade. (Source: NSF/NIH/USED/NEH/USDA/NASA, 1960-2005 Survey of Earned Doctorates.)

| Rank | Institution | 60's | 70's | 80's | 90's | 00's | Total | Avg. per Year |
|---|---|---|---|---|---|---|---|---|
| 1 | Teachers College-Columbia University | 44 | 80 | 67 | 77 | 41 | 309 | 7.02 |
| 2 | University of Georgia | 8 | 46 | 36 | 56 | 33 | 179 | 4.07 |
| 3 | The Ohio State University | 34 | 55 | 25 | 38 | 13 | 165 | 3.75 |
| 4 | University of Texas | 10 | 49 | 33 | 49 | 17 | 158 | 3.59 |
| 5 | Florida State University | 19 | 53 | 19 | 26 | 13 | 130 | 2.95 |
| 6 | New York University | 23 | 51 | 33 | 13 | 4 | 124 | 2.82 |
| 7 | Indiana University | 9 | 49 | 18 | 16 | 6 | 98 | 2.23 |
| 8 | Rutgers University | 10 | 34 | 16 | 21 | 14 | 95 | 2.16 |
| 9 | University of Maryland | 7 | 38 | 21 | 17 | 11 | 94 | 2.14 |
| 10 | University of Illinois | 25 | 41 | 9 | 6 | 8 | 89 | 2.02 |
| 11 | University of Northern Colorado | 14 | 50 | 3 | 12 | 9 | 88 | 2.00 |
| 12 | Oklahoma State University | 43 | 29 | 5 | 3 | 3 | 83 | 1.89 |
| 13 | Georgia State University | 0 | 14 | 25 | 33 | 7 | 79 | 1.80 |
| 14 | University of Wisconsin | 21 | 22 | 12 | 18 | 4 | 77 | 1.75 |
| 15 | University of Michigan | 33 | 26 | 2 | 10 | 2 | 73 | 1.66 |

*Continued on next page*

| Rank | Institution | 60's | 70's | 80's | 90's | 00's | Total | Avg. per Year |
|------|-------------|------|------|------|------|------|-------|---------------|
| 16 | Temple University | 4 | 21 | 21 | 13 | 9 | 68 | 1.55 |
| 17 | State University of New York-Buffalo | 3 | 23 | 12 | 17 | 7 | 62 | 1.41 |
| 18 | University of Oklahoma | 5 | 14 | 7 | 18 | 13 | 57 | 1.30 |
| 19 | Vanderbilt University | 9 | 24 | 6 | 13 | 4 | 56 | 1.27 |
| 20 | Michigan State University | 5 | 25 | 11 | 6 | 6 | 53 | 1.20 |
| 21 | University of Minnesota | 7 | 19 | 10 | 10 | 5 | 51 | 1.16 |
| 22 | North Carolina State University | 0 | 3 | 8 | 16 | 20 | 47 | 1.07 |
| 22 | University of Virginia | 14 | 14 | 5 | 6 | 8 | 47 | 1.07 |
| 24 | The Pennsylvania State University | 5 | 25 | 6 | 4 | 5 | 45 | 1.02 |
| 25 | Purdue University | 8 | 19 | 8 | 5 | 3 | 43 | 0.98 |
| 25 | University of Iowa | 2 | 4 | 18 | 14 | 5 | 43 | 0.98 |
| 27 | American University | 0 | 1 | 10 | 19 | 12 | 42 | 0.95 |
| 28 | Boston University | 3 | 8 | 18 | 11 | 1 | 41 | 0.93 |
| 28 | Illinois State University | 0 | 0 | 2 | 11 | 28 | 41 | 0.93 |
| 28 | University of Missouri | 5 | 7 | 12 | 6 | 11 | 41 | 0.93 |
| 31 | University of Pittsburgh | 0 | 11 | 14 | 12 | 3 | 40 | 0.91 |
| 32 | Syracuse University | 8 | 8 | 4 | 11 | 7 | 38 | 0.86 |
| 32 | University of California | 5 | 5 | 13 | 8 | 7 | 38 | 0.86 |
| 34 | Auburn University | 3 | 13 | 6 | 5 | 8 | 35 | 0.80 |
| 35 | Northwestern University | 4 | 21 | 6 | 2 | 0 | 33 | 0.75 |
| 35 | Oregon State University | 1 | 5 | 6 | 10 | 11 | 33 | 0.75 |
| 35 | University of Houston | 2 | 17 | 7 | 5 | 2 | 33 | 0.75 |
| 38 | Stanford University | 9 | 10 | 5 | 4 | 3 | 31 | 0.70 |
| 39 | University of Tennessee | 2 | 6 | 6 | 9 | 5 | 28 | 0.64 |
| 40 | University of Massachusetts-Amherst | 0 | 4 | 10 | 9 | 4 | 27 | 0.61 |
| 41 | University of South Carolina | 0 | 6 | 2 | 12 | 3 | 23 | 0.52 |
| 42 | University of Florida | 4 | 6 | 5 | 5 | 2 | 22 | 0.50 |
| 43 | University of South Florida | 0 | 1 | 6 | 9 | 5 | 21 | 0.48 |
| 44 | Cornell University | 3 | 4 | 2 | 11 | 0 | 20 | 0.45 |
| 44 | University of Colorado | 6 | 9 | 3 | 1 | 1 | 20 | 0.45 |
| 46 | University of Oregon | 3 | 9 | 5 | 1 | 1 | 19 | 0.43 |
| 47 | Wayne State University | 6 | 7 | 2 | 3 | 0 | 18 | 0.41 |
| 48 | Harvard University | 5 | 8 | 2 | 1 | 1 | 17 | 0.39 |
| 48 | University of Kansas | 8 | 2 | 0 | 2 | 5 | 17 | 0.39 |
| 50 | Arizona State University | 2 | 8 | 2 | 1 | 2 | 15 | 0.34 |
| 50 | Ohio University | 0 | 0 | 2 | 5 | 8 | 15 | 0.34 |

*Continued on next page*

| Rank | Institution | 60's | 70's | 80's | 90's | 00's | Total | Avg. per Year |
|------|-------------|------|------|------|------|------|-------|---------------|
| 50 | University of Connecticut | 1 | 9 | 3 | 0 | 2 | 15 | 0.34 |
| 50 | University of Massachusetts-Lowell | 0 | 0 | 0 | 11 | 4 | 15 | 0.34 |
| 54 | University of New Hampshire | 0 | 1 | 5 | 2 | 6 | 14 | 0.32 |
| 55 | Southern Illinois University | 0 | 4 | 2 | 6 | 1 | 13 | 0.30 |
| 55 | Texas A&M University | 0 | 5 | 2 | 4 | 2 | 13 | 0.30 |
| 55 | University of Alabama | 1 | 3 | 2 | 5 | 2 | 13 | 0.30 |
| 55 | University of Denver | 3 | 5 | 5 | 0 | 0 | 13 | 0.30 |
| 59 | University of Chicago | 2 | 2 | 0 | 7 | 1 | 12 | 0.27 |
| 60 | University of Pennsylvania | 1 | 10 | 0 | 0 | 0 | 11 | 0.25 |
| 60 | Washington State University | 2 | 1 | 0 | 7 | 1 | 11 | 0.25 |
| 62 | Montana State University | 1 | 0 | 1 | 4 | 4 | 10 | 0.23 |
| 62 | University of Southern Mississippi | 0 | 1 | 3 | 5 | 1 | 10 | 0.23 |
| 62 | University of Delaware | 0 | 1 | 1 | 8 | 0 | 10 | 0.23 |
| 65 | Kansas State University | 0 | 5 | 4 | 0 | 0 | 9 | 0.20 |
| 65 | University of Arizona | 0 | 2 | 0 | 3 | 4 | 9 | 0.20 |
| 65 | University of Nebraska | 2 | 5 | 1 | 1 | 0 | 9 | 0.20 |
| 65 | West Virginia University | 0 | 2 | 3 | 2 | 2 | 9 | 0.20 |
| 69 | Claremont Graduate School | 0 | 0 | 0 | 5 | 3 | 8 | 0.18 |
| 69 | University of Rochester | 0 | 3 | 3 | 1 | 1 | 8 | 0.18 |
| 69 | University of Toledo | 0 | 4 | 1 | 3 | 0 | 8 | 0.18 |
| 69 | Western Michigan University | 0 | 0 | 0 | 3 | 5 | 8 | 0.18 |
| 73 | University of North Carolina | 2 | 2 | 0 | 2 | 1 | 7 | 0.16 |
| 73 | University of California-Los Angeles | 4 | 2 | 0 | 0 | 1 | 7 | 0.16 |
| 73 | University of North Texas | 4 | 3 | 0 | 0 | 0 | 7 | 0.16 |
| 73 | University of Washington | 0 | 2 | 2 | 2 | 1 | 7 | 0.16 |
| 77 | State University of New York-Albany | 0 | 3 | 2 | 1 | 0 | 6 | 0.14 |
| 77 | University of Missouri-Kansas City | 2 | 0 | 0 | 3 | 1 | 6 | 0.14 |
| 77 | University of Southern California | 3 | 1 | 1 | 1 | 0 | 6 | 0.14 |
| 80 | George Mason University | 0 | 0 | 0 | 2 | 3 | 5 | 0.11 |
| 80 | Kent State University | 0 | 1 | 0 | 4 | 0 | 5 | 0.11 |
| 80 | San Diego State University | 0 | 0 | 0 | 2 | 3 | 5 | 0.11 |
| 80 | University of North Carolina - Greensboro | 0 | 0 | 0 | 5 | 0 | 5 | 0.11 |
| 80 | University of California-Davis | 0 | 0 | 0 | 2 | 3 | 5 | 0.11 |
| 80 | University of Kentucky | 3 | 0 | 0 | 2 | 0 | 5 | 0.11 |
| 80 | University of Mississippi | 2 | 0 | 0 | 3 | 0 | 5 | 0.11 |

*Continued on next page*

| Rank | Institution | 60's | 70's | 80's | 90's | 00's | Total | Avg. per Year |
|------|-------------|------|------|------|------|------|-------|---------------|
| 80 | University of North Dakota | 0 | 0 | 0 | 2 | 3 | 5 | 0.11 |
| 80 | University of Utah | 2 | 1 | 0 | 0 | 2 | 5 | 0.11 |
| 80 | Utah State University | 2 | 1 | 1 | 1 | 0 | 5 | 0.11 |
| 90 | Duke University | 3 | 0 | 1 | 0 | 0 | 4 | 0.09 |
| 90 | Emory University | 0 | 0 | 1 | 1 | 2 | 4 | 0.09 |
| 90 | Florida Atlantic University | 0 | 1 | 2 | 1 | 0 | 4 | 0.09 |
| 90 | Louisiana State U & A&M College | 1 | 1 | 0 | 2 | 0 | 4 | 0.09 |
| 90 | Nova Southeastern University | 0 | 0 | 1 | 1 | 2 | 4 | 0.09 |
| 90 | University of Cincinnati | 0 | 0 | 1 | 2 | 1 | 4 | 0.09 |
| 90 | Walden University | 0 | 0 | 0 | 2 | 2 | 4 | 0.09 |
| 98 | Boston College | 1 | 1 | 0 | 1 | 0 | 3 | 0.07 |
| 98 | Bowling Green State University | 0 | 0 | 2 | 0 | 1 | 3 | 0.07 |
| 98 | Clemson University | 0 | 1 | 0 | 1 | 1 | 3 | 0.07 |
| 98 | Florida Institute of Technology | 0 | 0 | 0 | 1 | 2 | 3 | 0.07 |
| 98 | Mississippi State University | 1 | 0 | 1 | 0 | 1 | 3 | 0.07 |
| 98 | Montclair State University | 0 | 0 | 0 | 0 | 3 | 3 | 0.07 |
| 98 | Northern Illinois University | 0 | 0 | 0 | 2 | 1 | 3 | 0.07 |
| 98 | Portland State University | 0 | 0 | 0 | 0 | 3 | 3 | 0.07 |
| 98 | Texas Tech University | 2 | 0 | 0 | 0 | 1 | 3 | 0.07 |
| 98 | University of Missouri-Saint Louis | 0 | 0 | 1 | 1 | 1 | 3 | 0.07 |
| 98 | University of Arkansas-Fayetteville | 1 | 1 | 0 | 0 | 1 | 3 | 0.07 |
| 98 | University of Central Florida | 0 | 0 | 0 | 0 | 3 | 3 | 0.07 |
| 98 | University of Idaho | 0 | 0 | 0 | 0 | 3 | 3 | 0.07 |
| 98 | University of Illinois-Chicago | 0 | 0 | 0 | 2 | 1 | 3 | 0.07 |
| 98 | University of Montana | 0 | 0 | 0 | 1 | 2 | 3 | 0.07 |
| 98 | University of New Mexico | 1 | 0 | 1 | 1 | 0 | 3 | 0.07 |
| 98 | University of South Dakota | 0 | 0 | 0 | 3 | 0 | 3 | 0.07 |
| 115 | Baylor University | 0 | 0 | 0 | 1 | 1 | 2 | 0.05 |
| 115 | Clark University | 0 | 0 | 1 | 1 | 0 | 2 | 0.05 |
| 115 | George Washington University | 1 | 0 | 0 | 0 | 1 | 2 | 0.05 |
| 115 | City University of New York | 0 | 0 | 0 | 2 | 0 | 2 | 0.05 |
| 115 | Indiana University of Pennsylvania | 0 | 0 | 0 | 0 | 2 | 2 | 0.05 |
| 115 | Lehigh University | 0 | 0 | 2 | 0 | 0 | 2 | 0.05 |
| 115 | Marquette University | 0 | 0 | 0 | 1 | 1 | 2 | 0.05 |
| 115 | University of Memphis | 0 | 1 | 0 | 1 | 0 | 2 | 0.05 |
| 115 | Morgan State University | 0 | 0 | 0 | 0 | 2 | 2 | 0.05 |

*Continued on next page*

| Rank | Institution | 60's | 70's | 80's | 90's | 00's | Total | Avg. per Year |
|------|-------------|------|------|------|------|------|-------|---------------|
| 115 | St. Louis University | 0 | 2 | 0 | 0 | 0 | 2 | 0.05 |
| 115 | State Univ of New York-Binghamton | 0 | 0 | 0 | 2 | 0 | 2 | 0.05 |
| 115 | Tennessee State University | 0 | 0 | 0 | 1 | 1 | 2 | 0.05 |
| 115 | University of Arkansas-Little Rock | 0 | 0 | 0 | 0 | 2 | 2 | 0.05 |
| 115 | University of California-San Diego | 0 | 0 | 0 | 0 | 2 | 2 | 0.05 |
| 115 | University of Colorado-Denver | 0 | 1 | 0 | 0 | 1 | 2 | 0.05 |
| 115 | University of Nevada-Las Vegas | 0 | 0 | 0 | 0 | 2 | 2 | 0.05 |
| 115 | University of Wyoming | 0 | 1 | 1 | 0 | 0 | 2 | 0.05 |
| 115 | Virginia Polytech Institute | 0 | 0 | 0 | 1 | 1 | 2 | 0.05 |
| 133 | Argosy University | 0 | 0 | 0 | 1 | 0 | 1 | 0.02 |
| 133 | Ball State University | 0 | 0 | 0 | 1 | 0 | 1 | 0.02 |
| 133 | Brandeis University | 0 | 0 | 0 | 1 | 0 | 1 | 0.02 |
| 133 | Brigham Young University | 0 | 0 | 1 | 0 | 0 | 1 | 0.02 |
| 133 | Colorado State University | 0 | 0 | 0 | 0 | 1 | 1 | 0.02 |
| 133 | Fairleigh Dickinson University | 0 | 0 | 1 | 0 | 0 | 1 | 0.02 |
| 133 | Fordham University | 1 | 0 | 0 | 0 | 0 | 1 | 0.02 |
| 133 | Georgia Southern University | 0 | 0 | 0 | 0 | 1 | 1 | 0.02 |
| 133 | Hofstra University | 0 | 0 | 0 | 1 | 0 | 1 | 0.02 |
| 133 | Iowa State University | 0 | 1 | 0 | 0 | 0 | 1 | 0.02 |
| 133 | Johns Hopkins University | 0 | 0 | 0 | 0 | 1 | 1 | 0.02 |
| 133 | Loyola University of Chicago | 0 | 0 | 0 | 1 | 0 | 1 | 0.02 |
| 133 | Massachusetts Inst of Technology | 0 | 0 | 0 | 1 | 0 | 1 | 0.02 |
| 133 | Miami University | 0 | 0 | 0 | 1 | 0 | 1 | 0.02 |
| 133 | Northwestern State University of Louisiana | 0 | 0 | 1 | 0 | 0 | 1 | 0.02 |
| 133 | Princeton University | 0 | 0 | 0 | 0 | 1 | 1 | 0.02 |
| 133 | South Carolina State University | 0 | 0 | 0 | 1 | 0 | 1 | 0.02 |
| 133 | Southern University & A&M College | 0 | 0 | 0 | 0 | 1 | 1 | 0.02 |
| 133 | State U of New York- Stony Brook | 0 | 0 | 0 | 0 | 1 | 1 | 0.02 |
| 133 | The University of West Florida | 0 | 0 | 0 | 0 | 1 | 1 | 0.02 |
| 133 | University of California-Riverside | 0 | 0 | 0 | 0 | 1 | 1 | 0.02 |
| 133 | University of California-Santa Barbara | 0 | 0 | 0 | 0 | 1 | 1 | 0.02 |
| 133 | University of Puerto Rico-Rio Piedras | 0 | 0 | 0 | 0 | 1 | 1 | 0.02 |
| 133 | University of Akron | 0 | 0 | 1 | 0 | 0 | 1 | 0.02 |
| 133 | University of La Verne | 0 | 0 | 0 | 0 | 1 | 1 | 0.02 |
| 133 | University of Miami | 0 | 0 | 0 | 1 | 0 | 1 | 0.02 |

*Continued on next page*

| Rank | Institution | 60's | 70's | 80's | 90's | 00's | Total | Avg. per Year |
|------|-------------|------|------|------|------|------|-------|---------------|
| 133 | University of New Orleans | 0 | 0 | 0 | 1 | 0 | 1 | 0.02 |
| 133 | University of Notre Dame | 0 | 0 | 0 | 1 | 0 | 1 | 0.02 |
| 133 | University of Rhode Island | 0 | 0 | 0 | 1 | 0 | 1 | 0.02 |
| 133 | University of St. Thomas | 0 | 0 | 0 | 0 | 1 | 1 | 0.02 |
| 133 | University of Texas-Arlington | 0 | 0 | 0 | 0 | 1 | 1 | 0.02 |
| 133 | University of Wisconsin-Milwaukee | 0 | 0 | 1 | 0 | 0 | 1 | 0.02 |
| 133 | US International University | 1 | 0 | 0 | 0 | 0 | 1 | 0.02 |
| 133 | Washington University | 0 | 0 | 0 | 1 | 0 | 1 | 0.02 |
| 133 | Wilmington College | 0 | 0 | 0 | 0 | 1 | 1 | 0.02 |
| Total: | | 494 | 1095 | 648 | 844 | 518 | 3599 | |
| Number of institutions with graduates: | | 70 | 86 | 85 | 118 | 115 | 167 | |
| Average number of graduates per institution: | | 7.1 | 12.7 | 7.6 | 7.2 | 4.5 | 21.55 | |

An examination of Table 4 shows that 17 institutions did not award a doctorate in mathematics education from 1990-2005. Eighteen institutions graduated doctorates only during the most recent decade (2000-2005). Thus, one might assume they are new programs or that graduates are better informed about providing the proper code for their major area of emphasis on the NORC survey.

## Summary

These NORC data indicate an increasing number of institutions are producing graduates with a doctorate in mathematics education. Although the 5 to 10 institutions producing the largest number of graduates have remained fairly stable over several decades, there are some relatively new doctoral programs (such as Illinois State University) that are now among the largest producers of doctoral graduates in mathematics education. It is noteworthy that 30 institutions produce nearly three-fourths of all the doctorates in mathematics education. While these largest producing institutions have several graduates each year, the majority of institutions produce less than one doctorate a year in mathematics education as their area of emphasis.

There has been a gender shift in recipients of doctorates from the 1960s and 1970s where males greatly outnumbered females, to more recently where about 60% of doctorates in mathematics education are awarded to females. While the number of minority graduates has increased over the past 45 years, the overwhelming majority of doctoral graduates in mathematics education are Caucasian with the ratio of Caucasian to minority graduates about 5 to 1 for the last decade.

*Robert Reys*
*University of Missouri*
*Columbia, MO 65211*
*reysr@missouri.cdu*

*Robert Glasgow*
*Southwest Baptist University*
*Bolivar, MO 65613*
*bglasgow@sbuniv.edu*

*Dawn Teuscher*
*Arizona State University Polytechnic Campus*
*Tempe, AZ 85287*
*dawn.teuscher@asu.edu*

*Nevels Nevels*
*University of Missouri*
*Columbia, MO 65211*
*nnnc4f@mizzou.edu*

CBMS Issues in Mathematics Education
Volume **15**, 2008

# Doctoral Programs in Mathematics Education in the United States: 2007 Status Report

## Robert Reys, Robert Glasgow, Dawn Teuscher and Nevels Nevels

Individuals with doctorates in mathematics education have many different career options, including positions in higher education, K-12 district supervisor, state departments of education, and the publishing industry (Glasgow, 2000). In higher education, the positions are about equally split between mathematics departments, and colleges/schools of education. In either case, the supply of faculty with doctorates in mathematics education falls short of the demand of such individuals (Reys, 2000; 2002, 2006). For example, over 40% of institutions of higher education searching for mathematics education faculty in 2005-06 were unsuccessful in filling those positions (Reys, 2006).

Doctoral programs in mathematics education have the responsibility of preparing students to enter any of these positions, and this need to prepare graduates for such a wide range of career choices makes designing and implementing a doctoral program in mathematics education challenging. Although the number of programs that award doctorates in mathematics education has grown over the past 4 decades, the production of doctorates in mathematics education has not increased significantly (Reys and Kilpatrick, 2001; Reys, Glasgow, Teuscher & Nevels, this volume). So what do we know about the nature of doctoral programs in mathematics education? This paper addresses that question and provides a summary of the current status of doctoral programs in the United States. It is based on a national survey of doctoral programs in mathematics education conducted in early 2007.

For this report we contacted a representative from each institution whose doctoral program was listed on the Association of Mathematics Teacher Educators [AMTE] website of doctoral programs (see www.amte.net). In addition, representatives from institutions that graduated at least three doctorates during each of the last two decades and institutions with recently initiated doctoral programs in mathematics education were contacted. The union of these groups produced an initial list of 95 different institutions. An email was sent to one faculty member in mathematics education at each institution asking her/him to complete an on-line survey (See the survey at http://matheddb.missouri.edu/surveys/dpsurvey/start.php). In response to the e-mail, eight institutional representatives reported their universities

---

A slightly modified version of this paper was published in the November 2007 issue of the *Notices of the American Mathematical Society.*

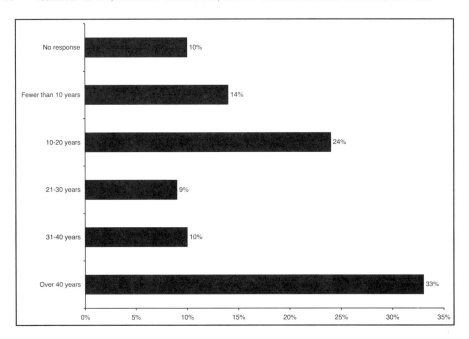

FIGURE 1. Percent of institutions reporting the number of years their doctoral program in mathematics education program has existed (N=70).

did not have a doctoral program in mathematics education. (e.g., American University, University of Chicago, Harvard University, University of South Dakota). The initial e-mail together with a follow-up to those not responding to the initial request produced information on 70 of the 87 remaining institutions for an 80% return rate. All results reflect the information self-reported by these institutional representatives. Taken collectively, the 70 institutions responding account for over 80% of doctorates in mathematics education in the United States from 1990 to 2005.

## Doctoral Programs within Institutions

Institutions award different doctoral degrees in mathematics education with over two-thirds awarding only a Ph.D. Thirteen percent award only the Ed.D. and about 15% award both the Ed.D. and Ph.D. Programs are housed within different colleges and departments across institutions. The majority of institutions (76%) report their doctoral program in mathematics education resides in a College/School of Education. Twelve programs (17%) are located in other colleges, such as the, College of Arts and Sciences, and four programs jointly administered by College/School of Education and Arts and Sciences.

Each institution reported how long its doctoral program in mathematics education has been in existence (see Figure 1). As noted, one-third of the institutions have had a program for over 40 years. On the other hand, 14% of institutions initialed new programs in the last 10 years.

## Doctoral Program Faculty

As noted earlier, a shortage of doctorates in mathematics education exists. In addition, previous surveys have indicated a large percentage of current faculty members in the area are approaching retirement age (Reys, Glasgow, Ragan & Simms, 2001).

**Faculty Size.** The 70 institutions had a total of 366 full-time faculty members, of which 201 (55%) were tenured. The number of mathematics education faculty at an institution ranged from 2 to 19, with the mode being four. Faculty members were predominately in the College of Education, but 25 institutions had at least one member of their faculty in the mathematics department. In fact, all or nearly all of the mathematics education faculty members at six institutions (Illinois State University, Montclair State University, Portland State University, Texas State University, University of Northern Colorado, and Western Michigan University) have an academic home in the mathematics department.

Sixteen institutions reported a post-doc position in mathematics education at their institution, and six of them reported having more than one post-doc. The majority of these post-doc positions are funded externally, but five institutions reported that internal funds were available to support post-doc appointments.

**Faculty Turnover.** Fifty-six institutions reported 115 faculty members either moved from their institution or retired during the last five years. Thirty-four institutions reported faculty members moving from their institutions. A total of 60 retirements from 38 different institutions were reported. While the majority of institutions reported one retirement, 10 institutions reported two retirements, one institution reported four, and another reported five.

**Projected Retirements.** In order to gather data about possible retirements, respondents were asked "How many of your faculty members are eligible for retirement in one or two years?" Twenty-eight institutions reported that collectively 42 faculty members were eligible for retirement within two years and an additional 34 more faculty members would be eligible for retirement within five years. These numbers reflect a combined projected loss of about 20% of current mathematics education faculty members in doctoral programs over the next five years.

Although the projected retirement rate is high, it is not as dramatic as the data reported in the 1999 survey. In the earlier survey, institutions were asked to make the same predictions of faculty eligible to retire. One of the stunning findings was that two-thirds of the faculty members in mathematics education in 1999 were eligible to retire by 2004 (Reys et al., 2001). A comparison of retirement information from 39 institutions that participated in the 1999 and 2007 surveys confirms that for the last 5 years mathematics education faculty have been retiring steadily as they become eligible to retire or perhaps a few years after they are eligible. Thus, the prediction from 1999 survey for a large number of retirements appears to be coming to fruition, even if a few years delayed.

**Hiring Faculty.** Given the faculty turnover in mathematics education positions, one would suspect that most institutions would be regularly searching for and hiring new faculty. In fact, over 90% (64/70) of institutions reported making at least one hire in mathematics education during the last 5 years. Eighteen institutions made one hire, 24 made two hires, nine made three hires, eight made four hires, four made five hires and one institution made six hires. The latter institution is in the process of establishing a new doctoral program in mathematics education.

Respondents were asked, "Do you have any unfilled positions in mathematics education for 2006-07?" About one-third of the institutional representatives reported that they currently had at least one unfilled position. In response to a question that asked respondents to "rate the current supply and demand for faculty with doctorates in mathematics education," over 95% said there would be "more or many more mathematics education jobs than qualified applicants." When asked to rate the future supply (in 5 to 10 years), almost 95% provided a similar response. It seems clear that the shortage of doctorates in mathematics education is recognized in the mathematics education community and that the shortage is likely to continue, given current graduation rates (Reys, et al., this volume).

Over 80% of the institutional representatives reported they would be searching for one or more positions in 2007, and 50 reported they would be doing a search for new faculty members in mathematics education in 2008. Of these institutions, over one-half reported searching for one position and another 20 said they will be searching for two or more positions.

## Admission Requirements

Admission requirements for entering a doctoral program in mathematics education vary depending on program emphasis and career goals of the candidates. For example, some institutions differentiate requirements according to whether the candidate seeks an elementary (K-8) or secondary (7-12) emphasis. The survey sought to collect information on all programs related to prerequisite mathematics content background and K-12 teaching experience.

Figure 2 displays the prerequisite mathematics content background for doctoral applicants who wish to pursue an elementary emphasis in mathematics education. Just over fifty percent of the institutions require or strongly encourage students to enter their program with a BS/BA in Mathematics or Mathematics Education, and about the same percentage of institutions require or strongly encourage students to enter the program with a MS/MA/MEd in Education.

Figure 3 displays the levels of teaching experience for doctoral applicants who wish to pursue an elementary emphasis in mathematics education. About one quarter of the institutions reported a requirement for elementary teaching experience and about one-half (47%) reported they strongly encourage students to have this experience. Although middle, secondary, and college teaching experience were not required, about one-third of the institutions strongly encouraged doctoral applicants to gain such experience. Only 11% of the institutions require doctoral students seeking an elementary emphasis to have an elementary teaching certificate; however, 40% strongly encourage students to have this certificate.

As one might suspect, a different level of mathematics knowledge is required for students who wish to pursue an emphasis in secondary or K-12 mathematics education. Figure 4 shows that over half of the institutions require entering students

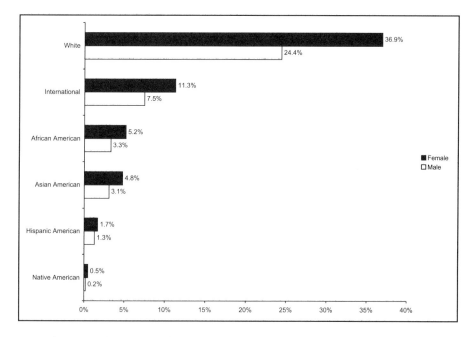

FIGURE 2. Levels of mathematics background for admittance to programs with an elementary mathematics education emphasis (N=70).

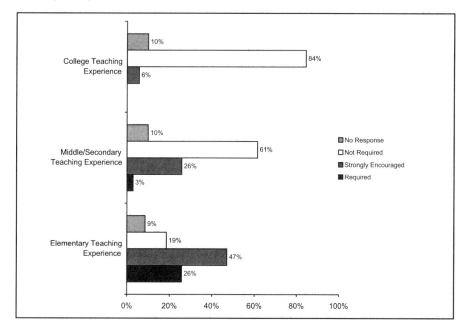

FIGURE 3. Levels of teaching experience for elementary emphasis (N=70).

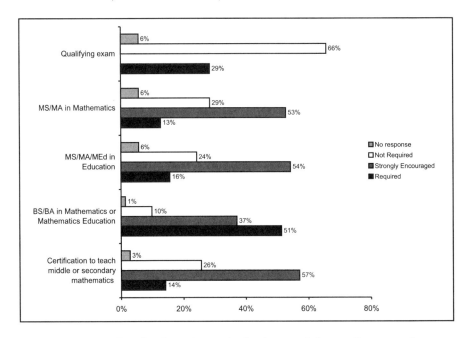

FIGURE 4. Levels of mathematics background for applicants seeking a secondary or K-12 emphasis in mathematics education
(N=70).

to have a BS/BA in Mathematics or Mathematics Education, and over half of
the institutions strongly encourage students to have either an MS/MA/MEd in
Mathematics Education or an MS/MA in Mathematics before entering the program.

In contrast to admittance requirements for applicants seeking an elementary
emphasis, nearly three-fourths of institutions require or strongly encourage entering
students seeking a secondary emphasis to have a teaching certificate at the middle
or secondary level. A little over a quarter of the institutions require entering students to take a qualifying exam, although no details were gathered regarding the
nature and scope of this exam.

Figure 5 displays information about teaching experience for doctoral students
wishing to pursue a secondary or K-12 emphasis in mathematics education. Twenty-
seven percent of the institutions require middle or secondary teaching experience
prior to entering their doctoral program, and over half (54%) report they strongly
encourage students to have this experience.

In addition to reviewing academic backgrounds and teaching experiences, most
institutions (87%) require applicants to take the Graduate Record Examination
(GRE). Additional requirements for entering doctoral students in mathematics education include letters of recommendation, writing samples, statement of purpose,
TOEFL score for international students, and faculty interviews. Other considerations noted in the selection process are depth of mathematics content knowledge,
evidence of research experience, and determination of whether the goals and interests of the applicant align with the institution's doctoral program in mathematics

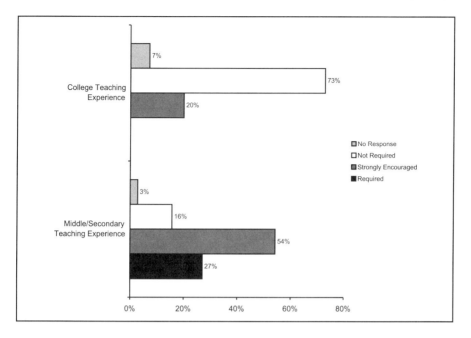

FIGURE 5. Levels of teaching experience for applicants seeking a secondary or K-12 emphasis in mathematics education (N=70).

education.

## Recruitment Strategies

Institutions differed greatly in the intensity of their recruitment efforts for doctoral students in mathematics education. Some institutions rely completely on 'walk-in' graduate students to enter their doctoral programs. Other institutions cast a wide net to attract potential doctoral students by recruiting nationally. Among the most cited local recruitment strategies was communication with former masters' students and local/regional teachers with encouragement to consider a doctoral degree.

Other strategies cited by respondents include posting information about doctoral programs on websites of professional organizations, such as AMTE, and also by being visible at conferences or professional meetings. Dedicating a web page to doctoral programs was also a commonly cited way to attract students. Advertising in professional journals was not generally cited as a common recruitment strategy.

The single most often mentioned recruitment strategy cited was word of mouth. That is, current doctoral students and past graduates were recognized as ambassadors for recruiting new students into a doctoral program. Therefore, institutions producing more graduates are also producing more ambassadors. These ambassadors may contribute to the success of large established doctoral programs continuing to attract large numbers of doctoral students in mathematics education.

When a student expresses interest in a doctoral program, personal follow-up from a faculty member was frequently cited as valuable in establishing an ongoing line of communication. Delegating one faculty member to provide continuous communication with potential graduate students appears to be an effective strategy. This arrangement places a heavier responsibility on one faculty member but it also insures a common source of information is provided to each student, and that students have individual questions answered in a prompt and consistent manner. Furthermore, the potential students know whom to contact when new questions arise.

Institutions serving full-time doctoral students listed the ability to offer substantial funding to their students as the single most effective recruitment strategy, while others indicated the lack of available funding as detrimental to their recruitment efforts. Institutions reported that financial support was about equally split among doctoral students for teaching assistantships and research assistantships. Teaching assistantships ranged from $11,000 to about $15,000 (median of $13,000) for the academic year, while research assistantships were slightly more, ranging from $11, 900 to about $16,000 (median of $13,500). In addition to assistantships, about one-third of doctoral students receive additional fellowships/scholarships. These fellowships/scholarships ranged from $300 upward to $10,000. Furthermore, 86% of the institutions reported a full-tuition waiver for students receiving a teaching or research assistantship. Two-thirds of the institutions also provided health insurance for full time graduate students.

## Demographics of Current Doctoral Students

Institutions reported that over one-half (56%) of the current doctoral students were full-time. It was also reported that 60% of the current doctoral students in mathematics education were female. Dominance of females continues a two decade trend of more females graduating with doctorates in mathematics education than males (Table 5, Reys, et al., this volume). The ethnicity of current doctoral students includes American Indian or Native Alaskan (0.6%), Hispanic Americans (3.0%), African Americans (8.4%), White (non-Hispanic) Americans (61%), and Asian Americans or Pacific Islanders (8.0%). The percent of minority groups represented is consistent with the data reported earlier (Table 6, Reys, Glasgow, Teuscher, & Nevels, this volume). Nearly one-fifth of the current doctoral students in mathematics education were international students (19%). Figure 6 provides information on both ethnicity and gender for all groups of doctoral students.

**Employment Graduates Pursue.** Respondents were asked to rank order positions taken by their students upon completion of a doctorate in mathematics education. Positions in higher education, either colleges/schools/departments of education or mathematics departments were the two most often cited positions. Joint appointments in education and mathematics were also ranked high. Over 85% of the respondents ranked a position in higher education as the number one type of position taken by their mathematics education doctoral program graduates. The popularity of jobs in higher education for graduates with doctorates in mathematics education reported here is consistent with earlier research done by Glasgow

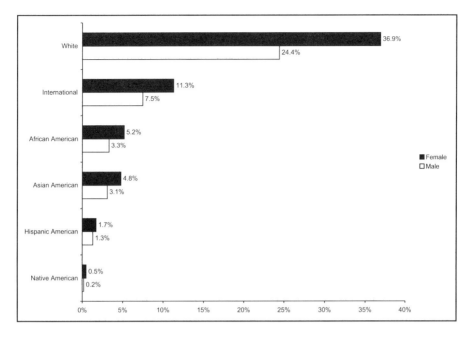

FIGURE 6.  Gender and ethnicity of current mathematics education
doctoral students (N=70).

(2000). While doctorates in mathematics education have many different job opportunities outside of academia, the overwhelming majority of doctorates are employed
in higher education. Another 13% of respondents ranked positions as K-12 classroom teachers or district/state mathematics coordinators as the top position taken
by their graduates. About 2% indicated some other type of position as their graduates' top ranked employment. When asked in the survey to describe these other
job opportunities for graduates, employment at junior/community colleges was the
most frequently mentioned.

## Program Requirements

About one-half the institutions reported a requirement of 81-100 graduate semester hours (post bachelors degree) to complete a doctorate, with more than
one-third of the institutions requiring fewer than 81 semester hours. In an effort to
determine how these hours were distributed across different areas, a question was
asked about course requirements in different areas. Figure 7 confirms that required
courses are distributed across different areas, with only two areas (Education Policy
and Cognitive Psychology) below the 50% level. Note that most, but not all of the
programs require coursework in mathematics.

In an effort to get another perspective of the emphasis placed on coursework,
respondents were asked to rate the attention given to courses in different areas.
Figure 8 shows the two areas with the strongest emphasis (major or moderate)
in doctoral programs are Research in Mathematics Education (98%) and Research
Methods (Quantitative and Qualitative) (97%), followed by Mathematics Content

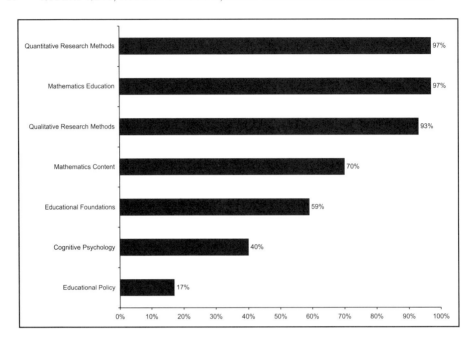

FIGURE 7. Percent of institutions reporting required courses in specific disciplines (N=70).

(90%), Learning Theories (83%), Teaching/Professional Development (83%) and Mathematics Curriculum (80%). In addition, a few institutions identified other program areas, such as Diversity/Multiculturalism, Equity and Cognitive Science as receiving moderate or major emphasis in their doctoral program.

In addition to coursework, most institutions require comprehensive examinations (89%) and residency (76%), although residence requirements vary across institutions. Several "beyond course" experiences were reported as required, with internships in research (31%) and college teaching (21%) being the most frequently cited. In addition, 16% of institutions required at least one presentation at a professional meeting, and three institutions required a published article as part of their program expectations.

As noted earlier, the emphasis on college mathematics within a doctoral program in mathematics education varies across institutions. Dossey and Lappan (2001) offered proposals to reflect different depths of mathematical knowledge for doctoral students seeking emphasis in elementary, middle and secondary school mathematics education. Figure 8 summarizes the level of mathematics content that would generally be attained as reported by institutions in this survey for elementary and K-16 emphasis.

Nearly one-half of the doctoral students who focus on elementary, graduate with a mathematics content background similar to a middle school teacher and the others have at least the equivalent of a major in mathematics. Whereas, upon completion of their doctoral program, students with a K-16 focus graduate with

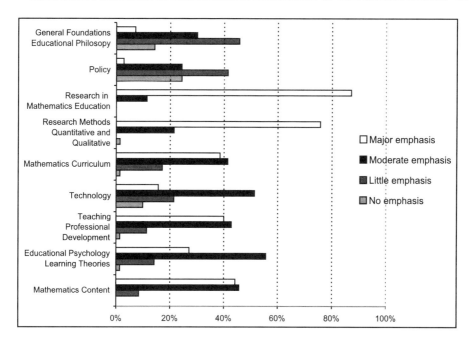

FIGURE 8. Percent of institutions reporting emphasis given to different content areas (N=70).

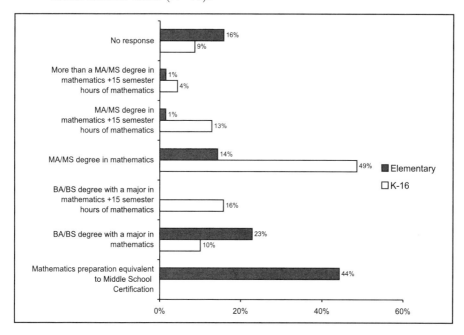

FIGURE 9. Percent of institutions reporting the level of mathematics coursework generally attained by doctoral students focusing on elementary or a broader K-16. (N=70)

a mathematics content background equivalent to a MA/MS in mathematics. The data in Figure 8 are generally consistent with the 'plus six' criterion offered by Dossey and Lappan (2001), namely that graduates have at least six educational grade levels above their teaching assignment.

## Changing Nature of Doctoral Programs

As a result of the 1999 Conference on Doctoral Programs in Mathematics Education, the AMTE established a task force to develop guidelines for doctoral programs in mathematics education. The task force produced *Principles to Guide the Design and Implementation of Doctoral Programs in Mathematics Education*. This document was endorsed by the AMTE and the National Council of Teachers of Mathematics (NCTM) in 2002.

In an effort to determine the extent to which this document was known and to examine its impact among institutions with doctoral programs in mathematics education, the following question was asked: "How familiar are you with *Principles to Guide the Design and Implementation of Doctoral Programs in Mathematics Education*?" Twenty-eight percent of respondents were unaware of the document. On the other hand, 72 percent of these respondents were either Somewhat Familiar (41%) or Very Familiar (31%) with the document. This latter group reported using the AMTE *Principles* to guide the development of a review or reshaping of their doctoral program or in the development of a new program. For example, one respondent said: "It served as a framework for us to develop new courses to provide a broader and deeper preparation of doctoral students." Another indicated, "We used the suggested guidelines for establishing requirements for the Ed.D. in Pedagogy with a Specialization in Mathematics Education." In addition, several respondents commented that they used the recommendations provided in the section 'Institutional Capacity Needed to Support Quality Doctoral Programs' to garner more institutional resources to support their doctoral program in mathematics education.

The 1999 Conference resulted in the publication of *One Field, Many Paths: U. S. Doctoral Programs in Mathematics Education*. This document provided a number of ideas and suggestions regarding doctoral programs. One survey question asked: "How familiar are you with *One Field, Many Paths: U. S. Doctoral Programs in Mathematics Education* (2001)?"

Over three-fourths of the respondents were either Somewhat or Very Familiar with *One Field, Many Paths*. Respondents reported using this document to shape their doctoral program. For example, "We used the information about shortages as a resource to the task force that recently wrote a paper for departmental discussion related to hiring a mathematics educator." Another said "It helped us implement internships and also led to annual progress reviews of our doctoral students that we designed to simulate what our graduates will experience if they pursue a tenure track position in higher education."

These two documents were developed to share with others involved in doctoral programs in mathematics education. The survey results underscore the impact of these documents on the field. The fact that one-quarter of the respondents was not aware of either of these documents suggests there is a continuing need to spread the word about these publications and their potential for informing and stimulating discussion about doctoral preparation in mathematics education.

Two survey questions were provided to gain information about the status of doctoral programs in mathematics education. One question asked about changes in the last five years, and another asked respondents to speculate on changes for the next five years.

In response to the question "Have the requirements in your doctoral programs changed in the last five years?" institutions were about evenly split. Slightly over half of the institutions (36/70) reported no programmatic changes. Of the other institutions, the common theme was that their doctoral program in mathematics education was "constantly evolving." Large established doctoral programs were represented in each group; whereas smaller and newly established programs dominated the institutions reporting change. The changes reported were diverse, ranging from establishing a new doctoral program (3 institutions) to replacing one doctoral program with another. For example, one institution reported replacing their Ed.D. program with a Ph.D., while another institution reported their Ph.D. program had been shifted from the Department of Mathematics to their College of Education.

While changes in entrance requirements were reported, the most frequently cited changes reflected expanding course offerings in mathematics education, or providing internship opportunities. There was a trend to expand or refocus course offerings to better serve doctoral students. Institutions reported developing specific courses for doctoral students in mathematics education in a range of areas, including foundations of mathematics education, equity, curriculum, learning, policy, technology, and professional development. Although mathematics content courses provide a common foundation for nearly all doctoral students in mathematics education, no institution reported making any substantial changes in mathematics content courses targeted toward graduate students in mathematics education.

In addition to creating specific courses, research was the area most singled out for change. More emphasis was given to strengthening research preparation. This was reflected in different statements such as:

> "Additional research methods are now required."
> "Increased research methodology requirements, to better prepare students to understand and use a variety of research methods."
> "Requiring a research apprenticeship."
> "We are moving from a program for practitioners to one that promotes high professional engagement in research and scholarship."
> "More emphasis on research, flexibility in core foundation courses, emphasis on presentations and publications."

High quality preparation of doctoral students in mathematics education must go beyond coursework (Blume, 2001; Golde & Walker, 2006; Levine, 2007). There was evidence that a number of institutions have initiated multiple "beyond coursework" experiences for their doctoral students in mathematics education. This idea was clearly captured by one institutional response that stated "We have completely redeveloped our program to emphasize a graduated series of research apprenticeship experiences that extends beyond formal courses." While this response focused on research apprenticeships, other institutions echoed a similar approach by providing teaching internships (where doctoral students co-teach undergraduate methods courses with regular faculty). Other internships cited included the art of editing, proposal writing, and co-authoring manuscripts for publication. All of these internships reflect an effort to provide opportunities for increased mentoring and closer working relationships with faculty members in mathematics education.

In looking to the future, over one-half of the institutions reported their doctoral program will be changing in the next five years. A central issue for 8 of these institutions was related to the degree designation. Institutions offering both the Ph.D. and Ed.D. were reviewing the nature of these degrees to determine if they were significantly different to justify offering separate degrees. Two institutions that offer the Ed.D. reported they were reshaping their program to offer the Ph.D. in lieu of the Ed.D. Several existing doctoral programs (whether Ph.D. or Ed.D.) were revising their program to better serve students. For example, one urban institution reported developing a doctoral program for part-time students who have a school-centered focus. Several institutions reported a change from a strong emphasis in mathematics content to more rigorous preparation in mathematics education.

The majority of changes described were specific with respect to an institution. However, among the litany of challenges being addressed by more than one institution were better accommodation of international students; strategies for preparing doctoral students who have little/no teaching experience in U.S. schools; reviewing residency requirements; developing graduate courses in mathematics to better serve doctoral students in mathematics education; establishing teams of doctoral students to work closely with individual faculty members; and providing an option of journal articles in lieu of a dissertation. These were offered as issues that are currently being discussed along with the realization that they are complex and their resolution remains a challenge.

Increasing course offerings by adding new required courses for doctorates in mathematics education was reported by many institutions. These course changes were similar to those mentioned earlier by institutions that have changed their programs over the last 5 years. In addition to the wave of expanding beyond course experiences (such as co-teaching, research, and grant writing), some institutions were specifically expanding requirements to have students take courses in other disciplines, such as cognitive science and learning theories, as well as sociology and urban studies.

Taking these two questions together (i.e., Has your program changed in the last 5 years? Do you anticipate changes in the next 5 years?) it is clear that doctoral programs in mathematics education are changing. Nearly 80% of the institutions reported change has been or will be taking place in their doctoral programs in mathematics education. Given the rapid changes in society and demands for leadership in mathematics education, such ongoing program review and changes are critical to the continued growth and strengthening of doctoral programs in mathematics education.

It is surprising that no institution identified the time required to complete a doctorate in mathematics education as an issue being considered among the many program changes that were implemented or were considered for the future. This is in contrast to the discussions reported by Golde & Walker (2006) where concern about shortening the time required to complete a doctorate was a common theme among many different disciplines.

In mathematics education, the majority of doctoral students acquire teaching experience prior to entering doctoral programs. That means these students must make significant financial sacrifices in their income to return as full-time graduate students. Every year spent as a full-time graduate student multiplies this financial sacrifice. Glasgow (2000) reported that doctorates in mathematics education average 18 years between earning their bachelor's and doctoral degrees. This means that generally they are near 40 years of age before they earn a doctorate in mathematics education. This is in comparison to many fields, such as mathematics, where doctorates are usually earned while a person is still in their twenties. For doctoral students in mathematics education, this translates into less time in their career prior to retirement. Given these situations and the shortage of doctorates in mathematics education, it seems reasonable that exploring ways of shortening the time to complete a doctorate in mathematics education should at least be on the radar screen for discussion.

How changes are initiated and implemented are unique to each institution. Learning from others can be a valuable teacher. Along that line, it is said imitation is the greatest form of flattery. Several institutions reported faculty members visiting other campuses with the specific purpose of learning more about their doctoral program in mathematics education. These experiences were used to revise and strengthen their doctoral programs. One institution reported it made "changes to reflect ideas ... from other strong doctoral programs in mathematics education." Since every institution is different, there is no single approach to strengthening or revitalizing a doctoral program. Nevertheless, it seems reasonable that faculty at each institution have a responsibility to be vigilant of their doctoral program, the faculty and resources available, and factor in the students being served to ask "Are we doing the best that we can with what we have?"

## "Particularly Strong" Doctoral Programs in Mathematics Education

In 2001, the AMTE created a website to allow institutions with doctoral programs in mathematics education to share common information. This resource remains available at www.amte.net. The institutional information is self reported and no effort was made to verify the information or to analyze the data in order to examine different qualities of doctoral programs. Some publications, such as the *U.S. News and World Reports*, provide annual rankings of undergraduate and graduate programs. Although some rankings are based on quantitative data, such as the number of scholarly papers published, often rankings are based on perceptions that have been established. In such cases, the beauty of a doctoral program is in the eye of the beholder.

We report here a slightly different approach. Respondents were asked to identify 'particularly strong' doctoral programs in mathematics education. The assumption in this effort is that faculty members involved in a doctoral program in mathematics education are aware of different programs around the country. Their familiarity may result from a variety of experiences, ranging from being a graduate of a program, working with colleagues in other programs, and knowing graduates of certain programs. It may also be influenced by the visibility of faculty members from specific institutions during professional meetings and via scholarly publications. Any and all of these factors are likely to influence the perception of a program.

This was the philosophy used in ratings of graduate programs generated by the National Research Council in its first report on the status of research-doctorate programs in the Sciences (including the broad fields of Biological Sciences, Physical

Sciences and Mathematics, and Social and Behavioral Sciences), Engineering, and Arts and Humanities in the United States (Jones, Lindzey, and Coggeshall, 1982). The ratings were updated in a second report published in 1995 (Goldberger, Maher, and Flattau, 1995). The process used to form ratings of graduate programs in various fields involved asking faculty members of other programs to rate an institution's program based on two criteria. The criteria were: (1) scholarly quality of program faculty, and (2) effectiveness in educating research scholars/scientists. To facilitate the raters' decisions, a list of faculty for a particular program was provided. The NRC ratings are still used by other organizations, such as the American Mathematical Society, to group graduate programs in particular academic disciplines. There has been no similar effort done with regard to identifying nationally recognized doctoral programs in mathematics education. And given the grain size of doctoral programs in mathematics education, this type of reporting is unlikely by national media.

The current survey collected data from representatives of 70 institutions with doctoral programs in mathematics education, and as mentioned earlier, these institutions account for more than 80% of doctorates in mathematics education. The programs range in size of faculty and the production of doctoral students. Some produce 2-10 doctoral students each year, but the majority graduate 1-2 doctoral students in mathematics education over several years. One respondent from each institution was asked to respond to the following question:

> Identify 6 institutions that you think are particularly strong and that you would currently recommend to a potential doctoral student in mathematics education (other than your own institution).

Seven respondents did not identify any institutions. An examination of the data revealed that all of the respondents honored the request to not make a self-nomination. About half the institutions listed six institutions, and the remaining nominated from one to five institutions. The data in Table 1 were compiled by tallying the number of times an institution was listed, and all institutions identified by at least two respondents were reported. Forty different institutions were nominated by 63 respondents, but only three institutions (University of Georgia, Michigan State University, and University of Michigan) were named by a majority of institutions. The University of Georgia is also the only institution among the top five producers of doctorates in mathematics education to also be named by a majority of institutions. In fact a number of the large producers of doctorates, such as Teachers College and Florida State University received only two nominations.

It is recognized that as faculty and resources come and go, programs change. This survey provides a current perspective of program visibility from one's peers. Hopefully, these data will be useful as institutions reflect on how their doctoral program in mathematics is perceived by others.

One limitation of this survey is that only one representative from each institution provided information. It is not known whether their selection of institutions was based solely on their own opinion or reflected discussions with other colleagues. Despite whatever limitations are associated with this effort, Table 1 provides a unique view of "particularly strong" doctoral programs in mathematics education.

TABLE 1. Institutions that were identified by at least two institutional representatives as a "particularly strong doctoral program and one you would recommend."

| Rank (by number of nominations) | Institution | Number of Nominations | Rank (by number of doctorates awarded) |
| --- | --- | --- | --- |
| 1 | University of Georgia | 50 | 2 |
| 2 | Michigan State | 37 | 20 |
| 3 | University of Michigan | 33 | 15 |
| 4 | University of Missouri | 29 | 28 |
| 5 | University of Wisconsin | 20 | 14 |
| 6 | University of Maryland | 18 | 9 |
| 7 | San Diego State University/UCSD | 17 | 80 |
| 8 | Pennsylvania State University | 15 | 24 |
| 8 | University of California-Berkeley | 15 | 32 |
| 10 | Indiana University | 12 | 7 |
| 11 | Vanderbilt University | 10 | 19 |
| 12 | Stanford University | 8 | 38 |
| 12 | University of Delaware | 8 | 62 |
| 14 | Arizona State University | 6 | 50 |
| 15 | Illinois State University | 5 | 28 |
| 16 | Ohio State University | 4 | 3 |
| 16 | University of Louisville | 4 | New Program |
| 16 | University of New Hampshire | 4 | 54 |
| 19 | North Carolina State University | 3 | 22 |
| 19 | Texas A & M University | 3 | 55 |
| 19 | UCLA | 3 | 73 |
| 19 | University of Texas | 3 | 4 |
| 23 | Florida State University | 2 | 5 |
| 23 | Portland State University | 2 | 98 |
| 23 | Teachers College, Columbia University | 2 | 1 |
| 23 | University of Tennessee | 2 | 39 |

## Summary

The information reported here was gathered from representatives of 70 institutions in the United States with doctoral programs in mathematics education. It provides current information on faculty and institutional program characteristics.

Both the Ph.D. and Ed.D. degrees are available, but the Ph.D. is offered by over 80% of the institutions, and exclusively by two-thirds of the institutions. Nearly

90% of the doctoral programs in mathematics education reside in the College/School of Education.

The majority of institutions offering doctoral programs in mathematics education were established for over 30 years, while about 15% of the programs are less than 10 years old. Regardless of the duration of their program, nearly four-fifths of the institutions reported their doctoral program in mathematics education was undergoing constant review and experiencing frequent changes. One of the most frequently cited changes from the program descriptions provided in the 1999 survey was the initiation of beyond-course experiences (such as co-teaching, research, and grant writing) into many doctoral programs.

Over half of the current full-time faculty members in mathematics education were tenured, and over 80% of them were in Colleges/Schools of Education. In some institutions, all of the mathematics education faculty members were in the mathematics department, yet over one-third of the institutions reported having at least one mathematics educator in the mathematics department.

All institutions were aware of the shortage of doctorates in mathematics education. Consequently, recruiting new faculty and retaining current faculty was recognized as a continuing challenge. During the last five years, four-fifths of the institutions reported losing one or more faculty members to either retirement or being hired by another institution.

As the need for more doctorates in mathematics education increases, the recruitment of doctoral students has become more intense. Word of mouth from prior graduates of doctoral programs was identified as one of the most effective means of recruiting new students. Support (financial, tuition waivers, health insurance) for full-time doctoral students varied among institutions, but the largest variance was in the number of scholarships/fellowships available and their range of financial support.

This survey provides some information on doctoral programs perceived as 'particularly strong' by faculty at peer institutions. These results suggest that some of the larger producers of doctorates were perceived as 'particularly strong' but other large producers were not frequently nominated. It is a reminder that doctoral programs in mathematics education are constantly changing, and as these changes occur, perceptions of these programs by their peers change.

Our hope is that this survey provides data that will be useful in reflecting on the nature of doctoral programs in mathematics education in the USA. It is only a snapshot, and it only reflects information gathered from 70 institutions. Nevertheless, it provides a current set of benchmarks to use for thoughtful discussion, and ultimately, action as our mathematics education community continues to work toward the never ending task of improving doctoral programs in mathematics education. We are in agreement with Lee Shulman who said:

> The Ph.D. is expected to serve as a steward of her discipline or
> profession, dedicated to the integrity of its work in the generation,
> critique, transformation, transmission, and use of its knowledge.
> (Golde & Walker, 2006, p. 122)

Our hope is that information reported here will facilitate institutional efforts to strengthen their doctoral programs in mathematics education and thereby prepare future stewards of our discipline.

*Robert Reys*
*University of Missouri*
*Columbia, MO 65211*
*reysr@missouri.edu*

*Robert Glasgow*
*Southwest Baptist University*
*Bolivar, MO 65613*
*bglasgow@sbuniv.edu*

*Dawn Teuscher*
*Arizona State University Polytechnic Campus*
*Tempe, AZ 85287*
*dawn.teuscher@asu.edu*

*Nevels Nevels*
*University of Missouri*
*Columbia, MO 65211*
*nnnc4f@mizzou.edu*

CBMS Issues in Mathematics Education
Volume **15**, 2008

# Report of a 2007 Survey of U. S. Doctoral Students in Mathematics Education

## Dawn Teuscher, Nevels Nevels, and Catherine Ulrich

This paper reports the results of a survey of current mathematics education doctoral students. It was conducted to gather information about their doctoral programs. One faculty member from each of the 70 institutions with doctoral programs in mathematics education that had responded to an earlier institutional survey (Reys, Glasgow, Teuscher, & Nevels, this volume) was contacted. These faculty members were asked to provide the names of three current doctoral students in mathematics education to participate in a survey. Faculty from 52 of these institutions (74%) provided names and email addresses for 157 current doctoral students. Four of the email addresses were undeliverable and three names submitted were no longer graduate students as they had recently graduated. We contacted the remaining 150 doctoral students representing 50 different institutions, inviting them to respond to a survey. Responses were received from 111 students (74%) representing 51 different institutions. The results reported here are based on information self-reported by these doctoral students.

Doctoral students were given the opportunity to disclose various aspects of their educational experience ranging from their reasons for choosing their institution to their career intentions upon degree completion. This information informs the decision-making processes of doctoral programs in several ways. Understanding what motivates students to choose a particular institution may aid doctoral programs in their recruitment process. Ascertaining the educational background and teaching experience of entering doctoral students may assist in determining how to design and develop programs that will best serve the students. Finding where new doctoral graduates seek employment may allow institutions to identify strong program areas as well as reveal areas in need of strengthening.

### Citizenship and Gender of Doctoral Students

Citizenship and gender data reported on this survey is consistent with data reported on the institutional survey (Reys et al., this volume). One doctoral student did not provide citizenship. About 90% of the respondents are citizens of the

---

This study was supported by the Center for the Study of Mathematics Curriculum that is funded by the National Science Foundation under Grant No. ESI-0333879. The opinions expressed are the authors and this article does not reflect any endorsement of the results by the National Science Foundation.

United States. Seven different countries were represented by the other respondents, and the percent of international students was consistent with an earlier study by Glasgow (2000). Sixty-six percent of respondents were female, consistent with the two-decade trend of more female doctoral students in mathematics education than males (Reys, et al., this volume).

The ages of the responding students ranged from 24-64 with an average age of 36 and a mode of 31. Nearly three-fifths (59%) of the doctoral students in the survey were married.

## Educational Background and Teaching Experience

Doctoral programs have varied requirements for admitting students. Some programs require teaching experience while others do not. On the other hand, some require a Master's degree in mathematics or mathematics education, while others do not stipulate a minimum standard for the study of mathematics content.

Students reported receiving undergraduate degrees in many different fields. Majors included: Education (e.g., elementary, middle, policy, special education, curriculum & instruction), Engineering (e.g., chemical, mechanical, computer), Mathematics (e.g., computational, applied, pure), and Science (e.g., microbiology, physics). Table 1 displays the percentage of students' first and second Bachelors' degrees across different content areas. Fifty-five (50%) doctoral students held a Bachelor's degree in mathematics while 17% of respondents held a Bachelor's degree in mathematics education.

Mathematics majors (57%) were dominant at the undergraduate level for current doctoral students, but their major course of study shifted to be more closely aligned to Education (e.g., teaching & leadership, curriculum & instruction, science education, mathematics education, middle, elementary) at the master's level. Table 2 displays students' content areas for first and second Masters' degrees. Mathematics education majors (35%) lead all categories for Master's degrees, while Education-related degrees (mathematics education, education, counseling, science education, technology in education) accounted for 58% of all majors at the master's level. Nearly one-third of the doctoral students held a master's degree in mathematics.

Teaching certification varied among respondents with the majority (77%) indicating they were certified to teach mathematics in some grade level K-12. Thirty-four percent of respondents indicated two certifications and 14% earned a third. The respondents received their teaching certification from some jurisdiction within six different countries (Colombia, Kenya, Puerto Rico, Slovakia, Turkey, and the USA). Respondents reported 31 different states as the grantor of their certification within the USA.

Six grade bands were coded to encompass the variety of grade level certifications. Figure 1 displays the percentage of students with each level of teaching certification. The majority (41%) of doctoral students were certified to teach at the secondary level prior to entering doctoral programs. On the other hand, 25 students did not indicate having a teaching certification. A single respondent indicated not having K-12 certification, but having 6 years of experience as a community college adjunct instructor.

TABLE 1. Bachelors' degrees of doctoral students in mathematics education reported in percent (N=111)

| Major | 1st Bachelor's degree | 2nd Bachelor's degree |
|---|---|---|
| Mathematics | 57% | 4% |
| Mathematics Education | 17% | 2% |
| Education | 7% | 2% |
| Engineering | 5% | |
| Psychology | 3% | 1% |
| Science | 2% | 1% |
| History | 2% | |
| Liberal Arts | 2% | |
| Computer Science | 1% | 1% |
| Administration | 1% | |
| Business | 1% | |
| Interdisciplinary | 1% | |
| Human Ecology | 1% | |
| Film and Media | | 1% |
| Music | | 1% |

TABLE 2. Masters' degrees of doctoral students in mathematics education reported in percent (N=111)

| Major | 1st Master's degree | 2nd Master's degree |
|---|---|---|
| Mathematics Education | 35% | 5% |
| Mathematics | 32% | 1% |
| Education | 25% | 3% |
| Business | 2% | |
| Counseling | 1% | |
| History | 1% | |
| Multimedia Systems | 1% | |
| Science Education | 1% | |
| Technology in Education | 1% | |
| Viral Oncology | 1% | |
| Statistics | | 2% |

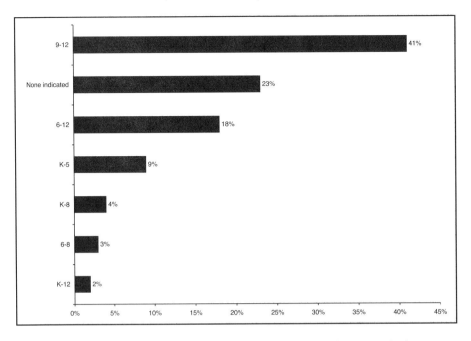

FIGURE 1. Teaching certifications of doctoral students in Mathematics Education (N=111)

When asked to specify the grade band for the majority of their teaching experience, students indicated the following: K-5 (8%), 6-8 (15%), 9-12 (43%), and 13+ (34%). About 77% of doctoral students had teaching experience at the secondary or college levels before entering their programs. The number of years doctoral students taught mathematics at the K-12 level varied from 0-31 years with a mean of 5.6 years. Nineteen of the respondents indicated they had no K-12 teaching experience. Of these nineteen respondents, seven were certified somewhere in the K-12 range. Additionally, six more did not respond to this question; however, the same six all indicated 1 to 10 years (3.8 years average) of teaching experience at the college level.

### Choosing Doctoral Programs

Research has documented the shortage of doctoral graduates in mathematics education (Reys, 2002, 2006). Institutions are continually searching for effective methods for recruiting quality students. In response to this issue, doctoral students were asked three questions:

(1) Why did you choose to pursue a doctoral degree in mathematics education?
(2) How did you learn about different doctoral programs?
(3) Why did you choose your current doctoral program?

Figure 2 displays six common responses for why students chose to pursue a doctorate in mathematics education. All but one student responded to this question and the most common reason cited was to advance their careers. For example, respondents wanted to become a better teacher, improve salary level, qualify for

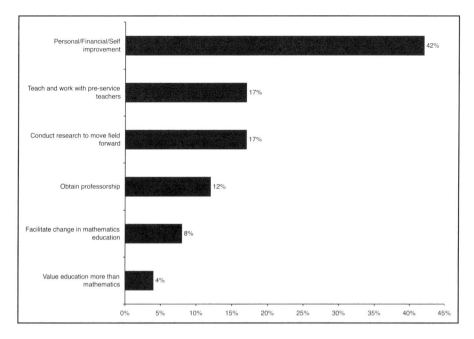

FIGURE 2. Six reasons given by doctoral students for choosing to
pursue a doctorate in mathematics education (N=110).

academic promotion, or make a change in career focus. Other reasons included the
desire to work with preservice teachers (17%) and conduct research that moves the
field forward (17%).

To assist in the recruitment efforts of institutions, this survey sought information about how prospective doctoral students learned about potential mathematics
education programs. This question was open ended; therefore, it was coded into
nine categories: prior association with the institution, proximity to home, internet
searches, personal recruiting, reputation of the school, journal ads, mathematics
conferences, information packet, and word of mouth. The three top categories used
to learn about various programs were internet searches, former associations with
faculty at the university, and word of mouth. A popular strategy used by many
institutions is to advertise in professional journals; however, only two respondents
reported using this method to search for graduate programs in mathematics education.

Respondents were asked to identify up to three reasons why they chose their
respective program from the following categories: family reasons, convenience, reputation of school, type of research, financial support, CLT, reputation of faculty,
personal recruitment, and other. The three top reasons cited by respondents were
reputation of faculty, convenience, and financial support. It was interesting that
the reputation of the mathematics education faculty outweighed the reputation of
the institution by nearly 3 to 1 in the selection process.

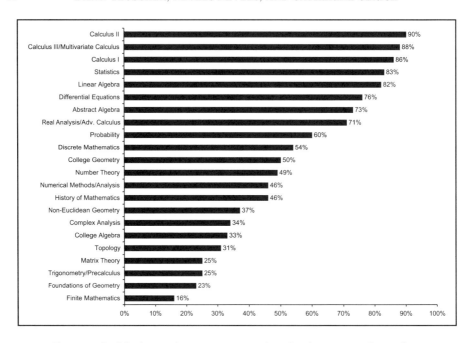

FIGURE 3. Mathematics courses completed prior to entering a doctoral program (N=111)

## Mathematical Preparation for Current Students in the US

To gain a better understanding of the mathematical preparation of students entering doctoral programs, respondents were asked to identify all collegiate mathematics courses completed prior to entry. Figure 3 displays the different courses and the percentage of students in our survey that took each course.

Most respondents (86-90%) entered their doctoral program having completed the calculus sequence (Calculus I, II, III). A large percentage of students had also completed Linear Algebra (82%), Differential Equations (76%), Abstract Algebra (73%) and Statistics (83%). However, fewer students entered with a background in geometry (only 50% of students completed a college-level geometry course, 37% completed a Non-Euclidean Geometry course, and 23% completed a Foundations of Geometry course). Thirty-six students responded that they had completed other mathematics courses not listed on the survey, which included Combinatorics, Differential Geometry, Graph Theory, and Mathematical Modeling.

Respondents were asked to list mathematics courses they had or would complete during their doctoral program. Figure 4 displays the most popular mathematics courses completed during doctoral programs. As might be expected, Statistics was the most popular area of coursework. This may be because students are required to complete at least one research methods (qualitative or quantitative) course. About a fifth (18%) of students had not taken a mathematics course during their doctoral program. It may be the case that these students entered with a Master's degree in mathematics; however, some students noted their institution did not have a requirement for mathematics courses. It is also interesting to note that

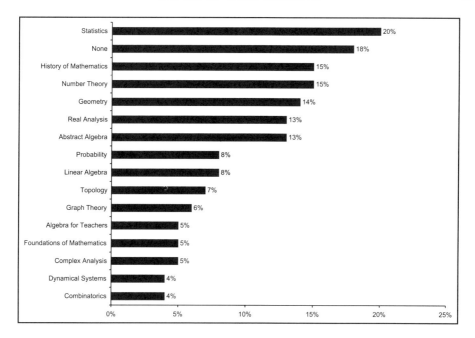

FIGURE 4. Mathematics courses students completed during their doctoral program (N=111)

the majority of students entered their doctoral programs with a limited, if any, knowledge of geometry at the collegiate level, and fewer (14%) were completing a graduate-level geometry course (see Figure 4).

Students were asked what level of mathematics course work they would obtain upon finishing their program. Figure 5 displays four different levels of mathematics course work. About one-half (51%) of the students will have obtained a MA/MS degree in mathematics or higher and only 15% of students will graduate with less than a BA/BS degree in mathematics. Eight students did not respond to this question, possibly because they are just began their program and were not aware of what mathematics courses they would take.

## Looking Forward

As institutions continue to prepare doctoral students to enter into the field of mathematics education, questions arise, such as: what will these new students bring to the field; what research will these graduates build upon; what new ideas will they develop; and how will these new professionals move the field forward? To address these questions respondents were asked about their current research interests at the as well as what type of job they would be interested in pursuing after graduation.

Current doctoral students in mathematics education are interested in a variety of research interests: student learning (32%), teacher knowledge and learning (23%), curriculum-based topics (21%) and equity (17%). Other research interests noted were elementary-school mathematics, manipulatives, professional development, and

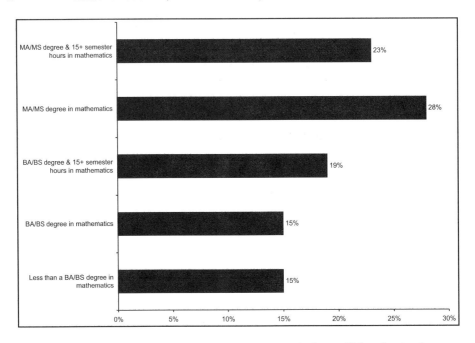

FIGURE 5. Level of mathematics course work that will be obtained
when doctoral students graduate (N= 103)

technology. Although these categories are quite broad, they provide some indicators
of current research areas of interest.

Respondents were asked to select the top two jobs they planned to pursue after
graduating. Figure 6 displays the responses. The majority of students plan to take
a job in higher education at doctoral (63%), master's level (42%), or bachelor's level
(24%) institutions, while few students plan to go into the K-12 system. Other job
possibilities noted by doctoral students were: educational policy, return to current
teaching positions, postdoc positions, and enter K-12 classroom teaching to gain
experience prior to accepting a position in higher education.

Finally, students were asked to identify if they were interested in obtaining a job
in a specific geographical region. Figure 7 displays the results with the majority of
those that have a preference being in the northeast region of the US. Ten percent of
respondents plan to work internationally. Of this 10%, five of the students are from
other countries and are planning to return to their home, while six other students
were looking at international jobs as a possibility.

## Strengths and Weaknesses of Doctoral Programs

As each institution evaluates its doctoral program in mathematics education it
may be of help to understand what current doctoral students believe are strengths
and weaknesses of their respective programs. Respondents were asked in open
ended questions to identify aspects of their program that were the strongest and
weakest. These responses were divided into two groups: the first group came from

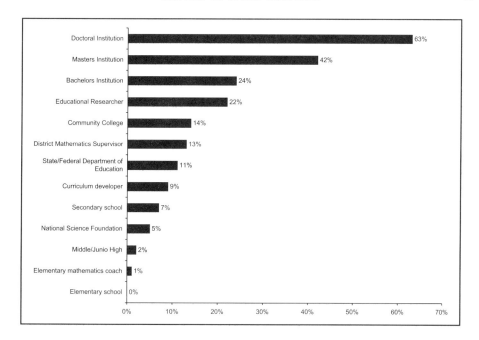

FIGURE 6. Job opportunities likely to be pursued after graduation (N=111)

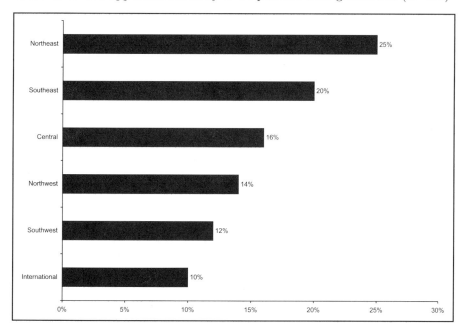

FIGURE 7. Geographical location doctoral students are interested in obtaining a job

TABLE 3. Top strengths of individual doctoral programs

| Strengths | Percent of students from larger doctoral programs (N=44) | Percent of students from smaller doctoral programs (N=67) |
|---|---|---|
| Faculty members | 36 | 40 |
| Being involved in research projects | 34 | 28 |
| Community of doctoral students | 14 | 4 |
| Course requirements and sequencing | 11 | 18 |
| Individualized programs | 7 | 9 |
| Balance between Mathematics and Mathematics Education courses | 5 | 7 |
| Many opportunities (conferences, manuscript writing, projects) | 2 | 7 |

doctoral students in programs ranking in the top twenty-five for number of mathematics education doctorates awarded during the years 1990-2005 (Reys, et al., this volume) and the second group came from doctoral students in a historically smaller program. The first group included 44 responses representing doctoral students at 18 different institutions and the second group included 67 responses representing 33 different institutions. Students provided multiple strengths of their doctoral program; however Table 3 reports only the seven most frequently cited strengths. Table 3 summarizes the top strengths across the two groups of doctoral programs. Collaboration with highly qualified and productive faculty members was a positive aspect of programs for both groups of doctoral students. The second most cited strength in both groups was the opportunity to be involved in research projects. In addition, students from the first group felt that the cohort of doctoral students at their institution was a strength; whereas, the other group of doctoral students felt their course requirements were a strength for their programs.

In a similar manner Table 4 provides a list of the six most frequently noted program weaknesses. The most frequently cited weakness for both groups was lack of coursework in mathematics, mathematics education, research (both general and specific to mathematics education), and other areas. Students in the first group expressed a need for more mentoring in writing skills for grant proposals and the dissertation process. These students also expressed the concern that there was a lack of communication between faculty and students, which, often led to a mismatch of expectations between individual faculty members and students. Eighteen percent of the students from smaller programs responded that a lack of resources, faculty or faculty expertise in specific areas were weaknesses of their programs. Thirteen

TABLE 4. Weaknesses of individual doctoral programs

| Weaknesses | Percent of students from larger doctoral programs (N=44) | Percent of students from smaller doctoral programs (N=67) |
|---|---|---|
| Course work available | 23 | 30 |
| Mentoring | 14 | 3 |
| Communication | 14 | 9 |
| Lack of resources and faculty | 14 | 18 |
| Opportunities to work on a research project | 11 | 13 |
| Lack of funding | 2 | 6 |

percent of students from both groups desired to have more experience working with faculty members on research projects before they began their dissertation or graduated.

This survey provides data directly from doctoral students. It is only a snapshot, and it only reflects information gathered from 50 institutions. However, it provides information that our mathematics education community may use as we work toward the never-ending task of improving doctoral programs in mathematics education.

*Dawn Teuscher*
*Arizona State University Polytechnic Campus*
*Tempe, AZ 85287*
*dawn.teuscher@asu.edu*

*Nevels Nevels*
*University of Missouri*
*Columbia, MO 65211*
*nnnc4f@mizzou.edu*

*Catherine Ulrich*
*University of Georgia*
*Athens, GA 30602*
*culrich@uga.edu*

# Part 2

# Developing Stewards
# of the Discipline: Core Elements

CBMS Issues in Mathematics Education
Volume 15, 2008

# Creating a Broader Vision of Doctoral Education: Lessons from the Carnegie Initiative on the Doctorate

## Chris M. Golde

The Carnegie Initiative on the Doctorate was born of the recognition that the world of doctoral education is changing. Two decades of research and reports have identified a number of stress points, some of which have been under discussion for a good deal longer than that.[1] Among the challenges are: high rates of attrition, ever lengthening time to degree, changing student demographics and related challenges in diversifying the graduate student population, knowledge structures that are becoming simultaneously more interdisciplinary and more global, diversifying career paths and escalating career demands, and changing funding structures and university organizations. These are of concern to those in all fields, including mathematics education. In the face of all of these challenges, a stance of complacency is dangerous.

Many of these reports provided recommendations and exhorted disciplinary communities and university departments to put them into practice. Too often, it seems these reports simply ended up collecting dust on administrator's shelves. The Carnegie Foundation for the Advancement of Teaching wished to put these ideas into action, and so the Carnegie Initiative on the Doctorate (CID) was born. With funding from the Atlantic Philanthropies, the CID was a five-year action and research project (2001-2005), the goal of which was for departments to carefully examine their doctoral programs and make changes they deemed appropriate.[2] One of the organizing principles of the initiative was to focus only on a small number of disciplines (chemistry, education, English, history, mathematics, and neuroscience) in order to understand them well, recognize and respond to disciplinary uniqueness, and have an impact within the field.

Instead of detailing the project further, or focusing on the many examples of interesting work undertaken by the participating departments (both topics reported in detail in *The Formation of Scholars: Rethinking Doctoral Education for the 21st*

---

[1]Among those particularly germane to mathematics educators are Board on Mathematical Sciences, 1990; Board on Mathematical Sciences of the National Research Council, 1992; Committee on Science Engineering and Public Policy, 1995; Ewing, 1999; National Research Council, 1984; Odom, 1998; Reys & Kilpatrick, 2001.

[2]The CID leadership team at the Carnegie Foundation included, in addition to the author, project director George Walker, senior scholar Laura Jones, and research scholar Andrea Conklin Bueschel. Many of the ideas in this paper come directly from the work of the CID and reflect the contributions of the entire team.

*Century* (Walker, Golde, Jones, Bueschel, & Hutchings, 2008), in this talk I want to focus on the legacy of ideas from the CID. Although the focus was on disciplines and departments, one of the most important outcomes of the project was learning how common the challenges actually are. Several of the most important legacies of the project are important ideas that seem to have traction and resonance in all of the disciplines.

## Stewardship

One of the framing ideas of the CID was that the purpose of doctoral education is to prepare "stewards of the discipline." By this we mean that every recipient of the Ph.D. should be someone who generates knowledge, conserves knowledge, and transforms that knowledge by teaching in the broadest sense of the word. The word stewardship was deliberately chosen for its intellectual and ethical overtones. A steward of the discipline is entrusted with the future of the discipline by those in the discipline. The phrase "steward of the discipline" does not resonate with all listeners, but it is an idea that has provoked debate about the purpose of doctoral education – whether or not it is the preparation of stewards.

The notion of stewardship is explored in greater depth in the first book that emerged from the Carnegie project. *Envisioning the Future of Doctoral Education: Preparing Stewards of the Discipline* (Golde & Walker, 2006) includes a chapter discussing the ideas of stewardship (Golde, 2006) followed by essays commissioned for the project written by leading scholars in each of the six participating disciplines.[3] Each of the authors analyzes the way in which current practices fall short and provides suggestions for rethinking doctoral education to better prepare stewards of the discipline.

## Intellectual Community

We fully expected the departments to focus on new ways to think about the dissertation, the qualifying exam, practices of advising and mentoring, and for incorporating new directions for the disciplines and interdisciplinary advances into the curriculum. We did not anticipate the importance that intellectual community would come to have in the project's work. CID faculty and students seized on intellectual community as an important framing concept.

A healthy intellectual community is vital for the core work of doctoral education, building knowledge. Intellectual communities can and should be deliberately designed and shaped. This should not be an afterthought, but rather an integral consideration in any aspect of departmental life. I suspect that most of you have been in a department where you say *"That* is an exciting intellectual community." Think about that department: what made you say that? These are features worth paying attention to and possibly emulating.

Certainly, intellectual community as an organizing principle for doctoral programs and doctoral education is not a new idea. "The extent to which the department is seen as a social network of relationships as well as a professional, discipline-oriented, community of scholars" was identified by the mid-1970s an important dimension of the departmental environment that can positively or negatively affect the nature and quality of the graduate student experience (Hartnett, 1976, 71).

---

[3]There are two addressing the field of education (Berliner, 2006; Richardson, 2006) and two written by mathematicians (Bass, 2006; Chan, 2006).

Precisely because healthy intellectual communities have long been recognized as crucial to doctoral education, today we must carefully consider their defining characteristics. Following are five mutually reinforcing features that emerge and suggestions for how to promote them.

**Purposeful and Knowledge-Centered.** A department that is a vital intellectual community embraces the shared purpose that the department exists in the service of the creation and transmission of knowledge. The department shares more than an agenda for how to operate; there is a community-wide commitment to help students develop into the best scholars possible so that they, in turn, may contribute to the growth and creation of knowledge.

Intellectual community is visible. People can be seen having hallway conversations. There are conference poster presentations on the wall. It is enacted on a daily basis in seminars that encourage respectful habits of debate, or labs where all members are invited to critique a hypothesis or argue about the significance of new data. By debating the ideas that shape our disciplines, we both solidify what we value and move beyond what is no longer relevant. These exchanges bring vitality and energy to a community.

**Broadly Inclusive.** An intellectual community should be broadly inclusive and diverse along several dimensions of difference. It must include people of broadly different experiences and backgrounds. Likewise it must be welcoming of different points of view. Departments that deliberately seek out a wide representation of backgrounds in their students and faculty are more likely to ensure a broad range of intellectual perspectives. Far from requiring agreement on everything, true intellectual exchange must include a wide range of opinions that can challenge and inform thinking. In addition, a vibrant intellectual community is multigenerational. It includes graduate students, postdoctoral fellows, and faculty. This raises the important question of how junior members are brought into the community. Students can play important roles and learn about contributing to the disciplinary community throughout their careers by serving on committees, hosting outside scholars, and planning events.

**Flexible and Forgiving.** The most productive intellectual community is one that provides opportunities for experimentation and risk taking. Learning, after all, means making mistakes and testing inchoate ideas. It is important for every member of the community to recognize that it is not only acceptable, but necessary, to make mistakes and learn from them. Every scholar must learn how to learn from failure.

**Respectful and Generous.** An intellectual community and an academic department should support interaction rather than isolation. Clearly communities are strengthened by close personal relationships, and the general atmosphere ought to be civil, respectful, and generous. Members of a vibrant intellectual community are generous with their time, ideas, and feedback. Generosity derives from the assumption that all members of the community ought to be helped to succeed, and, indeed, that other community members bear a measure of responsibility for helping foster that success.

**Deliberately Tended.** Like all highly functioning workplaces, these communities must be created, nurtured, fostered, and tended. Active participation in collegial intellectual activities must become routine: well-attended seminars, journal clubs, job talks, alumni panels. Social components are the lubricant: coffee machines, kitchens, places where students (especially those who do not have on-campus offices) can connect with others and keep in touch with the activities of the department. Events that are academic should also include unstructured time that allow people to connect at a more individual, one-on-one level.

## The Challenge of Preparing Researchers

A third theme running through the work of the CID departments was the necessity of thinking hard (and it is very hard work) about the preparation of researchers. Most reports start with the assertion that the US leads the world in doctoral education. The prevailing assumption is that doctoral programs are highly effective at preparing researchers and scholars, however much they may fall short in preparing students to teach, or develop capacity to actively engage a full range of professional roles and responsibilities. And yet, by the conclusion of the CID, it became clear that this assumption deserves to be critically probed and perhaps challenged.

We found evidence that research preparation is falling short. The evidence was not definitive, but it was indicative. We conducted surveys of faculty and graduate students. Table 1 shows data about how proficient students are perceived to be as researchers by the end of their doctoral studies. The data suggest that most students reach acceptably high levels of proficiency. Nevertheless, we are troubled by the relatively large group (perhaps as much as a quarter) that may not. Likewise, discussions at the CID convening among faculty and students revealed that those in fields as seemingly different as mathematics, English, and neuroscience all struggle with questions of how to foster creative thinking, how to keep students' passion alive, or how to teach the ability to ask a good research question.

These data suggest that the central tasks and assignments that doctoral students encounter may not be as effective as they could be. Perhaps this is because they have gone pretty much unchanged from generation to generation. In many cases, they are inherited practices and emulation of that which went before. "What worked well for me probably works well for my students," is a common approach. These strategies may work well for some students but poorly for others. One problem that results from assuming that prior practices continue to serve is that the underlying theory of how to prepare researchers goes unspoken. Indeed it may not even be clearly understood.

We began to use the term "pedagogy of research" to describe the theory and practice of developing researchers. I argue that there are several prevalent theories, although they are largely implicit.

*The osmosis theory.* Students learn by reading good research and being near faculty who are doing high-quality research. Then they absorb what they need to know.

*The sink or swim theory.* Students are thrown into their initial teaching experience—or research assignment—and thrash their way to completion of the assignment with little guidance. Those who succeed may know something about

TABLE 1. Perceived Research Proficiency of Students at End of Program

| Rating of doctoral students by Faculty | High proficiency | Low-mid proficiency | Unable | Don't know /NA |
|---|---|---|---|---|
| Ask a good research question | 76% | 16% | 0% | 9% |
| Independently analyze and interpret data (or text) | 76 | 14 | 0 | 10 |
| Proficiently employ research techniques | 81 | 10 | 0 | 9 |
| **Self-rating by doctoral students at dissertation stage** | **High proficiency** | **Low-mid proficiency** | **Not at all** | |
| I can design AND carry out research of my own devising | 75 | 24 | 1 | |
| I can generate interesting questions worth investigating | 78 | 21 | 1 | |

swimming by virtue of their prior undergraduate or master's studies or by coming from academic families.

*The talented-students-will-self-discover theory.* Capable students will figure out everything that they need to know and go get it. Doctoral programs get out of the way of students' self-development. Those without the internal resources, the skills, or self-confidence to learn what they need are likely to abandon the process.

*The high-pressure crucible theory.* A doctoral program is a high-pressure crucible that proceeds as a set of high-stakes tests and hurdles. Throughout the process the stakes are high, and students are expected to perform at a very high level. Surviving the tests makes them stronger. Those who are less capable are weeded out.

These are all very Darwinian approaches. A cogent critique was offered by Ronald G. Douglas, then Executive Vice President and Provost at Texas A&M University, at a Workshop on Actions for the Mathematical Sciences sponsored by the National Academy of Sciences. "For people who view the profession as a kind of priesthood, is appealing to reduce numbers by keeping out all but the most worthy. However, there might be several negative consequences to such an approach. First, there would be the terrible human waste of labeling a large group of our most talented people as failures and choking them out. ... Second, while Darwinian selection ... [seems to be] a fair way to choose those who succeed, the playing field is often not as level as many would like to believe. In many cases, it's as though someone taught some of the animals how to use weapons and accepted the outcome of which animals survived as having been dictated by nature" (Board on Mathematical Sciences, 1997, p. 43).

Perhaps the most prevailing organizing principle is the apprenticeship theory. This too has many downsides. For one, it encourages conformity and stunts students' ability to develop independent voice and line of thought. For another, students may be dependent on one faculty advisor who may neglect or exploit the student. When this happens students usually feel they have few avenues of recourse.

## New Vision of Apprenticeship

Despite these shortcomings, we argue that apprenticeship *does* have a place. As a result of the Carnegie Initiative on the Doctorate, we want to re-appropriate the term "apprenticeship". The critical move is to shift from seeing students as apprenticed *to* masters, to recognizing that they are apprenticed *with* several mentors. Such apprenticeship relationships are reciprocal relationships in the service of learning. The Darwinian models described earlier do little to actively promote learning or take a deliberate guiding hand in the formation of scholars. The cognitive sciences have shown us that most people learn more and develop further in a more purposefully constructed environment (Bransford, Brown, & Cocking, 2000). In this framing, apprenticeship is a pedagogical theory based on learning theory.

How does this work? It is not unlike craft apprenticeship. As expert practitioners, the masters or faculty mentors must understand and explain the constituent parts of expert practice and demonstrate how the parts fit together in a whole. Mentors devise assignments so that students can practice components in low stakes, carefully designed situations. These might be simulations (defending a grant proposal to a mock panel review), or problems with known solutions (as is done in mathematics), or well designed small components of a larger work (a course on scholarly publication or dissertation proposal writing).

The student engages in repetitive practice with coaching and feedback. By sequencing tasks and using scaffolding appropriately, students are guided to the expert performance, transferring their knowledge and understanding to increasingly diverse settings. Mentors must provide many opportunities for the novice to practice the skill being developed. With repetition and success, students move from simple to complex tasks, from low to high risk situations, and to settings of increased ambiguity in which they must exert independent thinking and decision-making.

As support is removed, the mentor fades, and the student takes increased responsibility. Students are encouraged to reflect on what they are learning and to compare their work with that of experts. They are expected to develop a schema for their own expertise.

This model expects much of faculty and students, and will require many people to behave quite differently than they are currently accustomed to. Mentors must:

- be expert;
- understand their expertise well enough to be able to model the whole;
- break the whole apart into constituent components;
- develop strategies for teaching the pieces;
- help students integrate them back into the whole;
- know when to offer guidance, and when to let students try and fail;

- have an internal model of the typical apprentice's development over time;
- have experience with the kinds of scaffolding and coaching that will move students along the trajectory towards expertise, independence and inter-dependence; and
- customize learning experiences for each student, whom they know well.

Students for their part must:

- adapt to a new way to learn, especially unfamiliar in the context of formal schooling;
- practice, practice, practice (research as craft);
- take active responsibility for their own learning;
- reflect on what they have done;
- develop models and patterns;
- generalize to other contexts; and
- take risks and be willing to fail.

This vision of apprenticeship learning has four other characteristics that are important to note.

**Multiple Relationships.** Vital to this rich vision is multiple mentoring re-lationships for every student. There are too many arenas for development for one super-mentor to serve each student. This is especially true with increased inter-disciplinary studies and research projects, which is particularly relevant fields like mathematics education. As with other aspects of re-envisioned apprenticeship, ex-pecting students to engage in multiple mentoring relationships requires rethinking customary practices. It is important to recognize that not all the mentoring must be provided by faculty members. Students can mentor each other. And groups—courses, research labs, writing groups, cohorts—are important mini-communities for learning.

**Characterized by Respect, Trust and Reciprocity.** Apprenticeship re-lationships are more likely to flourish when they cultivate the qualities of respect, trust and reciprocity. These qualities set the conditions that foster learning. Recall they are characteristics of vibrant intellectual communities.

Mutual respect, which does not require affection for friendship, is necessary. How are the mentor's ideas and feedback incorporated into the student's work in a way that recognizes the teacher's greater experience, but also respects the student's growing intellectual independence? How are the student's ideas given room to grow and develop? Personal respect (which does not presuppose affection or friendship) can build from respect for ideas. Trust grows over time from interactions based on respect.

Such relationships are not power neutral, but reciprocal. Students get training, advice, sponsorship, funding, support, encouragement, feedback. Faculty members get new ideas, infusions of energy and excitement, the satisfaction of seeing students succeed, and intellectual legacy.

**Share, Learn, Improve and Recognize.** In the survey of CID faculty mem-bers, we asked "Is there someone whose advising you try to emulate?" Most re-spondents identified their own primary adviser as a model (38 percent), but the most striking finding was that "no one" was the second most common response (33

percent). We did not ask how many had an "anti-role model," although several survey respondents volunteered that fact. Being a good mentor is not an innate talent,
or a function solely of "chemistry." These are techniques that can be learned. It is
important to create occasions for faculty members to learn about and discuss one
another's advising philosophies and strategies. Opportunities to discuss challenging
moments might be particularly useful. And to continue a positive feedback loop, it
is necessary to make effective mentoring a focus for recognition and reward.

**Collective Responsibility.** A functioning community requires collective responsibility for student success. This requires setting clear expectations regarding
expected progress through the program, a timeline for informally and formally identifying mentors, customary speed of response to draft papers and chapters, and the
like. Holding one another accountable means integrating checking up on students'
progress into daily life. The baseline expectation should be for shared, rather than
abdicated, responsibility. Formally, the department should provide every student
with annual reviews at a minimum. By the same token, it is important to provide
formal and informal safety nets.

## Pedagogy of Research

Even if we accept a version of apprenticeship as the theory for how to best
develop researchers, it leaves many questions unanswered. And these questions
are tremendously fertile arenas for inquiry. The term "pedagogy of research" is
intended to capture the theory and practice of how to prepare researchers. As with
other aspects of the scholarship of teaching and learning, the assumption is that
we can turn our scholarly skills and habits inward to look at how to best prepare
our students. Obviously doing these well shouldn't be a matter of luck. Instead,
developing effective practices can be something tested and investigated. Here you
have a considerable advantage coming from the field of mathematics education.
These are researchable questions quite similar to your own scholarship.

**Examples of Pedagogy of Research Questions.** With little effort it is
possible to generate questions in several categories.

1. Questions about program elements.
   - How should courses be structured, or are courses even the best for-
     mat?
   - Do collaborative dissertations teach students more or less about how
     to conduct research than solo-authored efforts?
2. Questions about effective strategies.
   - When should students learn from observation and carefully constructed
     assignments, and when is it necessary to leap into the thick of things,
     to try, and to risk failure.
   - What kinds of assignments are most effective for helping students
     advance?
3. Questions about achieving desired outcomes.
   - Are there regular opportunities for intellectual risk-taking, creativity,
     or interdisciplinary thinking?

## A Concluding Invitation

I began by describing the CID as a project that invited departments to debate purpose and critically examine existing requirements and practices; to decide what works and should be kept, and what can and should be changed. I will close with an invitation for you to join this movement. Do you subscribe to the vision of the Ph.D. that the purpose of doctoral education is preparing stewards of the discipline? If not, then what is the purpose of your program? Regardless of how you describe the purpose, what specific knowledge, skills, dispositions should Ph.D. recipients exhibit? To other faculty and students in your department agree? What is the underlying theory of developing researchers to which you subscribe? And which practices in your department comport with your theory and yield the results you desire? Which are ripe for investigation and change?

These are big, important, and difficult questions. They deserve the best of your intellect and talent. I submit that you and your students deserve nothing less.

*Chris M. Golde*
*Stanford University*
*Palo Alto, CA 94305*
*golde@stanford.edu*

CBMS Issues in Mathematics Education
Volume 15, 2008

# What Core Knowledge Do Doctoral Students in Mathematics Education Need to Know?

## Joan Ferrini-Mundy

The problem of addressing what knowledge should form the core of the preparation of a doctoral student in mathematics education is challenging. This response addresses three questions:

- What are the purposes of doctoral education more generally?
- What is entailed in the professional practice of mathematics educators?
- What are the relevant current and future contexts and trends in education and policy?

Doctoral study of mathematics education is situated within the broad arena of doctoral preparation in education (and sometimes mathematics), both in the United States and beyond. Mathematics education doctoral programs are located in colleges and universities that sponsor graduate education across a wide spectrum of disciplines and fields of study. Thus the norms, practices, traditions, and pressures in graduate preparation in education generally need to be considered in the discussion of core knowledge for mathematics education doctoral students.

In K-12 education one approach to the planning of curricula and course requirements involves "backward design" (Wiggins & McTighe, 1998), where the goals and outcomes drive the design of the preparation or instructional experience. In mathematics teacher education, the work of Ball, Hill, and Bass (2005) has focused on analyzing the mathematical demands entailed by teaching practice through "close examination of the actual work of teaching elementary school mathematics" (p. 17). Presumably such an approach can lead to considerations about the elements needed in the preparation of mathematics teachers. Similarly, analysis of the practice of mathematics education as enacted by Ph.D.-level participants, even informally, might suggest components for the preparation of doctoral mathematics educators.

Finally, along with other fields of scholarship that are associated with application, mathematics education doctoral program planning and revision should be mindful of the external contexts that affect the field. And, because the field is quite dependent on external funding to continue research and development efforts,

---

This material was based on work supported by the National Science Foundation, while working at the Foundation. Any opinion, finding, and conclusions or recommendations expressed in this material are those of the author and do not necessarily reflect the views of the National Science Foundation.

watching and anticipating trends in practice and policy seems important, even in considering the core knowledge of mathematics educators.

## The Broader View of Doctoral Education

Discussions about the purposes of doctoral education have been reinvigorated by the work of the Carnegie Foundation for the Advancement of Teaching through the Carnegie Initiative on the Doctorate (Golde & Walker, 2006). The perspective of this initiative is that the purpose of doctoral education is "... to educate and prepare those to whom we can entrust the vigor, quality, and integrity of the field... a scholar first and foremost, who will creatively generate new knowledge, critically conserve valuable and useful ideas, and responsibly transform those understandings through writing, teaching, and application... a 'steward of the discipline'..." (Golde, 2006, p. 5). This view of a "steward of the discipline" is interesting to consider in mathematics education, when in fact there is debate about whether our area constitutes a discipline, or a field of study. Stewardship in the case of mathematics education may also involve responsibility for building and shaping the development of the discipline, and for making arguments about the viability and necessity of the field of study.

The matter of how mathematics education compares to other academic disciplines was addressed by Fey (2001). He wrote "... I believe that a professional field like ours is different from traditional academic disciplines. It requires different talents and different kinds of knowledge, and it makes different kinds of contributions to society. Ours is an appropriately eclectic field. It requires advanced study and skills comparable to those in other professional fields that award doctorates, but a narrow focus on research isn't the right thing." (p. 57). Indeed, there is an applied component of mathematics education, and in the view of some, a need for advocacy of particular approaches to improvement and change of mathematics teaching and learning. This may mean that mathematics education has some similarity to areas that address complex practical problems and advance areas of studies through professional schools (e.g., engineering, medicine). In any case, Fey is direct about the view that mathematics education doctoral preparation is about more than research. In contrast, Ball and Forzani (2007) argue that schools and departments of education must make the development of knowledge (from research) in education their "primary reason for being", and to "embrace unapologetically the worlds of both practice and scholarship." (p. 537).

Another contemporary perspective on the evolving nature of doctoral education is provided in the National Science Foundation's solicitation for the Integrative Graduate Education and Research Traineeship Program (IGERT) (NSF, 2007). The IGERT program is designed to provide funding to universities for interdisciplinary programs to prepare "... U.S. Ph.D. scientists and engineers who will pursue careers in research and education, with the interdisciplinary backgrounds, deep knowledge in chosen disciplines, and technical, professional, and personal skills to become, in their own careers, leaders and creative agents for change... [who will] understand and integrate scientific, technical, business, social, ethical, and policy issues to confront the challenging issues of the future..." (http://www.nsf.gov/pubs/2007/nsf07540/nsf07540.htm.) This view of doctoral education implies an even more ambitious sense than the "steward of the discipline" view. It emphasizes leadership and serving as a change agent. Richardson, in her essay for the Carnegie Initiative on the Doctorate (Richardson, 2006), helps by reminding us that education is both a field of study and an enterprise. She argues that "stewards of education have duties related to communicating and engaging in decisions concerning the practice of education... they communicate normative as well as epistemic theory, research, and analyses to very different audiences so that decisions about the enterprise are made within strong analytical and morally defensible frameworks." (p. 254), and that the preparation of such scholars requires formal knowledge, practical knowledge, and beliefs and misconceptions, along with a willingness to be self-critical and possibly change one's own beliefs. This may be closer to a view expressed by the Council of Graduate Schools (CGS), who also emphasizes an application component when they claim that doctoral education should prepare students "to be scholars capable of discovering, integrating, and applying knowledge." (CGS 1990, cited in NSF 2006). More recent formulations (e.g., the mission statement of the Council of Graduate Schools (2007), which says "ensure the vitality of intellectual discovery and to promote an environment that cultivates rigorous scholarship") also raise the issue of rigor in scholarship.

The duality that Richardson highlights presents an interesting challenge in doctoral preparation in mathematics education. People electing to pursue PhDs in mathematics education often have substantial experience as teachers of mathematics, or in other applied areas such as curriculum development or teacher professional development, and are familiar with education as an enterprise. Doctoral education faces an interesting challenge: to simultaneously build on such experiences while at the same time developing the objective, scholarly side of the practitioner (capable of cultivating rigorous scholarship, as CGS maintains). Richardson notes that it "is also important to help students who have spent considerable time in schools as teachers or administrators to learn how to move to a different level of analytic scholarship than the experiential level with which they enter the program." (p. 266). Wilson (2003) reflects on this in his own experience: "My years at Stanford were a time for tearing down and rebuilding my ideas of mathematics education... I think all of us were learning something more fundamental: to be able to adapt high quality mathematics education practices to whatever context we found." (p. 1793-94). How should mathematics education doctoral programs be structured to celebrate our students' experiences and idealistic hopes, and at the same time build their growth as scholars who can be objective in the questions they ask and the interpretation of the evidence they gather?

The multiple views of doctoral preparation –to prepare stewards of the discipline, leaders, change agents, and scholars who can do rigorous work and make groundbreaking discoveries - may even conflict in some ways. Mathematics education doctoral programs face challenges in deciding which of these many facets they wish to feature and promote, and then build programs accordingly.

## The Professional Practice of Doctoral Mathematics Educators

Some of the most potentially helpful work underway in mathematics education, in my view, examines the nature of the professional practice of particular groups and then maps backward, or infers from the apparent demands of that practice, the nature of the preparation that might be needed. This approach has limitations, of course; there is inference about what knowledge, skills, and dispositions are needed, and in what combinations, to be effective in complex practices. And, given the dynamic nature of education, the demands and nature of practice by professional mathematics educators with doctoral preparation are varied. It might be reasonable to undertake systematic research to better understand the practice of mathematics education as conducted by professionals prepared with doctoral degrees.

The analysis that follows is in no way formal, rigorous, or based in the literature; it is designed for a talk and thus should be seen with all of the appropriate caveats. I propose that the professional practice of doctoral mathematics educators includes: research, teaching, service, curriculum design, and teacher education, practiced in a variety of institutions. Mathematics educators work in higher education (doctoral, masters, bachelors and community colleges), K-12 schools and districts, government (state and federal), business and industry (training, publishing, assessment), research and development think tanks, consulting firms, and curriculum development and teacher professional development firms. The practice for some mathematics educators might include interpreting and responding to inquiries from the press (Richardson, 2006). Coincident with the conference for which this talk was prepared, the report "Important, But Not for Me: Parents and Students in Kansas and Missouri Talk about Math, Science, and Technology Educatio"" (Public Agenda, 2007) was released. The study found that, although parents and students evidently will acknowledge the importance of mathematics, science, and technology in general, they do not see these areas as being important for themselves. What helps prepare a professional mathematics educator to be ready to discuss the implications of this with local school district leaders, or with teachers, or their own students?

A team of researchers at Michigan State University undertook a project called "Developing Leadership for Mathematics and Science Education"[1] , a retrospective study of leaders in mathematics and science education that examined their characteristics and what led to their leadership and influence. The theoretical model that guided the study was drawn from literature on leadership, and is shown in Figure 1.

In this interview study of 71 leaders, we found their early experiences were pivotal in their pursuit and eventual success in mathematics and science education. They often cited very early interest, the influence of a parent or a teacher, and a strong commitment to change and improvement. Within doctoral study they noted the importance of their mentors, apprenticeships in research and teaching, and the connections they established with faculty, students, and leaders in the field as the most important influences. Few mentioned their formal coursework as having been essential. Through descriptions of their participation in significant career episodes, our analyses indicated that the following knowledge skills and dispositions recurred among these leaders. They displayed clear vision and commitment to long-term goals; there was an element of good citizenship, where leaders would undertake leadership roles because they were asked and felt a level of responsibility. They noted the importance of good interpersonal skills, ability to collaborate, readiness to learn new ideas, and having a focus on results. The leaders highlighted the importance of being willing to take risks and be flexible, and the need to be able to deal with controversy. A majority indicated that they had not started their careers with expectations of being leaders, but that they did have a vision for improvement

----

[1]PI Jim Gallagher; other senior staff included Robert Floden, Joan Ferrini-Mundy, Charles Anderson. This project was funded through NSF ESIE award number 010110.

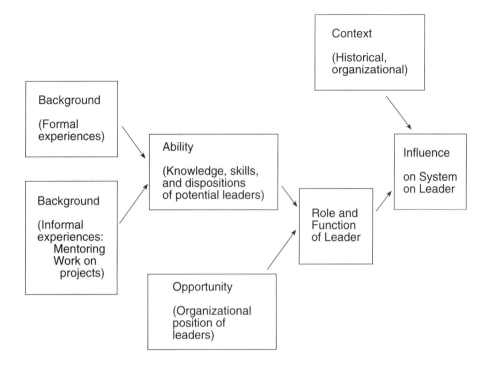

FIGURE 1. Leadership Development Model

and a belief they could make a difference. During the interviews leaders also were asked to report on sources of opportunity. They talked about serendipity (being in the right place at the right time with the right people), and about getting engaged with mentors and professors who were current leaders. We did not find any single clear pathway that led to leadership; their experiences and backgrounds were varied. For most, however, they had an early experience that brought them visibility where their potential could be recognized. They mentioned that NSF summer institutes were important, and that participation in funded projects helped them select graduate programs and provide opportunity to work with their mentors and connect to others in the field.

## Contexts and Trends

It seems important to place mathematics education doctoral preparation in context. Data in the NSF report US Doctorates in the 20th Century (2006) highlight how small a fraction of the full field of doctoral recipients is comprised by mathematics education. Between 1920 and 1999 there were 1.3 million PhDs awarded in the U.S., with about 800 thousand of these in science and engineering. There were 256,014 PhDs awarded over this period in education, and 3,084 in mathematics education.

The problem of capacity in mathematics education has been reported by Reys (2000). The NSF's Centers for Learning and Teaching (2000-2005) program was a recent effort to help boost capacity in the field, and its goals included offering "graduate students the broad range of knowledge, skills, and tools they will need to become leaders in the field." (CLTNet, 2006, p. iii). Fourteen centers were funded,

and as of May 2006 nearly 60 new graduate courses had been established and
support had been provided for more than 300 doctoral students (CLTNet, 2006, pp.
1, 23). The impact of such programs on both the national capacity in mathematics
education, and ultimately on the ability to make progress on significant problems,
remains to be seen. However, the knowledge and experience gained from such
programs could be potentially useful in the ongoing formation and improvement of
doctoral programs in mathematics education.

Other trends in the current context are worth noting as well. There is a convergence, due in part to federal policies and activities, on the importance of educational
research that can demonstrate effectiveness through causal claims. For instance,
the new Society for Research on Educational Effectiveness has been formed to "advance and disseminate research on the causal effects of education interventions,
practices, programs, and policies. To increase the capacity to design and conduct
investigations that have a strong base for causal inference"
(http://www.educationaleffectiveness.org/). Analyses of whether graduate education in mathematics education is preparing students who have both the mathematics education knowledge and the research design and analysis knowledge, as
well as the inclinations to study questions of effectiveness, are needed. At the
National Science Foundation, emphases on the integration of research and education, potentially transformative research, innovation, and rigorous research are
major focal topics. The public is far more engaged in issues of mathematics teaching and curriculum today, and the work of the National Math Advisory Panel,
(http://www.ed.gov/about/bdscomm/list/mathpanel/index.html) will likely influence that discussion further. There are issues involving heightened accountability,
local and national policy debates, focus on mathematics learning across the lifespan
and in all settings, globalization, and workforce issues that need to be addressed.
Are doctoral programs in mathematics education keeping pace with these issues,
or better yet, anticipating them? Are we preparing generations of scholars who
will be motivated to play a proactive role in these arenas of communication and
educational practice?

## Finally, Core Knowledge for Doctoral Mathematics Education

With all of this as backdrop I now will address the actual topic of my talk; what
should be the core knowledge for doctoral mathematics education? Reys, Glasgow,
Teuscher & Nevels, (2007) have provided very useful descriptive information about
the status quo. Their data suggest that more than 90% of programs require courses
in quantitative research methods, mathematics education, and qualitative research
methods. Mathematics content, educational foundations, cognitive psychology, and
educational policy are required in some programs. We see from the same survey that
the two program areas of greatest emphasis are research in mathematics education
and research methods (both quantitative and qualitative). So it appears that there
is consistency at a rather general level about what is offered as core in doctoral
programs.

There also have been many lists provided from various sources about the potential emphasis areas for doctoral education. For instance, the Association of

Mathematics Teacher Educators, in its *Principles to Guide the Design and Implementation of Doctoral Programs in Mathematics Education* (2003) specifies the following areas: mathematics content, research, educational contexts, learning, teaching and teacher education, technology, and curriculum and assessment. Fey (2001) at an earlier conference on doctoral programs in mathematics education, offered a different list: mathematics and its applications; how people learn; experience as a teacher; broader educational and social context; teacher candidates, in-service teachers, and schools, research basis for practices; and scholarly skills to contribute to the improvement of mathematics education. And, at the current conference, the areas are defined by the organization of the program as mathematics, curriculum, policy, teaching, diversity, and technology. When Richardson (2006) provided categories, she used a broader frame: formal knowledge, practical knowledge, and beliefs and misconceptions. It might also be helpful to look at the view from educational psychology, provided by Berliner (2006) in his essay for the Carnegie Initiative on the Doctorate, given the proximity of many of the research questions in mathematics education to this field, and the reliance on similar research approaches. Berliner called for a rethinking of the methods course, as well as consideration of the rationale behind whatever "big idea" would be presented. He highlights the need to "introduce doctoral students to the sites where students live and learn" (p. 279), presumably to encourage classroom-based studies and awareness of the real questions that practitioners face. He also notes the importance of providing research internships in complex environments and the need to develop an understanding of educational policy. Both suggestions seem applicable in the preparation of mathematics education doctoral students also.

To address the matter of core knowledge, in addition to considering the various categories of emphasis that have been proposed, it seems reasonable to consider the context of an institution and a program as well. First, the institutional capacity of the university that houses the program needs to be considered. Faculty and program leaders might ask themselves such questions as:

- What is the nature of your intellectual community?
- What is your institutional capacity to mentor well?
- What are your potential hiring plans or faculty demographic shifts in the faculty over the next 5-10 years?
- What resources and allies does the program have outside of the cohort of mathematics educators involved and the sponsoring department?

Addressing the first question frankly is essential, I believe. Unless a program is very large and has a faculty with quite diverse strengths and interests, it seems reasonable to design a program that has some consistency with the traditions of faculty interest and expertise, which could vary from basic, fundamental research in mathematics learning, to design and development of instructional materials, to the practice of mathematics teacher education, or to the improvement of undergraduate mathematics teaching and learning. Similarly, in an institution with a nationally and internationally active faculty who have major research programs, consideration must be given to the commitment and availability of the faculty for providing sustained mentoring and advising time for students in deciding on the nature of the program and the size. If the plans of the university include growing the mathematics education faculty in coming years then the design and refinement of the program should consider how that might enable the program to grow. And finally, given

that mathematics education is interdisciplinary, access to and strong relationships
with faculty members and resources in mathematics, education, philosophy, psychology, sociology, cognitive science, and other fields within the university should
have bearing on program elements.

There are additional questions a program might contemplate, such as:

- How dynamic and responsive to changing context do you want your program to be?
- Is the program trying to prepare a particular type of scholar?
- Where is the program on the stewardship-discovery-leadership-application
  terrain?

And finally, questions of the history and genesis of the program can be addressed,
especially as new faculty join:

- What kind of students are attracted to your program?
- Does the program have a large contingent of international students?
- What do you know about the career pathways of the graduates of the
  program?
- Can you describe the portfolio of dissertations that the program has pro-
  duced?

Levine, in his 2007 report on graduate programs in education, pursued the
question of whether "current preparation programs have the capacity to equip researchers with the skills and knowledge necessary to carry out research that will
strengthen education policy, improve practice, or advance our understanding of how
humans develop and learn?" (p. 15.) The template that Levine and colleagues used
for judging graduate programs had the following dimensions: purpose, curricular
coherence, curricular balance, faculty composition, admissions, graduation and degree standards, research, finances, and assessment. (pp. 15-16). This template
offers additions ideas for self-examination questions.

## Conclusion: Comments on Core Knowledge

If pressed to name some core of knowledge that I believe is essential in the doctoral preparation of mathematics educators, I would call for focus on mathematics,
on learning, and on research , with some of the preparation to occur in the inter-
sections of these areas. I believe that to study questions of mathematics teaching
and learning, having as part of one's graduate preparation the experience of doing
mathematics at a level close to what research mathematicians experience is useful;
it provides a sense of the span of the discipline that gives perspective in the study
of teaching and learning questions. And, a focus on what is known about learning
- generally, and in mathematics in particular, including emphasis on the continuing
dynamic nature of this area, will serve doctoral students well. Finally, a focus on
research: its purposes, its methodologies and designs, and its interpretations, in
education generally, and in mathematics education in particular. Within research
I include specific and deep focus on research design and methodology, particularly
the importance of a strong understanding of statistical experimental design and
quantitative approaches as they can be applied to pressing research questions in
mathematics education, along with qualitative methodologies, including analytic
approaches.

However, I believe also that a doctoral program should be dynamic, responsive to context, and forward looking in the preparation experiences it offers its students. So, I would expand the core to include a dynamic, context and contemporary-issue-based "core plus", to include focus on the following: resources for learning (e.g., instructional materials, technologies, tools); contexts (e.g., public response, international comparisons); diversity and equity (e.g., understanding of changing demographics in schools and universities, theory and research on reaching all students in mathematics); ethics (e.g., issues in human subjects research, advocacy and objectivity, research sponsorship); teacher education (e.g., research, theory, practice); teaching (e.g., research, theory, practice); policy (e.g. federal, state, and local); technology (e.g. new opportunities for mathematics learning); and international issues (e.g., assessments, educational practices).

Mathematics education is a complex, challenging and rewarding field for study and practice. I appreciate the opportunity to reflect and comment on the most critical processes of preparing the next generations of doctoral scholars in mathematics education.

*Joan Ferrini-Mundy*
*National Science Foundation*
*Arlington, VA 22230*
*jferrini@nsf.gov*

Breakout Sessions

CBMS Issues in Mathematics Education
Volume **15**, 2008

# The Mathematical Education of Doctorates in Mathematics Education

## Daniel Chazan and W. James Lewis

This paper focuses on mathematics that doctorates in mathematics education need to know. To frame the discussion, we asked participants to respond to these questions:

- What mathematics should doctorates in mathematics education know?
- How can we design, tailor and focus mathematics courses to ensure that doctoral students in mathematics education have this knowledge?
- What are some existence proofs where this is done well and can these examples be transported to other institutions?

While this first question is closely related to discussion at the first National Conference on Doctoral Programs in Mathematics Education (1999), the second and third questions are stimulated by several "Centers for Learning and Teaching" funded by the National Science Foundation that have provided opportunities for exploration of specially created experiences and courses. This development is a new one on the landscape and deserves attention.

The questions one might tackle related to doctoral programs in mathematics education are complicated because there is no clear definition as to what constitutes a doctoral program in mathematics education. Among those questions are: What constitutes a doctorate in mathematics education? Who pursues a doctorate in mathematics education? Why is a doctorate in mathematics education being pursued?

The paper, *Doctoral Production in Mathematics Education in the United States: 1960-2005*, (Reys, Glasgow, Teuscher & Nevels, this volume) reports data published by the National Opinion Research Center (NORC). NORC collects self-reported data provided by students at the time they earn a doctorate. Since 1960, 3599 doctorates identified their degree as being in mathematics education. A total of 167 institutions were credited with producing at least one doctorate in mathematics education, but over half produced 5 or fewer such doctorates. One-third of the institutions awarded their first doctorate in mathematics education since 1990.

Despite the large number of institutions credited with at least one doctorate in mathematics education, 15 institutions have awarded over 50% of the degrees and 40 institutions have awarded over 81% of the degrees. Twenty-three of these "top 40" universities have posted data about their mathematics education program on the Association of Mathematics Teacher Educators (AMTE) web site, www.amte.net.

Most of these programs award the mathematics education doctorate in a College of Education, while in four cases the degree is awarded by a Department of Mathematics within a College of Arts and Sciences. Of those institutions where the degree is awarded by the College of Education, most degrees are awarded by a department that generally fits the description of a Curriculum and Instruction Department. In only five cases is the degree awarded by a department focused on mathematics and science education. In a few institutions, more than one department awards the mathematics education doctorate.

Most mathematics education doctorates are awarded by a department with a broader mission than just mathematics education. Therefore the data reported by Reys et al. (this volume) is almost certainly an undercount as many new doctorates may report their degree as being in curriculum and instruction, elementary education, mathematics, or some other area. However, even if one takes into account that these data represent an undercount, most doctoral programs in mathematics education are small. While the three largest doctoral programs have awarded, on average, about 6 doctorates per year over the last decade and a half, the rest of the "top 10" awarded only about 2.5 doctorates per year and the next thirty departments awarded, on average, one doctorate per year.

Another perspective on the size of doctoral programs in mathematics education can be obtained by looking at data on the AMTE web site. Again, setting aside the three largest programs, the average size of doctoral programs in mathematics education among the 40 most productive universities is 13 full time students and 5 part time students. Of course, the remaining programs would typically be even smaller.

The issue of size can have an impact on the courses that a program offers to doctoral students. A small mathematics education program in a mathematics department may require substantial mathematics and a relatively few education courses. At the other extreme, if a student's mathematics education coursework is viewed as only a small part of a broader doctoral program in curriculum and instruction, much of the coursework may emphasize broader education issues and only a small part of the doctoral program will be in mathematics or mathematics education. In small programs, it may not be feasible to offer many specialized courses of any kind for doctoral students.

Given this diversity, are both degrees mathematics education doctorates? The answer may depend on the eye of the beholder. Certainly, doctoral students pursue coursework in mathematics education as part of preparing for a wide variety of careers. Some pursue a doctorate to become academic researchers in mathematics education. But good research in mathematics education is inherently interdisciplinary. Many scholars whose expertise is not centered on mathematics make important contributions to research in the teaching and learning of mathematics. Thus, faculty designing programs for students interested in mathematics education research must balance the need to learn mathematics with the need for other expertise that will enable students to become skilled researchers.

Other doctoral students may set as their career goal becoming a teacher educator or teaching mathematics in a four-year college or a community college while focusing on working with future mathematics teachers. Still others seek expertise that will enable them to become K-12 teacher leaders, curriculum developers, or district leaders. These varied careers may have different mathematical needs. In particular, those who want to be teacher educators often focus their preparation on working with teachers in elementary schools, middle schools, high schools, or at the collegiate level. Thus, it is difficult to analyze the role of mathematics in the work in such a range of positions and develop a well-defined sense of a common body of mathematical knowledge needed by all doctoral students in mathematics education.

At times, the desire to ensure that doctoral students in mathematics education have a deep knowledge of mathematics may be at odds with the need to ensure that future educators have other expertise. Take, for example, the need for elementary mathematics educators. Ideally, faculty who prepare students to be elementary mathematics teachers should themselves have substantial experience inside an elementary school classroom. But, people with experience teaching in elementary schools seldom come to graduate school with a strong mathematics background. What mathematics and how much mathematics is needed by these students is a special challenge for mathematics education programs. (Kirshner & Ricks, this volume).

Despite the different mathematics needed to prepare doctoral students for a variety of careers, participants in the conference expressed general agreement with Dossey and Lappan (2001) that doctoral programs should seek to develop individuals in mathematics education:

- who will know mathematics deeply;
- who will be focused on content in the areas in which they have the responsibility to prepare or support teachers; and
- who will [be able to "do mathematics" at an appropriate level given a range of professional careers] (p. 71).

Dossey and Lappan go on to specify that to "do mathematics" at an appropriate level, a doctoral student should be able to:

- appreciate the rules of evidence within the discipline;
- outline and connect the major ideas of the discipline;
- analyze and apply the major algorithms and procedures;
- describe the ways of thinking through which the discipline itself expands;
- use disciplinary knowledge to solve problems;
- see the connections among and between ideas, concepts, structures, and methods (p. 67).

## The "Plus Six" Proposal

In light of the range of potential student professional career goals, in *One Field, Many Paths*, Dossey and Lappan (2001) suggest a "plus six" criterion for mathematics learning requirements for mathematics education doctoral programs. Essentially, they suggest that mathematics education doctorates should be able to know and use mathematics (i.e. reason, solve problems, communicate, etc.) in situations that are at least six grade levels above that of their teaching assignment. Elaborating on this proposal, Dossey and Lappan went on to suggest that "... a mathematics educator preparing to teach prospective elementary teachers ought to have a command of mathematics at a level equivalent to that of the first three years of undergraduate work in mathematics (Grade 9 + 6). Teachers of prospective secondary school teachers ought to have a grasp of mathematics through an M.S. +30 in mathematics (grade 12 +6)" (p. 68).

At the first National Conference on Doctoral Programs in Mathematics Education (1999) some participants were outraged at the idea of a mathematics requirement at all. Faculty from smaller colleges tended to argue that education courses were more valuable to their graduates and some faculty from research universities did not support the notion that to do excellent research in mathematics education one needs to know mathematics well beyond the grade level of the target students. Some of the heat in this discussion seems to have turned on the notion of setting requirements for doctoral programs. Stepping away from the question of requirements, our own view is that this recommendation is reasonable in considering guidelines for the mathematical knowledge needed by different doctoral students, especially if one refines the idea to think of elementary teachers as being those who teach in grades K-6 and the (overlapping) middle grades as being grades 5-8. With this refinement, the elementary teacher educator should have a strong command of the K-12 mathematics curriculum; the middle level educator should have at least a strong minor in mathematics; those who teach future high school mathematics teachers should have the equivalent of a masters degree in mathematics; and those who will do research in undergraduate mathematics education should reach the M.S. +30 level in mathematics.

Just as a doctoral student's career goals has an impact on the mathematics they need to know, the location of the doctoral program surely influences the mathematics expectations. Further, for those who seek an academic career, the kind of department in which one wants to work should influence the doctoral student's mathematical goals. For mathematics education programs within mathematics departments, there is a natural push to require a level of mathematical competence that will allow mathematics education doctoral students to experience full membership in the department. Such programs often require that students complete qualifying exams in mathematics. In the same vein, if one aspires to work, and earn tenure, in a mathematics department, they should seek a graduate education that prepares them for full membership in that department.

Similarly, within colleges of education, there is a natural push to require a host of educational competences that will allow mathematics education doctoral students to experience full membership as an educator. But, since most doctoral programs require less than 20 courses plus thesis hours, such a push often leaves little room in a program of reasonable length for numerous courses in mathematics.

## Reviewing Current Requirements and Course Taking Patterns

To consider further the issue of the mathematical knowledge needed by doctoral students in mathematics education and the related issue of determining mathematics requirements for a doctoral program, we review current information on who enters doctoral programs in mathematics education, program requirements, information on future mathematics educators' experience in these courses, as well as trends in the development of special coursework for future mathematics educators.

Another chapter in this book, *Report of a 2007 Survey of U.S. Doctoral Students in Mathematics Education*, surveyed 111 current doctoral students in mathematics education representing 45 universities (Teuscher, Nevels & Ulrich, this volume). Respondents were asked for information on their education background, their teaching certifications, and the level of education in mathematics that they anticipate achieving prior to earning their doctorate.

Of those surveyed, 89% reported information on their undergraduate degree with 50% (of the 111 students) reporting a first undergraduate degree in mathematics and another 15% reporting mathematics education as their undergraduate degree. A small number (6%) of the students reported a second degree in mathematics or mathematics education. Further, 92% of the students reported having a master's degree at the time of the survey with 29% (of the 111 students) reporting a first master's degree in mathematics and another 32% reporting a master's degree in mathematics education. When asked for information on their teaching certification, 80% reported that they held a high school certification. (For some, the certification included the middle school grades.) Another 15% reported an elementary certification, while only 4% reported a middle level certification. When asked for information on the level of mathematics course work they would obtain by the time they earned their doctorate, the students responded:

- 23% MA/MS degree & 15+ semester hours in mathematics
- 28% MA/MS degree in mathematics
- 19% BA/BS degree & 15+ semester hours in mathematics
- 15% BA/BS degree in mathematics
- 15% Less than a BA/BS degree in mathematics

These data seem to imply that, for many students, their mathematics background prior to entering a doctoral program in mathematics is sufficient to place their course work in the general ballpark of the "plus six" standard. If meeting this standard is based on the number of mathematics courses taken, then most doctoral students would be judged to have cleared this hurdle. Still, this standard begs the question of what mathematics doctoral candidates should study and when this study should take place. At the conference, comments from the audience indicated a strong push to have mathematical experiences for everyone in their programs including continued attention learning of mathematics as a necessary part of the doctoral experience. For some, however, such mathematical experiences did not have to be part of formal course work in mathematics. For example, faculty at the University of Delaware reported that preparing to teach mathematics content courses for pre-service elementary teachers – a regular assignment for their doctoral students – was a rich venue for mathematical learning.

On this point, the views being expressed by participants in our session were consistent with the Mathematics Content Principle put forth in the *Principles to Guide the Design and Implementation of Doctoral Programs in Mathematics Education* (2003) and adopted by the AMTE and the National Council of Teachers of Mathematics: "Mathematics educators need broad and deep mathematical knowledge both to identify the big ideas in the pre-K-14 mathematics curriculum and to examine how those ideas develop throughout the curriculum. Regardless of the entering level of mathematical knowledge they bring to a doctoral program, students should continue to study mathematics while in the program. Although each student may follow a different program of study, all should exit the program with some graduate study of mathematics and a deep and broad understanding of pre-K-14 mathematics." (www.amte.net) The AMTE/NCTM statement goes on to offer a caution, "Standard courses in advanced mathematics ... are seldom consciously designed or delivered in ways that enhance the knowledge or understanding of pre-K-14 mathematics."

Examination of the mathematics requirements in the mathematics education doctoral programs at several major universities offers examples of how institutions deal with the variety of backgrounds students may have as well as students' different career goals. For example, the Mathematics and Science Education Department at The University of Georgia (second only to Teachers College Columbia in the production of doctoral students in mathematics education) says that "The amount of coursework in mathematics depends on previous work and the interests of the candidate. Substantial study of mathematics is expected." Program goals include a breadth of study through 1st year graduate sequences in mathematics and a depth of study that includes at least one advanced sequence in mathematics. At the University of Maryland, students are expected to enter with a standard calculus experience in their background. When this is not met, a requirement to complete coursework through sophomore level mathematics is added to program requirements. All students are expected to take at least two mathematics courses, typically at the level of seniors/beginning graduate work. This requirement includes a specially designed Foundation of Math course.

The University of Arizona and Michigan State University are two institutions where a student can pursue a doctorate in mathematics education in both the mathematics department and the College of Education. At Arizona, students in the Department of Mathematics must meet highly selective admission requirements, earn a masters degree in mathematics, and pass the department's standard Qualifying Exam. Over in the College of Education, the degree focuses more on education coursework and preparation for research in education. There are no mathematics admission requirements and mathematics coursework for doctoral students can vary from one to six courses.

At Michigan State, there have been four different places where a student can earn a doctorate in mathematics education, two in the College of Natural Sciences and two in the College of Education. For the two College of Education programs, there are no explicit mathematics requirements. In the CNS, students who pursue their degree in the Division of Science and Mathematics Education must take four courses at the senior level or above, while in the Department of Mathematics, students must pass the Qualifying Exam in mathematics.

## Specialized Course Development

Advocates of the viewpoint that doctoral students in mathematics education need a deep understanding of mathematics and that all doctoral programs should include continued opportunities to learn mathematics are not necessarily endorsing the status quo in mathematics departments. The AMTE/NCTM statement, for example, says that advanced mathematics courses "are seldom consciously designed or delivered in ways that enhance the knowledge or understanding of pre-K-14 mathematics." The challenge for mathematics educators is to determine what kinds of mathematics courses will prepare doctoral students for the range of work they will do as mathematics educators and how to ensure that their students have such opportunities.

Dossey and Lappan (2001) say that "Faculty involved in doctoral programs in mathematics education and in mathematics must work together to establish sequences of course work that do not replicate the status quo. ...The task is to design new sequences of courses for doctoral students in mathematics education."

(p. 71) Recent funding opportunities have allowed the profession to begin to gain experience with such specialized courses as will be outlined below.

Mathematics educators designing programs for doctoral students or mentoring particular doctoral students need to carefully consider the mathematical knowledge that their students need to prepare for the jobs they hope to get, their past opportunities to learn mathematics and the experiences that should be part of their doctoral education. In the course of their professional work, graduates of doctoral programs in mathematics education will use mathematical knowledge, whether they are teaching, designing curriculum, examining student learning or issues of teacher knowledge, working with pre-service or in-service teachers, or consulting on educational policies.

The first author discussed his own experiences as a teacher entering a masters program and then his opportunities to learn more mathematics (and the history of mathematics) as a doctoral student. Consistent with the concern expressed by the AMTE/NCTM statement, formal course opportunities to learn mathematics often did not meet his needs as a future mathematics educator.

As a professor of mathematics education, he also has encountered students who wanted to pursue a doctorate in mathematics education but who did not appear oriented to learning more mathematics, nor did they pursue opportunities to learn mathematics. This resulted in a desire to communicate to doctoral students the importance of being a life-long learner of mathematics if one is to be a teacher of mathematics and certainly if one is to be a mathematics educator. Indeed, the need to develop this point of view among doctoral students in mathematics education is a good justification for taking additional mathematics courses as part of a doctoral program, even if a student has satisfied the "plus six" standard prior to beginning a doctoral program.

Partly because of the attention that NSF-funded Centers for Learning and Teaching have focused on the mathematical knowledge needed by mathematics education doctoral students, some new models for courses have been created since 1999. Three examples were highlighted in the sessions we organized.

Sarah Sword, a mathematician who works at the Educational Development Center (EDC), described a two-semester experimental course that she and Chazan created with support from the Mid-Atlantic Center for Mathematics Teaching and Learning while she was on a postdoctoral appointment at the University of Maryland. A primary goal of their courses was to help mathematics education doctoral students develop strategies for continued lifelong learning of mathematics; particularly of mathematics related to their professional work.

To do this, their courses had two principal components: in-class mathematics explorations and individual research projects of the students' own choosing. Often, their students "knew" the answers to the questions they posed, but sought some kind of new understanding. For example: one doctoral student in the course encountered the following problem while tutoring a middle school student:

> Arrange the digits 5, 6, 7, 8, and 9 into a three-digit number and a
> two-digit number so that their product is as large as possible.

The doctoral student could find the answer by trial and error, but she spent a semester understanding and proving several generalizations of the problem (Graybeal, 2007).

Another student who had taught calculus posed the following problem:

> The derivative of the area of a circle in terms of radius is the circumference of a circle. The relationship is seemingly not true for polygons. Why?

Similarly, in-class explorations investigated questions originating in (but not limited to) K-12 mathematics. For example, one exploration launched from a *Balanced Assessment* task on square-ness originally designed for high school students (Chazan et al., 2007). This task was used to launch into an exploration of continued fractions as an alternative to place value systems for representing real numbers.

The National Science Foundation funded the Center for the Scholarship of School Mathematics at Education Development Center to disseminate the course, which is currently being taught at universities around the country. (More info on this is available at http://cssm.edc.org.)

Ira Papick reported on four graduate level mathematics courses that he and his colleagues have developed at the University of Missouri. The development of these courses was funded by the Center for the Study of Mathematics Curriculum, an NSF-funded Center for Learning and Teaching. The titles of the courses are:

- Polynomial Algebra Underlying the Study of Polynomials in the Secondary Curriculum;
- Arithmetic and Algebra of the Integers and the Rational Numbers;
- Linear Algebra Underlying the Secondary Curriculum;
- Analyzing Curriculum From a Mathematical Perspective and Exploring Some Related Mathematics.

Papick elaborated on the Polynomial Algebra course that includes a curriculum review where students are asked to:

(1) Catalogue and analyze key polynomial concepts appearing in a wide variety of high school curricula; and
(2) Collect a wide spectrum of mathematical or "real world" applications of polynomials appearing in the secondary curriculum.

The course includes an in-depth study of polynomial rings and includes many familiar topics such as the arithmetic and algebra of the integers and the integers modulo $n$, basic ring theory, and polynomials in one variable over a field or over a commutative ring. Doctoral students are responsible for presenting some lectures and they prepare three papers: a curriculum analysis of current high school textbook treatments of polynomials; a detailed lesson plan and presentation of higher degree polynomial applications for secondary teachers; and a paper on a polynomial topic not covered in the class. An example of a possible content analysis might be: How are the concepts of indeterminate, polynomial, and polynomial function defined in current secondary textbooks and are these workable definitions? For example, using the definitions you find, is it straightforward to show that $2^x$ is not a polynomial function?

Carl Lee, a professor of mathematics at the University of Kentucky, reported on courses that he and his colleagues have created as part of the Appalachian Math Science Partnership and ACCLAIM, the Appalachian Collaborative Center for Learning, Assessment, and Instruction in Mathematics, two NSF-funded initiatives. In particular, Lee reported on Topics in Geometry, a course for mathematics education doctoral students in the five campus ACCLAIM program. Lee has offered the course as a summer course and he is currently offering the course as an online distance education course (via Moodle and Adobe Connect).

Many topics covered in the course (axiomatic systems, incidence, coordinates, distance, area, volume, angles, polyhedra, dimension, congruence, and symmetry) will be familiar to those who have taught a geometry course. The course is especially beneficial to mathematics education doctoral students because it is designed and delivered in a manner designed to:

(1) Increase their awareness and understanding of the scope and nature of geometry, including history, recent developments and applications, and connections to other contexts.
(2) Allow them to follow selected fundamental themes and concepts in geometry as they unfold in sophistication, paralleling their appearances in the middle school, high school, and college curriculum.
(3) Approach geometry in an investigative manner, using such techniques as a selection of sequenced problems, collaborative learning, exploration and problem solving to formulate, test, and prove or disprove conjectures; and written and oral arguments to develop effective communication skills; and such tools as physical manipulatives; models; and software.

## Future Mathematics Educators' Experience of Doctoral Coursework

In addition to presentations about specially developed courses, in the sessions we organized, Anne Marie Marshall, a doctoral student at the University of Maryland, presented some initial results of her dissertation study of doctoral students' experience of doctoral coursework (2008). In her preliminary analysis of the data collected from six participants, she distinguishes between conventional coursework and novel coursework. While her analysis confirms some of the earlier comments about formal mathematical coursework, it suggested particular aspects of the novel courses that seemed to be important to her respondents. It is important to note that some of the courses she labels novel were specially designed courses and others were regularly scheduled mathematics courses that incorporated some of the features listed below.

In communicating her understandings of her participants' experience as adult learners of mathematics, Marshall made reference to Golde and Walker's (2006) work on intellectual communities, communities that are knowledge centered, broadly inclusive, flexible and forgiving, respectful and generous, and deliberately tended. She drew a parallel between these aspects of intellectual communities and the classroom practices her respondents appreciated in what she calls the novel courses. In particular, her respondents felt better served by mathematical experiences where:

- Instructors shared authority in what was to be studied, student voice was critical, and course projects that allowed student initiative were central.
- A high level of interaction existed among students, between students and instructors, and between students and the mathematics.
- After a prompt, or problem, the mathematics evolved from the students working together and from students' experiences and questions.
- The expressed purpose of the course was two-fold, both an opportunity to really *do* mathematics and a model of interactive mathematics teaching and learning aimed at deep understanding of the content.

Examples of courses with these dimensions, as reported by participants, were the experiences that provided mathematics education doctoral students with mathematical experiences that felt particularly important to their doctoral preparation.

## In Closing

While the "plus six" proposal seems to articulate reasonable goals for the preparation of mathematics educators, in our sessions, the proposal did not generate much interest or controversy and does not seem to offer much guidance for those seeking to design programs. Many potential doctoral students seem to come to graduate school with background that is at least this strong. Nevertheless such seemingly well-prepared doctoral students often express dissatisfaction with their preparation in mathematics. While it is desirable to have doctoral students continue to learn mathematics throughout their programs; program requirements are to a large extent a zero sum game, increasing requirements in mathematics means specifying what else can be foregone. Currently there is no body or group that could effectively promote guidelines for requirements across the range of programs currently producing doctorates in mathematics education.

That said, there was much interest in the group about how to create appropriate mathematical experiences for the wide range of doctoral students in mathematics education, and in particular for future elementary mathematics teacher educators. With only a very small number of dissenting voices, the groups did seem to desire development of specialized mathematics coursework. Such specialized coursework seemed desirable because of its greater focus on "habits of mind" (Cuoco, Goldenberg & Mark, 1996), rather than on content coverage preparatory for more advanced study in mathematics. It also seems to be well suited to the needs of doctoral students as adult learners with specific career goals. Though there was some discussion of difficulties providing mathematics graduate credit for the examination of content that might be deemed undergraduate materials, there also was a sense that development of such coursework provides opportunities for substantive and useful collaboration between mathematicians and mathematics educators.

Practically speaking, however, there are limits to the possibilities for creating such coursework. The Centers for Learning and Teaching program that funded much of the current experimentation is reaching its concluding years. Many mathematics education doctoral programs are not large enough to generate enrollments that would justify such specialized courses. Finally, even in places that can generate small classes, mathematics departments already teach many services courses and may be reluctant to create small courses for a limited audience of doctoral candidates in mathematics education.

Stimulated by these issues, there was interest in the model Carl Lee presented of on-line courses, as well as in the exploration of other possibilities, like providing doctoral students with one credit courses to go along with conventional coursework in a mathematics department class or mathematical examination of the statistical methods studied in courses often required of doctoral candidates in education. As noted by one contributor to the session, these pragmatic issues around specialized coursework also raise a question about whether the field of mathematics education would be better served by greater consolidation of opportunities for doctoral study in the field and the development of more programs with enough students to support more specialized doctoral preparation.

*Daniel Chazan*
*University of Maryland*
*College Park, MD 20742*
*dchazan@umd.edu*

*W. James Lewis*
*University of Nebraska*
*Lincoln, NE 68588*
*wlewis1@math.unl.edu*

CBMS Issues in Mathematics Education
Volume **15**, 2008

# Curriculum as Core Knowledge

## Rose Mary Zbiek and Christian R. Hirsch

The 1999 National Conference on Doctoral Programs in Mathematics Education revealed considerable diversity in the goals, components, and expectations of mathematics education doctoral programs in the U.S. (Reys & Kilpatrick, 2001). In their conference paper (pages 73-75), Presmeg and Wagner (2001) summarized the sentiment of participants that there ought to be a core of knowledge that is common across doctoral programs, and that mathematics curriculum ought to be part of that core. But what was important for all doctoral students to know about mathematics curriculum was left as an open question.

A subsequent Task Force of the Association of Mathematics Teacher Educators chaired by Robert Reys prepared a report, *Principles to Guide the Design and Implementation of Doctoral Programs in Mathematics Education* (2003), which identified a curriculum knowledge base that students should acquire across a range of experiences, including courses, seminars, and clinical experiences. The report posited that:

> Doctoral students need experiences in curriculum analysis, design, and evaluation. As a result of these experiences and study, doctoral students should acquire:
> - Knowledge of the role and influence of local, state, and national curriculum frameworks and standards on the design and implementation of school programs.
> - Knowledge of how curricula, technology, and instructional strategies mesh to support mathematics learning.
> - Knowledge of the relative importance of mathematical topics in the curriculum and options for how these topics could be developed across grade levels. (p. 5)

This paper elaborates on the core knowledge related to curriculum that should be expected of doctoral students in mathematics education.

## Curriculum as a Central Component of Doctoral Experiences

Mathematics curriculum, what it should be, what it is, how it is organized and sequenced, how it is taught, and what students learn is the core around which school mathematics revolves. It is the commonly recognized mathematics of mathematics education. But curriculum in terms of design and enactment also draws from, and contributes to, theories of learning and our research knowledge base. An

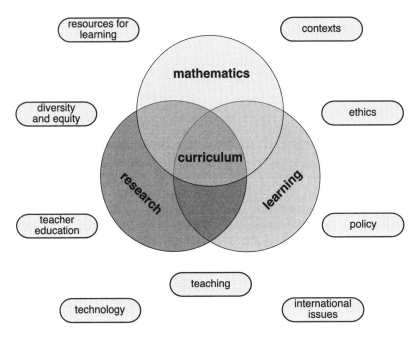

FIGURE 1. Expanded core knowledge for doctoral students (Adapted from Ferrini-Mundy, this volume).

examination of the broader mathematics education landscape today suggests that curriculum could be conceived as the center of core knowledge for doctoral students. (See Figure 1.)

Because of the ubiquitousness of curriculum-related matters in mathematics education, conference participants reported a variety of ways in which their doctoral students encounter curriculum issues. They do so within courses and beyond courses, although within courses seemed to be the more common way of thinking about the curriculum. Courses vary in foci, from courses that examine particular sets of national/state curriculum standards, to courses on the history of school mathematics curriculum, to courses on curriculum design. Often, and not surprisingly, what is emphasized in a course (elective or required) depends on who teaches the course. There was consensus among participants that we should think about what doctoral students should know about curriculum as something that is developed across a range of experiences. How it fits into a program may be unique to institutions. Regardless of where and how doctoral students encounter curriculum, they need to wrestle with the question of what is curriculum. It is more than textbooks or materials. It has different phases or manifestations: ideal, intended, written, enacted, assessed, and achieved.

## Historical Issues, Trends, and Forces that Shape Curricula

Doctoral students should know about historical issues, trends, and forces that shape curricula. Intense discussion clarified goals for including a historical perspective on curriculum in doctoral programs while simultaneously addressing the breadth of that coverage and the role of evidence in discussions of curriculum history.

**Goals and Scope of a Historical Perspective on Curriculum.** One generally agreed upon reason for viewing curriculum from a historical approach, including issues and trends, was that a study of history provides a perspective for looking at today's curricula. A second reason was the study of curriculum from a historical perspective allows for the political and social nature of curriculum to become apparent. This provides an important lens for looking at contemporary curricula and curriculum materials. These goals for including a historical perspective on curriculum within a doctoral program had implications for how we thought about common tasks in doctoral programs, such as tracing curricular treatment of a topic over time. Beyond being simply interesting (to us, at least), such tasks help doctoral students to understand why curricular reforms arise, to communicate across the generations of colleagues in mathematics education, and to understand research studies conducted in the context of curricula from different eras that make sense only when considered within their curricular time period.

The group spent considerable time on the related questions of how far back in time doctoral students need to go and with which particular historical curriculum movements they need to be familiar. For example, some programs began historical consideration with Sputnik and others went back to the *Report of the Committee of Ten on Secondary School Studies* (National Education Association, 1894), while some opted to begin with the National Council of Teachers of Mathematics *Curriculum and Evaluation Standards* (NCTM, 1989) or perhaps *An Agenda for Action* (NCTM, 1980).

**Factors Influencing Curriculum.** The purposes of studying curriculum from a historical perspective suggested a need for doctoral students to understand forces affecting intended, written, enacted, and assessed curriculum. Doctoral students should know what factors have influenced curriculum conceptualization, development, dissemination, and enactment over time. For example, technology—both that for learning and doing mathematics and that available to students in their everyday life—has changed greatly in recent years and has continually emerged over centuries. Our doctoral students need to consider questions about how today's learners may think about mathematical experiences in light of the new technologies that students encounter in everyday life and in mathematics classrooms. For example, given the prevalence of video games, one might ask, do students now see manipulatives and mathematics learning technology in terms of what they need to "win" the game? We also need to make sure that our programs are preparing doctoral students to adapt to technology-influenced changes in research and teaching, which can greatly affect intended and enacted curriculum. Another factor affecting the nature and enactment of curriculum are parents' views and roles. Parents interface with learners and can serve as advocates for or against changes in curriculum. Doctoral students need to know how to have conversations with prospective teachers and current teachers about how to collaborate with parents within different curricular contexts. Language and culture are examples of factors that we understand affect how curriculum is conceptualized, developed, and enacted. Doctoral students should consider such issues as how the structure and syntax of the English language, such as noun and adjective placement and use of numbers as either nouns or adjectives, may affect how curriculum enactments unfold and materials appear.

**Curriculum over History as Source of Evidence.** In keeping with the idea that curriculum is only part of the doctoral program experience, doctoral students should see the study of curriculum over time as one way to elicit evidence of policy, teaching, and learning during different periods. Careful study of curriculum materials can suggest the effects of policy, such as the relative impact of state and national standards in textbooks of the 2000s compared to those of the 1970s. Doctoral students can use comparisons of curricular materials from a particular era to infer which beliefs and instructional practices dominated thought about teaching and learning at the time. In addition to looking at curriculum materials, doctoral students should study policy documents from different time periods. Evidence of what mattered during the time can be found not only in the content of the documents but also in the collaborations manifested in the writing team, the organization of the report, and the significance of the report as evidenced in textbooks and other venues. The 1980s and 1990s were a time in which many documents were produced, and we discussed strategies for engaging doctoral students with these documents in productive ways that honor the breadth and depth of the documents as well as the time and other constraints of a doctoral program. One example of a strategy involved a class discussion around focusing questions about a set of documents and for which each student or small group of students became an expert on one or more of these documents. It was noted that a useful set of resources supporting document analysis is available at the Center for the Study of Mathematics Curriculum (www.mathcurriculumcenter.org/curriculum _ course _ resources.php).

### Understanding Challenges to Curriculum Change

To understand the challenges to curriculum change, doctoral students first need to understand the reality in which curriculum change is attempted. One reality issue is the impact of various standards. The presence of these standards and the tendency to refer to them as "the curriculum" suggest the importance of these standards. Doctoral students should consider how differences in state standards, such as whether integrated approaches to mathematics are accepted, might affect the enacted curriculum directly and the intended curriculum indirectly. State standards impact publishing houses as publishers work across states with dissimilar expectations and balance this combination of expectations with priorities suggested by other voices. Textbooks with different ISBNs for different states provide evidence of these policy ramifications.

A second element of reality is awareness of what is happening in schools. Doctoral students should consider evidence of the extent to which curriculum change fits the reality of schools. For example, knowing what teachers and others in the school setting consider to be "curriculum" might help us to understand how textbook selection might be viewed as the totality of curriculum change. Doctoral students should explore the connection between the curriculum and teaching strands of their programs.

Consideration of state and school as part of the reality in which curriculum change occurs should fit within doctoral students' understanding of the levels of curriculum decision making. Decisions made by curriculum developers clearly affect curricula. Decisions about "curriculum adoption" and policy documents at the national, state, and local levels matter. Students have a role in curriculum decision making. Parents have a voice in curriculum decision making. Doctoral students should be aware of the combination of decisions made by these various stakeholders and ways to study how these potentially incongruent decisions might contribute to productive and counterproductive differences between the ideal curriculum and the achieved curriculum. With the power to empirically, theoretically, and experientially examine and explain these differences, doctoral students are better positioned to understand these differences. This kind of understanding allows emerging mathematics educators to reject change for the sake of change and stagnancy for the sake of what we "have always done."

## Curriculum Evaluation as Part of Doctoral Experience

It is very natural to think about curriculum evaluation when thinking about scholarly work related to curriculum. This tendency might be particularly alluring for doctoral students in a time when they feel a societal push for studies that attempt to compare curricula. A goal of doctoral programs should be to understand challenges of evaluating curricula and various approaches and techniques used to conduct curriculum evaluation studies that serve both curriculum generation and refinement needs and advance the broader field of mathematics education.

Doctoral students need to understand how common practices that are considered "evaluation work," such as textbook evaluations and state textbook adoption practices, are not the same as evaluation studies. To understand curriculum evaluation and research around curriculum requires probing sticky issues and knowing viable avenues taken by this work. For example, doctoral students need to know different techniques useful in studying how a curriculum is enacted and why it is difficult to "know" what students learn from curriculum materials. They also need to know what school mathematics curriculum can be and should be in terms of policy making. Here is a point at which various strands of a doctoral program (e.g., teaching, learning, technology, equity) merge as doctoral students develop greater understanding of what happens in the reality and complexity of a school classroom. They also need to distinguish between curriculum evaluation and discovery of what would characterize an ideal curriculum.

## Other Scholarly Matters Related to Curriculum

Curriculum plays a role in research and scholarly work beyond curriculum evaluation. Doctoral students need to see and distinguish between research in which curriculum is the object of interest and research in which curriculum has an important but less central role, and they need to see the various roles of curriculum in empirical work. For example, a particular curriculum may be an essential aspect of the setting in which researchers explore constructs that extend beyond a given curriculum, such as the effects of teacher questioning or supporting student reasoning. Doctoral students also need to see how a research team may develop a curriculum in the interest of studying a particular phenomenon, such as the effects of a particular type of technology in classroom learning or the effects of focusing on measure in the primary grades on arithmetic and algebraic reasoning in the later grades. In addition, doctoral students should explore the relationship between curriculum development and research design and methods. For example, they should consider how conducting a teaching experiment relates to curriculum conceptualization and development.

**Curriculum through Scholarly Lenses.** Throughout their study of curriculum history, curriculum evaluation, and other research and scholarship around curriculum, there are several lenses through which doctoral students should consider curriculum, including those lenses that take students beyond familiar settings and experiences. For example, doctoral students should see how one may value a curriculum differently or simply see different features of a curriculum if one approaches curriculum from a learning perspective (focus on what learners experience and what understandings they develop), a mathematics perspective (focus on what mathematical ideas are included and how they unfold), or a philosophical perspective (focus on the question of whether the goal is to perpetuate society or to change society). Noting differences between developing or viewing a curriculum from a learner view and from a mathematics view might be one way to understand some current curriculum debates. Doctoral students also should see how, even from the same perspective, one may see different things over time, across nations, and across policies. These lenses should be applied not only to a "textbook" but also to all of the tangible and intangible elements of a curriculum, as exemplified with the use of policy documents in the discussion of curriculum from a historical perspective.

One lens that participants suggested might be of particular interest and usefulness is an international perspective. Acknowledging that our doctoral students include individuals whose schooling may have occurred outside the United States and beyond North America, we need to ask what doctoral students gain from looking at curricula from other countries (e.g., Singapore). Simply looking at curriculum from other countries and describing what is there is not sufficient. Doctoral students need to look at those curricula for a purpose, such as seeing how very different perspectives and influences may be apparent in the curricula of particular countries. For example, a Vygotskian-influenced Russian curriculum builds mathematical ideas in elementary mathematics in a totally different sequence than is common in the U.S. There are implications of these influences on curriculum design. Examining curricula from other countries, such as looking carefully at how German curricula value both skills and concepts while focusing on what is a good problem, might call into question common practices in the U.S. Doctoral students also need to know how U.S. curricula have been impacted by and have had impact on mathematics education outside of this country. Examples include knowing how U.S. curricula (e.g., New Math) have influenced curricula in other countries. Among other things, the study of curricula from an international perspective should help doctoral students understand similarities and differences in U.S. curricula that arise from different perspectives and influences.

**Participation in Curriculum Work.** One curriculum-related activity beyond coursework for doctoral students is participation in projects that conceptualize and develop curriculum [materials]. These projects may vary in expected ways, such as the grade levels they address and the models they employ. The projects also may vary in the extent to which they strive to create a broadly used curriculum or to create a prototype of a curriculum with a particular feature. There was a sense that we want our doctoral students to be involved in the development of curriculum beyond, for example, a lesson or short sequence of lessons as the students might have done in their own teaching or in a teacher preparation program. Unlike a course assignment or lesson development, participation in a curriculum development project is an extended apprenticeship within an intellectual community. The experience problematizes curriculum and curriculum development and deeply engages doctoral students with key issues in conceptualizing curriculum. Among other things, curriculum project work brings attention to curriculum design as a process. While it may not be possible for all doctoral students to have this experience, it should be encouraged whenever possible, expected of doctoral students who plan to make curriculum a major part of their scholarly agenda, and required of those on a path to being the next generation of curriculum developers.

**Curriculum Design.** As former students and possibly former teachers or other leaders in mathematics education, doctoral students enter our programs aware of textbooks and familiar with the word *curriculum*. Through participation in curriculum development experiences, if not through courses, we want doctoral students to understand curriculum development and design as a process that is far more demanding than writing a textbook. Doctoral students should be aware of models for curriculum development, such as backward design (Wiggins & McTighe, 2005) and extended design experiments (cf. Gravemeijer, 1994). They should contrast the thinking and processes needed to implement backward design or another curriculum development model with, for example, the thinking process that one undertakes to develop and articulate a mathematical proof or to recount a story of what happens in a particular classroom. We want students to acknowledge and struggle with crucial questions and situations encountered within curriculum development. One example of a crucial and challenging situation is how developing curriculum forces one to ask the question of what are the most important ideas in mathematics that should be encountered by the student audience. Other examples include when and how these ideas should be encountered and sequenced.

While our focus was primarily on mathematics curriculum for students in prekindergarten through grade 12, participants were sensitive to the fact that doctoral students need a preparation that allows them to engage in curriculum development in a broader sense and with other groups of learners. Doctoral students likely will need to draw on their understanding of curriculum and curriculum development in many other circumstances as they, for example, develop undergraduate and graduate programs and courses, write learner materials and ancillary products, and mentor emerging teachers in their creation of lessons and units that need to exist within the guidelines of state and local expectations. To be contributors in and beyond the arena of mathematics curricula requires an understanding of curriculum development beyond knowledge of a few curricula and an experience in conceptualizing curricula beyond writing a few lessons.

## Acting on Shared Values and Goals

The combined values and goals expressed by conference participants create high expectations for the role of curriculum within doctoral programs. Examples of shared visions and programmatic changes within and across institutions are useful. Collaborative efforts to address these questions and develop shared goals as recommended by Hiebert, Kilpatrick, and Lindquist (2001) have recently been undertaken by two of the NSF-funded Centers for Learning and Teaching. The Mid-Atlantic Center for Mathematics Teaching and Learning (University of Maryland, University of Delaware, and Penn State University) and the Center for the Study of Mathematics Curriculum (University of Missouri, Michigan State University, and Western Michigan University) have each focused doctoral program improvement in the area of curriculum. The following goals are offered as a part of a continuing conversation on reaching consensus on core knowledge with respect to curriculum.

- Knowledge of the historical evolution in practice and thinking about school mathematics curricula–professional recommendations, approaches that have been tried, experiences with development and implementation of those approaches, and the professional and political interests that shape curriculum decisions.
- Knowledge of mathematical concepts, principles, techniques, and reasoning methods that are central to school curricula, and critical understanding of the ways that this mathematics is developed and evaluated by standard and innovative curriculum.
- Knowledge of the relationships between theories of teaching and learning and the content, organization, pacing, and presentation of mathematics curriculum topics.
- Knowledge of the implications of calculator and computer technologies for goals, structure, and presentation of mathematics curricula.
- Ability to examine critically the research and evaluation literature on mathematics curriculum issues and to design and conduct high quality research on mathematics curriculum variables.
- Knowledge of research findings directly related to developing conceptually oriented K-16 mathematics curriculum materials from a research perspective.
- Ability to conceptualize, design, conduct, and report *research* on a mathematics curriculum development effort.
- Disposition to examine critically both existing and proposed mathematics curricula to determine whether they value important mathematics and organize and present that content in ways that reflect understanding of student learning, effective teaching, and assessment of knowledge.

The above goals represent a step toward building a shared set of goals with respect to core knowledge and dispositions related to curriculum. We believe that building consensus on goals can be an important part of doctoral program improvement.

## Concluding Comments

The participants in the curriculum sessions generally agreed that there are several configurations of courses and experiences through which curriculum might fit into a doctoral program in mathematics education. Variations across universities naturally capitalize on the expertise of faculty within and beyond mathematics education. Beyond the details of where and how doctoral students encounter and engage with curriculum matters, participants expressed commitment to preparing doctoral students to develop their own reasoned responses to key questions. The questions embraced by the groups might be articulated as follows:

- What is curriculum? What is curriculum development?
- What is good curriculum? Who weighs in on this decision?
- What influences curriculum policy?
- What influences curriculum implementation?
- What research is done around curriculum? What challenges and techniques are involved in this work?

As one participant noted, we are part of a continuing line of doctoral educators in mathematics education with the ongoing task of engaging doctoral students in understanding, generating, and studying mathematics curriculum. We became participants in the ongoing conversation around curriculum. Perhaps the two questions that we must ask about our own programs are, to what extent do our current doctoral programs prepare students to take part in this conversation, and in what ways might we help students to become strong voices to be heard across the decades to come?

*Rose Mary Zbiek*
*The Pennsylvania State University*
*University Park PA 16802*
*rmz101@psu.edu*

*Christian R. Hirsch*
*Western Michigan University*
*Kalamazoo, MI 49008*
*christian.hirsch@wmich.edu*

CBMS Issues in Mathematics Education
Volume **15**, 2008

# Making Policy Issues Visible in the Doctoral Preparation of Mathematics Educators

Edward Silver and Erica Walker

At the first national conference on doctoral programs in mathematics education in 1999, the agenda offered no opportunity to explicitly consider the treatment of policy issues in the doctoral preparation of mathematics educators. In contrast, at the second conference in 2007 policy research was prominent on the agenda, with two breakout sessions on the first full day of the conference. This change reflects a growing awareness in the field of mathematics education regarding the importance and impact of policy enactment on the mathematics teaching and learning, and it is mirrored in the contents of research handbooks on the field. No chapter devoted to policy issues appeared in the first *Handbook of Research on Mathematics Teaching and Learning* (Grouws, 1992), but there are two chapters devoted to the discussion of policy issues in mathematics education (Ferrini-Mundy & Floden, 2007; Tate & Rousseau, 2007) in the second handbook (Lester, 2007).

Although the influence of policy on mathematics education has long been clear—one need only consider, for example, the flurry of federal programs spawned by the *Sputnik* launch in 1957 that changed the landscape with respect to school mathematics curriculum, teaching, and learning—the place of policy in doctoral preparation has not. For example, Reys, Glasgow, Teuscher, & Nevels (2007) surveyed 70 institutions offering doctoral programs in mathematics education and found that only 17 percent required any coursework on education policy; whereas, at least 50 percent required coursework on educational foundations.

Given that graduates of doctoral programs in mathematics education assume positions of leadership in the field-as researchers, teacher educators, state or district mathematics supervisors, and so on-and given the likely influence of policy on them and their work, it is important to consider how policy issues can reasonably be treated in their doctoral preparation. Prior to the 2007 conference we offered the following framing for the sessions related to policy:

> Given that we are not training scholars who will study policy enactment and implementation, what and how should mathematics education doctoral students learn about education policy and its effects not only on mathematics teaching and learning in schools but also on research, teacher education, curriculum and assessment, and other professional activities? How might we prepare future leaders in mathematics education so they can be successful

in the future in shaping policy at the local, state, and national
levels?

To organize our work in the conference breakout sessions, we posed three questions
for participants to consider:

- What are some key policy issues affecting mathematics education?
- Why do doctoral students in mathematics education need to know about
  policy?
- How might doctoral students in mathematics education learn about policy
  and be prepared to contribute to its development?

During the breakout sessions participants considered these questions as they identified and discussed policy issues associated with a specific case drawn from experience in New York State (see Figure 1) and with a more general matrix that
provided a framework for thinking about policy issues in relation to both the level
at which a policy might be made or enacted and the core area(s) of concern to
mathematics educators that the policy might affect (see Table 1).

> The New York State Education Department has decided that use of
> graphing calculators will continue to be permitted on the various Math
> A tests given in 2004. That includes pretests, field tests and the final
> Regents Exams, which were given this month and will be given again in
> June and August.
>
> For now, at least, SED has rejected a recommendation of its Math A
> panel that no students be allowed to use calculators unless they are
> available to all students statewide. The panel said calculators provide
> a definite edge to students who can afford them or whose districts can
> afford to provide them.
>
> SED officials said they will continue to study the issue with the Math
> Standards Committee the Regents and SED convened late last year to
> revise math standards.
>
> "We have analyzed the test questions and believe that while there is
> no advantage for students who use such calculators, we do not want
> to disadvantage students who have been using them regularly in the
> classroom," SED said in a statement posted on its Web site.
>
> Retrieved December 3, 2004 from www.nysut.org.

FIGURE 1. A Case of Policy from New York State

## Discussion of the Case

Because policy can be viewed from several perspectives-including development,
intent, enactment, implementation, impact, and/or consequences (Ferrini-Mundy
& Floden, 2007)—rich examples can be used to spur doctoral students' thinking
about many interacting issues in mathematics education. For example, a single
case can not only provide a source of discussion of how policy—both explicit and
implicit—is created and enacted, but also may incorporate issues of technology,
assessment, curriculum, research, among others. This can provide students with

TABLE 1. Matrix: Course/Experience Theme-by-Policy Level

| | School or District | State | National |
|---|---|---|---|
| Mathematics Teacher Education | | | |
| Mathematics Teacher Professional Development | | | |
| Mathematics Assessment | | | |
| Mathematics Curriculum | | | |
| Instructional Technology | | | |
| Mathematics Education Research | | | |

ideas about how the theories they are reading about and learning are enacted in the real world. Incorporating policy in doctoral studies can prepare students to address, as well as acquaint them with, issues that arise within a larger context.

To illustrate these points, we asked participants to read a short policy case (Figure 1) and to identify issues, especially mathematics education issues, evoked by their reading of the case. Although the case is not very detailed, it nevertheless sparked a lively discussion about policy and its relation to other key issues in mathematics education.

Among the points raised by the participants were the following:

- What is/was the *evidence base* for this (or any other) policy decision? How are the standards of evidence related to those we consider in relation to research in the field?
- Whose voice is/was heard in the policy-making process? What are/were the qualifications of those invited into the conversation?
- What are/were the intended consequences of this specific policy decision? What were/might have been the *unintended consequences*?
- With respect to this specific policy, what view of *equity* underlies this decision?
- With respect to this specific policy, what view of the *relation between testing and instruction* underlies this decision? For example, what does the design of a "calculator-neutral test" imply regarding the role of technology in instruction? What about the issue of testing under conditions similar to those found in instruction?
- What is the place of calculators in the mathematics curriculum - supplemental frills or core tools with which students should gain testable proficiency?

- How does this specific policy fit within a nexus of other related policies and conditions? For example, to what extent is the policy driven by academic concerns or financial ones?

As the list suggests, the case provoked a number of policy-related questions and concerns that are closely relate to issues that are commonly treated in mathematics education doctoral programs — evidence, equity, testing students' mathematics learning, the relation between testing and instruction, and technology. One of the key points made in our discussion of the case was that instances, like this one, of the design or enactment of educational policies can serve as a stimulus for conversations that link policy issues to other matters that we consider to be more "mainstream" issues in mathematics education. This then served as the backdrop for a consideration of the matrix shown in Table 1.

## Incorporating Policy into Doctoral Studies: Working with the Matrix

How might the consideration of policy issues become more prominent in mathematics education doctoral programs? One approach would be to require a course that specifically treats policy issues. Given the findings of Reys, et al. (2007) regarding the infrequency of policy-related coursework in doctoral programs in mathematics education, it is not clear that this suggestion could be easily implemented on a large scale. Yet, most doctoral programs in mathematics education do commonly require coursework and apprenticeship experiences related to many other topics (e.g., curriculum, learning, teaching, research, assessment, teacher education). Therefore, one sensible approach would be to find ways to give more explicit attention to policy issues in the context of these other courses/experiences. Toward that end, we asked participants to work with a matrix (Table 1) that crossed commonly treated mathematics education themes/topics with several levels at which policies might be enacted or implemented.

Participants were asked to work with selected themes/topics and to generate examples of policies and policy-related issues associated with different cells in the matrix. As with the case, the matrix sparked a rich discussion among the participants. It is not possible in the space available to give a full accounting of the rich array of ideas generated in the session, but a few examples drawn from the discussion should be illustrative:

- Related to *curriculum*, states typically have curriculum expectations or frameworks that shape decisions at the state and local levels. Nationally, the NCTM standards and NAEP frameworks have influenced states' policies regarding curriculum expectations. Some states have formal textbook adoption lists and processes that also influence which curriculum materials are likely to be used by local school districts.
- Regarding *teacher education*, state officials make policies regarding certification requirements, which influence (determine in many cases) the design and content of university programs. Policy recommendations made by national organizations (e.g., NCTM, NCATE, TEAC) often influence state policies. Policies related to alternative certification routes are also relevant here.
- Regarding *teacher professional development*, NCLB's requirement regarding "highly qualified teachers" is a case of national policy being enacted by

states in different ways, with implications for the design and implementation of professional development programs for mathematics teachers. State or district policies related to recognition from the National Board for Professional Teaching Standards, and school district policies regarding whether instructional time can be made available for professional development are also relevant here.

- Regarding *assessment*, policies regarding the frequency, nature, and use of student achievement testing are usually set at state and local levels — sometimes in response to federal policy requirements — and they often have a major influence on the teaching and learning of school mathematics. Policies related to the testing of teacher knowledge and professional qualifications are also relevant here.
- Regarding *technology*, the New York State case provides an interesting example of one set of policy issues related to testing, curriculum, and instruction. Policies related to the purchase of technological tools for teaching/learning are also relevant here.
- Regarding *research*, national and state agencies may establish funding priorities for research based on policy-related initiatives. University and school district IRB policies are also relevant here.

## Conclusion

Meeting attendees who chose to participate in the policy breakout sessions generally agreed that it was important to give more explicit attention to policy issues in mathematics education doctoral programs. Though many participants expressed the view that a special course on this topic would be a desirable addition to a doctoral program, there was strong resonance with the idea that increased attention could be given in existing required courses using tools like the case and the matrix. Given the growing attention to policy in our field, we look forward to the third national conference on doctoral programs in mathematics education, where we can see how the ideas discussed in these breakout sessions are enacted in the coming years.

*Edward Silver*
*University of Michigan*
*Ann Arbor, MI*
*easilver@umich.edu*

*Erica Walker*
*Teachers College*
*Columbia Univesity*
*New York, NY 10027*
*ewalker@exchange.tc.columbia.edu*

CBMS Issues in Mathematics Education
Volume **15**, 2008

# Preparing Teachers in Mathematics Education Doctoral Programs: Tensions and Strategies

Patricia S. Wilson and Megan Franke

Most students seeking mathematics education doctoral degrees have had teaching experience in schools. Regardless of whether they have had a few years experience or a full career in teaching mathematics, they have developed some expertise and confidence in teaching mathematics to a subset of students at some level from PreK through the undergraduate years. This is an important set of understandings and skills. However, preparing doctoral students in mathematics education for teaching requires complex levels of expertise broader than the expertise needed for teaching mathematics.

As university mathematics educators, doctoral students will be expected to teach mathematics to students who are or will be teaching mathematics themselves. *Teaching mathematics to teachers* involves an additional layer of complexity. Preparing teachers requires an enhanced set of knowledge and skills – the learner is a teacher of mathematics as well as a student of mathematics. The context of teaching becomes not just the classroom where teachers and students interact but also the school, the local community, and the community of mathematics teachers. Shifting from teaching mathematics to teaching teachers is challenging. Murray and Male (2005) discuss the phenomenon of "expert become novice" (p. 135) and other tensions associated with this critical shift in identity from being an expert teacher to a novice teacher educator.

Doctoral programs need to be structured to help students challenge their teaching practices, their notions about student learning and their understandings of schooling. In addition, they will need to help students consider ideas of teaching and teacher education in relation to potentially different populations than those they have taught. Students need to struggle with issues of culture, race, and equity, and integrate their new knowledge with previous ideas about teaching and teacher education.

We want to prepare teacher educators who will be able to plan, conduct, and assess courses and programs for teachers. We want them to learn the skills needed to conduct research related to learning and teaching mathematics. In addition, we want doctoral students to be prepared to work with both preservice teachers and practicing teachers, and we want to prepare them to work with teachers at multiple grade levels. Doctoral programs need to provide experiences for our doctoral students that will help them prepare teachers to work with increasingly diverse groups of mathematics learners including significant numbers of low-income students or students of color. As we take on the additional challenges of designing and implementing a doctoral program, we need to draw on our experiences as *mathematics teachers* and our experiences as *mathematics educators preparing teachers*, but we must realize that we are at yet another level of complexity when we address the work of *preparing mathematics educators*. We are responsible for preparing those who will work as colleagues and prepare future mathematics educators and conduct research in mathematics education.

As we add more layers, we rarely leave previous responsibilities behind. For example, as we move from teaching mathematics in grades PreK-16 to preparing teachers, we are still *teaching mathematics* and, in addition, we are teaching a *specialized knowledge of mathematics needed for teaching* (Ball, 2003; Cuoco, Goldenberg & Mark, 1996; Even, 1993). As we move to teaching mathematics to teacher educators, we need to teach *mathematics, specialized mathematics for teaching*, and mathematics *that is applied to preparing mathematics teachers* (Knuth, 2002; Schifter, 1998; Schoenfeld, 1988: Sfard & Linchevski, 1994). As we take on the responsibilities of preparing colleagues to teach, we need to take seriously ideas collected and proposed by Chris Golde (this volume) when she challenged us to prepare stewards of the discipline by engaging doctoral students in *apprenticeships with* rather than *apprenticeships in*.

Much of what we know about teacher learning applies to supporting doctoral students in mathematics education as they learn to teach at the university level. The research of Jean Lave and Etienne Wenger draws our attention to learning as a social practice, where identities shape participation and participation shapes identities. Communities of practice are social sites where people participate together in activities that shape who they are and what they know (Lave, 1996, Lave & Wenger, 1991; Wenger, 1998). Studies of such communities in mathematics education support the argument that learning to teach is enhanced by social interaction (Zaslavsky & Leikin, 2004; Wilson, Bismarck, & DuCloux, 2006). This perspective on learning leads us to a set of principles in which to consider creating learning opportunities: (a) learning occurs as novices participate with each other and experts on meaningful tasks, (b) joint participation enables participants to draw upon one another's particular knowledge and expertise, thereby expanding their shared repertoire, (c) dialogue provides participants with opportunities to make their knowledge explicit, to argue and challenge one another's beliefs, and to forge new ways of making sense of existing practice, (d) learners take on new dispositions, skills, and beliefs as they become more competent in practice, and (e) learning through mutual engagement in a joint enterprise enables participants to develop socially valued work-products-for example, stories, texts, and presentations that promote further learning (Oakes, Franke, Quartz, Rogers, 2002).

Creating opportunities within doctoral programs for students to learn more about this complex set of ideas requires apprenticeship situations with faculty, in certain settings, around particular mathematical work. Making sure these opportunities exist while at the same time maintaining the research apprenticeship creates a series of tensions. Our breakout sessions addressed many of the tensions that reside in all of our programs even though the program sizes and goals vary. We argue that it is important to acknowledge tensions, to see relationships between tensions, and to find strategies that begin to alleviate the tensions or actually use the tensions to build a better program. The majority of the time in each breakout session was used to discuss existing and potential strategies related to preparing doctoral students to successfully to fulfill the broad range of teaching responsibilities that they will assume as mathematics educators.

## Tensions and Strategies

We identified a series of tensions that the session participants supplemented. All identified tensions are shown in Table 1. The italicized rows in Table 1 identify three of the most-discussed tensions. The paragraphs following Table 1 provide some strategies participants offered to address them.

**Tension 1: Accommodating Both Fieldwork and Coursework.** In preparation for educating teachers (preservice and inservice), doctoral students need courses taught on campus as well as field experiences in schools and communities where they have the opportunity to engage in "teaching apprenticeships." Working in schools and with teachers imposes specific constraints on location and schedule often forcing doctoral students to choose between an exciting opportunity to do fieldwork and critical courses that are needed in their programs. In addition, there is disagreement about where this type of fieldwork fits within a doctoral program. Some see field work as central and ongoing while others see it following prerequisite coursework. How do fieldwork and coursework fit together?

Strategies:

- Create internship programs that integrate practice and research in local classrooms.
- Place students in schools with opportunities to learn about concurrent course content.
- Be explicit about how a doctoral program addresses the coursework and field work components.
- Merge the teaching and research components for greater impact (i.e., create "research on teaching" field experience).
- Doctoral students teach mathematics or content courses for preservice elementary while taking research in mathematics education and learning theory. They take a 1-hr coordinated seminar to help reconcile what they learn in their courses and what they experience in their teaching.
- Require a two-semester teaching internship and a three-semester research internship. Teacher prep courses can be taught in the field (at schools).

The conversations about strategies to address Tension 1 focused on intentionally shifting our doctoral programs so that teaching is more central in learning and connects to both coursework and research. Most participants saw learning to teach as a necessary part of the doctoral program and there was a sense that the best way to address this was to integrate learning to teach into existing opportunities. Some felt they could accomplish this through their research work if research experiences that involved schools and teaching were available. Others felt that they could do this through teaching opportunities at the university. Many programs had existing classes in teacher education or undergraduate programs that could serve as sites for communities of doctoral students and professors to design, implement, and study the courses. There are examples of this approach occurring at some of the sites

TABLE 1. Tensions in Preparing Mathematics Educators to Teach

| Tension | Description | Questions |
|---------|-------------|-----------|
| 1 | *Accommodating both fieldwork and coursework* | *How do fieldwork and coursework fit together? Can you manage both in a reasonable length of time?* |
| 2 | Providing optimal apprenticeship experiences in both teaching and research | How do you balance the needs of students and needs of department or research project? |
| 3 | Selecting communities where students and doctoral students can learn to teach and conduct research | How do we get our students to think about the challenges of low-performing schools? How do we prepare our students to work with students of color or with varying ethnicities, languages, economic resources, and cultures? |
| 4 | Helping doctoral students to move from a personal view of teaching to a broader view of teaching | How do we help doctoral students shift from a teacher identity to a teacher educator identity? |
| 5 | *Planning a program that serves a diverse population of doctoral students* | *How does a doctoral program support international students, part-time students, students with no teaching experience, or students entering from another field?* |
| 6 | Preparing doctoral students to work with teachers in PreK-16 and gaining expertise at a particular grade band | Should all students be prepared to take a position preparing mathematics teachers in grades PreK-16? Should students focus on a specific grade band range? |
| 7 | *Implementing a program with limited faculty, community access, students or other resources* | *How do you make decisions about resources? What resources can be shared across institutions? What are particular issues in urban and rural settings?* |

represented. We heard about programs where students engaged with faculty in teaching mathematics courses. They plan together, teach and learn from their experiences. In addition, this can serve as a site for research for the doctoral students. The point is to take advantage of these situations to create communities of learning around supporting those learning to teach in the field.

Finding opportunities for both research and teaching apprenticeships can be challenging, but there are ways to leverage each apprenticeship to support the other. If faculty are teaching particular courses, doctoral students can work with them to learn to teach and can use the work on the course as a site for research regardless of whether this is the faculty member's research agenda.

An additional theme that emerged around addressing Tension 1 related to creating opportunities in courses for learning to teach. Courses could address theory and research related to teaching as well as connecting these ideas to field work. For example, a course addressing research on teaching could embed field work or include an assignment to design a research-based course on teaching. Implementing these strategies requires those teaching the graduate courses to be knowledgeable about research and theories of teaching as well as teaching itself.

**Tension 2: Planning a Program that Serves a Diverse Population of Doctoral Students.** Doctoral programs are enriched by a diverse population of doctoral students who bring a wide variety of experiences to share. Diversity within the doctoral student population also makes it hard to plan a program that will benefit all students. Students come with different mathematical knowledge, teaching experiences, interests, native languages, cultures, and visions. Should there be entrance requirements such as a level of mathematics or teaching experience, or should these be exit requirements? How do we attract and serve underrepresented populations? How can we use the diversity of the doctoral student population to prepare teachers to work with diverse students of mathematics?

Strategies:

- Make explicit the focus of their program and what they are looking for in their students.
- Consider the program focus and requirements in light of who they want to attract.
- Consider how the structure and the content of the program meet the needs of the students you want to attract and serve.
- In working with part-time students, use technology and virtual faculties to implement courses and create a community for doctoral students.
- In working with international students, utilize the different skills and understanding students bring (e.g., language, schooling experiences, culture and mathematics) to enhance courses. Also, use these perspectives to help international students become familiar with teaching in the United States.

Tension 2 raised some questions and disagreement in the discussion groups about whom we want or need to attract to our doctoral programs. There were concerns about making sure we were attracting the best and brightest students, students with significant mathematical knowledge, students with diverse backgrounds, and students with a variety of relevant experiences. The issue was one of priority and whether programs need to make diversity, particularly around race or ethnicity, a priority. While many in the group looked for opportunities to diversify their doctoral programs and actively recruit, there are few programs that have made this an explicit priority in their admissions. If programs want to include a diverse population of doctoral students, they need to be prepared to meet the wide range of needs and interests of the students. This kind of support is particularly important if we expect doctoral students to learn through field experiences or situations that are different from their previous experiences.

Although international students may not know about the variety of curricula and teaching traditions in the United States, they know about teaching from their perspectives. A number of students come with extensive teaching and professional development experiences, while others have none. Suggested strategies included using the experiences that our doctoral students bring as a resource (not a deficit) and organizing opportunities for students to learn from each other as well as from faculty and field experiences.

**Tension 3: Implementing a Program with Limited Faculty, Community Access, Students or Other Resources.** Focusing on the learning-to-teach aspect of doctoral education requires resources. Often these resources must come from existing funding sources, which means that faculty time, expenses, and faculties need to be re-crafted or re-negotiated. New priorities need to be determined. How can universities address the range of resource issues (e.g., money, expertise, equipment, travel funds, space) as we move towards a different kind of doctoral education? How do you make decisions about resources? What resources can be shared across institutions?

Strategies:

- Be intentional and strategic in building a community of mentors for doctoral students around teacher education.
- Intentionally plan multiple, related tasks as part of mentoring doctoral students (e.g. plan to write an article on co-teaching a course, plan a presentation by mentor and doctoral student related to teaching).
- Have intentional learning goals for doctoral students around teacher education.
- Seek external funding to support teacher education and learning.
- Start small and build.
- Build mentoring of doctoral students into teaching goals of the doctoral program.
- Utilize (even notice) opportunities in specific localities for doctoral students to collaborate with school, district, and state leaders in mathematics education.
- Build practicums, internships, small scale apprenticeships, large scale mentoring groups into funding and programs for teaching assistants.

The resource issues are significant. Addressing the demands of supporting doctoral students to learn to teach requires money, expertise, courses, field experiences, coordination, and so on. The resource requirements depend on the particular institution and its history for supporting teaching. There was significant discussion about how a lack of resources can keep institutions from moving forward on any new plans around learning to teach. Programs need faculty with experience in using both theoretical and practical perspectives to inform their scholarship. Programs need students with diverse experiences. The consensus was that institutions can no longer neglect these requirements. Institutions and the people in them must find ways to start small and begin to build their programs around learning to teach. There are ways to draw on money and expertise from both inside and outside the institution. Programs can begin with modest adaptations, but mathematics teacher educators must focus on preparing doctoral students to teach in a way that is sustainable and becomes part of the overall institutional program. Institutions can look within and find ways to adapt what they already do without making substantial changes, by rethinking existing internships or turning teaching assistantships positions into learning opportunities.

## Summary

Overall there were a number of consistent recommendations. There was extensive conversation around learning through apprenticeship and how taking that seriously requires thinking differently about learning to teach in doctoral programs. There was little opposition to the conceptual idea. The difficulties come in trying to figure out how to make this work within the confines of our current doctoral programs.

One recommendation focused on starting "small". Starting small has to do with choosing something you can actually do and jumping in, rather than waiting until a complete package can be adopted or funded. A program can achieve small changes with only a few resources and clever adaptations.

The other overarching suggestion was around focus. We cannot accomplish all changes at once and we need to pick a systematic and careful place to begin and carry through with the work. The most challenging overarching suggestion had to do with integration. We can leverage our resources, our expertise, the expertise of the schools and communities and the expertise of our doctoral students in better ways than we are currently doing. If we are going to take more seriously the work of teaching as part of doctoral education, we will need to find ways to integrate this work with the work we are already doing - in our research, our coursework, and our field work.

*Patricia S. Wilson*
*University of Georgia*
*Athens, GA 30602*
*pswilson@uga.edu*

*Megan Franke*
*University of California-Los Angeles*
*Los Angeles, CA 90095*
*mfranke@ucla.edu*

CBMS Issues in Mathematics Education
Volume 15, 2008

# Doctoral Programs in Mathematics Education: Diversity and Equity

## Edd V. Taylor and Richard Kitchen

Issues related to diversity and equity in mathematics education have become a national concern in the United States during the past 25 years. The focus on diversity and equity in mathematics education, though, did not necessarily stem from a general concern for individual students and families. Instead, the supposed national shortcomings in mathematics education stemmed from the perception that the nation needed to increase the number of graduates in mathematics and science, specifically to address sustaining U.S. military and economic superiority (National Commission on Excellence in Education, 1983). Despite the initial motivation for examining success for "all" students, documents like *A Nation at Risk* (National Commission on Excellence in Education, 1983) and *Everybody Counts* (National Research Council, 1989) brought attention to the neglect of schools to prepare "all" students to learn mathematics and science. Indeed, the inclusion of the *Equity Principle* as a core concern of NCTM's *Principles and Standards* document (2000) underscores the need to address the needs of an ever-changing student population.

A question pertinent to doctoral education and related to diversity and equity in schools is "To what extent have PhD programs in mathematics education changed to address the needs of a diversifying population?" In recent years, doctoral programs have been modified to include coursework to prepare students to understand new theories about how children learn and this knowledge has transformed mathematics curriculum and instruction. Considering the changes in doctoral programs that were needed to give PhD students the knowledge underpinning such reforms, we believe that accompanying changes must be made in terms of the philosophies, values imparted, and coursework offered by doctoral programs to support the learning of a diverse student population.

Before providing a summary of themes that emerged related to issues of equity and diversity, we believe it is worth noting the contrast in the racial/ethnic background of three important groups: the PreSchool-12 (P-12) students in the United States, (2) the PreSchool-12 teaching force, and (3) graduate students enrolled in mathematics education doctoral programs.

*P-12 Students* (Fry, 2007)

- Nationally, 43% of public school enrollment consist of students of color
    - 19.8% are Latino/Latina.

    – 17.2% are African-American.

*P-12 Teachers* (National Center for Education Information, 2005)
- Nearly 90% of teachers in the U.S. are White.
- White teachers are 73% of the teaching force in urban schools.

*Mathematics Education Doctoral Students* (Reys, Glasgow, Teuscher, & Nevels, this volume)
- 11% minorities in the 1990s.
- 21% minorities in the 2000s.

We believe that the contrast between the racial/ethnic background of students in U.S. schools and those prepared to address their educational needs offers compelling evidence for the need to explicitly address issues related to diversity and equity in doctoral programs. Many graduates of PhD programs in mathematics education will work as mathematics educators. Given that many will be working to prepare P-12 educators who will be teaching in highly diverse school districts, PhD mathematics educators need to be prepared to train prospective teachers for the challenges they will be facing. For example, it is well-documented that teachers hold lower expectations for students of color and those from poor families than they do for White middle class students (Ferguson, 1998; Grant, 1989; Knapp & Woolverton, 1995; Zeichner, 1996). Low expectations are believed to be at the root of ineffective pedagogy with students of color and the poor. To counter low expectations, mathematics educators must be equipped to prepare prospective teachers to be reflective practitioners who hold high expectations for all students and actively work to support the learning of all students.

## Summary of Themes Related to Diversity and Equity

The themes that follow emerged from responses to two questions:

- What should doctorates in mathematics education know to be advocates for teaching for diversity and equity in mathematics?
- What common experiences should doctorates in mathematics education have to be advocates for teaching for diversity and equity in mathematics?

We were able to summarize the big ideas into five themes that emerged from posing these questions. What follows is a summary of the big ideas that materialized along with what we believe are the most vital recommendations that need to be made in order to implement these suggestions.

**Theme 1: There is a need for PhD students in mathematics education to learn about diversity/equity in all of their coursework and to develop national leaders in this area.** Diversity/equity should be central within all coursework and experiences of PhD students in mathematics education. From this perspective, courses in diversity/equity should not just be "add-ons" to the required program of studies. Instead, the study of diversity/equity should be integrated throughout the required program of studies for PhD students in mathematics education. In addition, creating leaders with expertise in diversity/equity in mathematics education should be a priority of doctoral programs throughout the country. This is *a must* given the highly diverse population of the United States and the changing demographics of the nation.

**Theme 2: There is a need for PhD students in mathematics education to learn "core knowledge" and have common experiences related to diversity/equity across institutions with doctoral programs in mathematics education.** In PhD programs across the United States, students need to learn specific knowledge that is directly related to diversity/equity in mathematics education. A very preliminary list–not meant to be exhaustive–of knowledge that should be included in this core include: (1) How diverse students learn (Banks, Cochran-Smith, Moll, Richert, Zeichner, & LePage, 2005), (2) Effective curriculum and instruction for diverse populations (Moses & Cobb, 2001 and Boaler, 2002), (3) Knowledge about and how to provide access to challenging curriculum and instruction for diverse learners (Boaler, 2006; Lipka, 2005; Moschkovich, 1999), (4) Strategies for supporting struggling learners (Bottge, 1999), (5) Mathematics curriculum/instruction that is infused by concerns related to social justice (Gutstein, 2005; Ladson-Billings, 2001), (6) The role of parents in mathematics education (Civil & Andrade, 2002), and (7) Strategies for preparing prospective teachers of mathematics to work with diverse learners (Rodriguez & Kitchen, 2005).

In PhD programs across the United States, students also need to have common experiences related to their training in diversity/equity in mathematics education. These common experiences could include: (1) The use of technology to connect faculty and others (e.g., classroom teachers) working directly in the area of diversity/equity, (2) Assignments given in doctoral courses in which PhD students conduct interviews and classroom observations in P-12 classrooms and in out-of-school contexts (e.g., community centers) to learn about diversity/equity, and (3) Seminars that value the expertise of faculty across departments and colleges on issues related to diversity/equity.

**Theme 3: There is a need for PhD students in mathematics education to have professional experiences in a diversity of settings.** Instead of simply reading articles about diversity/equity, PhD students need to have a significant field experience in a setting that is unfamiliar to them. PhD students in mathematics education need experiences different from what may be familiar to them (e.g., Middle-class Latina students from the suburbs need professional experiences in poor, rural schools). These experiences could be in the P-12 classroom, out-of-school contexts (e.g., community center), and include the study of video cases. There was broad agreement that these experiences need to be carefully reflected upon by participants, specifically to avoid reifying people into rigid categories by race, ethnicity, class, gender, sexual orientation, religion, etc.

Field experiences may assist PhD students in contextualizing their research projects vis-á-vis diversity/equity research, rather than providing little or no information about how their research was socially, culturally, or politically situated. The question was raised about how to affect change and create diverse experiences for PhD students at universities with just one faculty member and where diversity/equity may not be part of the institution's mission.

There was also discussion concerning the merits of PhD students in mathematics education developing the sense of being of service to others as well as of developing thoughtful notions of service with regards to their scholarship. Pragmatically put, there was agreement that PhD students in mathematics education should view their research as a means to serve others, as opposed to a means simply to promote their research agendas.

**Theme 4: There is a need for PhD students in mathematics education to develop an appreciation of diversity/equity issues even if diversity/equity is not central in the research that they undertake.** First, PhD students in mathematics education need to develop an appreciation of diversity/equity issues in general because of how their views of diversity/equity will influence their research methodology. This is the case even for studies that are not directly investigating issues related to diversity/equity in mathematics education. Second, there was concern that many PhD students in mathematics education may themselves hold deficit views of people different from themselves. To counter this, participants believe that all PhD students in mathematics education must be actively engaged in reflecting upon their views of people from diverse backgrounds. Third, participants expressed apprehension that researchers in mathematics education could over-generalize their research findings without a strong grounding in theoretical perspectives on diversity/equity in mathematics education. Lastly, there needs to be particular emphases placed on preparing PhD students in mathematics education to learn about diversity/equity so that these PhDs do not essentialize either prospective P-12 teachers and P-12 students in their research into rigid categorizations (e.g., all African American students believe that).

**Theme 5: There is a need for PhD students in mathematics education to develop an appreciation of theoretical frameworks related to diversity/equity and have knowledge of the research that has been undertaken that relates to diversity/equity in mathematics education.** PhD students in mathematics education need to investigate alternative theoretical frameworks and alternative interpretations of phenomena. At the doctoral level, students should study a wide array of theoretical frameworks and this includes theories related to diversity/equity. For example, PhD students should learn about theoretical frameworks that provide insight into how different mathematical assessment formats impact diverse students. For example, socio-cultural perspectives have shed light on how changing context and the language of mathematical tasks can impact the performance of students of color (Gutirrez, Baquedano-López, & Tejada, 2000; Ladson-Billings, 1997; Moschkovich, 2002). As part of their training, PhD students should also develop a propensity to interpret a broad array of phenomena from a variety of perspectives. Engaging in the study of diversity/equity will support PhD students in mathematics education to understand institutions and social structures and how they affect teaching and learning. For example, PhD students could study how tracking in mathematics classroom has disproportionately affected minority students negatively (Oakes, 1990). Alternatively, they could investigate how an emphasis on a technology-heavy mathematics curriculum may differentially impact low-income schools that may be unable to purchase the materials needed to successfully implement such a program (Apple, 1992).

## Challenges and Questions Related to Diversity and Equity

While many programs are concerned with preparing doctoral students who have the knowledge, dispositions, and skills to address issues related to diversity/equity, there may be inadequate knowledge at some institutions to develop courses, support projects, or modify programs that would result in appropriate preparation in this area. This issue becomes increasingly problematic as greater and greater numbers of doctoral students graduate from programs with little or no emphasis on diversity/equity and then go on to take positions at colleges and universities, thus perpetuating this deficit in the field.

A tension exists with regards to how teaching and learning about specific groups could lead to reification (i.e., rigidly classifying people and their beliefs/practices in terms of their racial group membership). There was also a concern that faculty with limited understanding of the complexity of issues related to diversity and equity may "do more harm than good" in trying to address these issues having only surface level exposure to research, programs, and communities relevant to issues of equity and diversity in mathematics education. PhDs in mathematics education need guidance in terms of learning about and reflecting about themselves and their beliefs vis-á-vis diversity/equity as well as across diverse groups, and within groups that they may claim membership (e.g., middle-class).

There were also concerns about the lack of role models among faculty, doctoral students, and P-12 teachers in the area of diversity/equity. There continues to be a shortage of people nationally with special expertise and passion to lead in this area. Bearing in mind the great challenge for programs with PhD programs in mathematics education to find faculty prepared to address issues of equity and diversity is not to argue that some programs should not address these issues. To the contrary, included in the definition of a successful PhD degree program in mathematics education should be criteria related to the program's ability to prepare doctoral students to effectively address issues of equity and diversity. Considering the *Equity Principle*, we should be cautious in lauding doctoral programs in mathematics education that produce teachers that fail whole populations of low-income and ethnic or language minority students despite their success with White and middle class populations. We must change our ideology of success. This highlights, yet again, the need to make the preparation of doctoral students in mathematics education with expertise in diversity/equity a national priority.

There are multiple opportunities for investigations into equity in the P-12 classroom as "reform" mathematics curriculum and instruction are implemented. Issues concerning diversity/equity are even more relevant as a diversity of students are challenged to engage in problem solving approaches that demand a high level of written/oral comprehension in English. Doctoral students' and others' research on curricular implementation and effectiveness should be designed and conducted bearing in mind issues related to diversity and equity.

## Recommendations for Addressing Challenges Related to Implementing Reforms

In the subsequent section, we provide some recommendations to address the challenges associated with the five themes to reform doctoral programs in mathematics education.

**PhD programs in mathematics education must place a priority on recruiting and retaining candidates with successful experiences in teaching a diversity of students.** The ways that individual programs address this may vary, but could include:

- recognizing course work and experiences related to issues of diversity in admissions.

- placing priority on teaching experiences in underserved communities for programs that value prior teaching experience before entering the doctoral program.
- emphasizing curriculum that addresses research related to issues of diversity from individual, community, and society level.

**PhD programs in mathematics education must foster the creation of faculty that is prepared to address diversity/equity.** We should consider the critical need for new mathematics educators in the next decade as a problem ripe with opportunity to change the overall composition of mathematics educators in regards to their ethnicity/race and their preparation to address issues of equity/diversity. If nearly half of mathematics educators will retire in the coming decade (Reys, Glasgow, Ragan, & Simms, 2001), then producing mathematics education doctoral graduates ready to engage in these issues as new hires may drastically impact the ability of PhD programs to implement change successfully. This requires, though, that competence related to issues of diversity/equity be prioritized during the hiring process.

**Considering the challenges in implementing the themes listed previously, PhD programs in mathematics education should consider the following recommendations:**

- Partnerships should be developed between universities that are developing their diversity/equity knowledge-base and universities with greater expertise in this area.
- Efforts should be undertaken to develop post doctoral opportunities and to sponsor graduate fellowships focused on research and support of a national effort to prepare PhD programs in mathematics education to address diversity/equity.
- Collaborations should be pursued in which technology could be used not only to connect mathematics education doctoral programs to P-12 schools and districts, but also to other universities in order to share specific expertise related to diversity/equity. Some National Science Foundation funded Centers for Learning and Teaching successfully implemented such models and developed models that others can learn from.

*Edd V. Taylor*
*Northwestern University*
*Evanston, IL 60208*
*edd-taylor@northwestern.edu*

*Richard Kitchen*
*University of New Mexico*
*Albuquerque, NM*
*kitchen@unm.edu*

CBMS Issues in Mathematics Education
Volume 15, 2008

# Using Technology in Teaching and Learning Mathematics: What Should Doctoral Students in Mathematics Education Know?

M. Kathleen Heid and Hollylynne S. Lee

The doctoral student in mathematics education in the 21st Century has unprecedented need for knowledge of technology. Most doctoral students, whether or not they are in mathematics education, use technology for communication, library research, and data gathering and processing. The doctoral student in mathematics education, however, has a unique set of additional technological needs arising from the singular role that technology has in the teaching and learning of mathematics. This paper shares ideas about the knowledge of technology needed by those graduating from a doctoral program in mathematics education.

The need for knowledge of technology by graduates of doctoral programs in mathematics education is substantiated in the Technology Principle in NCTM's *Principles and Standards for School Mathematics* (2000): "Technology is essential in teaching and learning mathematics; it influences the mathematics that is taught and enhances students' learning" (p. 24). If technology is essential for students in grades K through 12, it is certainly essential for their teachers, as well as for the teachers of their teachers. In their *Principles to Guide the Design and Implementation of Doctoral Programs in Mathematics Education*, the Association of Mathematics Teacher Educators (2003) described the knowledge and understandings of technology needed by doctoral graduates in mathematics education:

> Technological tools are vital to the development of mathematical concepts and processes, and their availability is changing mathematics at all levels. Consequently mathematics educators need both knowledge of and an ability to use such tools effectively. Graduates of doctoral programs in mathematics education should understand and be able to utilize technology as a tool of inquiry that has implications for teaching and learning mathematics. Although technology offers opportunities to present and explore mathematics in new ways, it is critical that doctoral students understand the potential and limitations of technology. They should be able to design learning experiences for students and teachers at various levels that utilize technology to enable and support mathematics exploration and learning. Fluency is expected with technology tools that support teaching, learning, and research. Knowledge

of research related to the interaction of technology and mathematics teaching and learning should be a specific focus of study within a doctoral program. (Retrieved December 10, 2007 from http://www.amte.net/resources/Doctoral_Studies_position_paper.htm).

To further develop our understanding of the knowledge and experiences needed by those completing a doctorate in mathematics education, we gathered information from attendees at the 2007 conference on mathematics education doctoral programs. What follows is a description of our efforts and recommendations that have emerged from our work.

## Method

Prior to the conference, we administered a brief e-mail survey polling conference attendees on technology-related goals and practices. Of the 140 participants to whom we sent a survey, 20 responded. Those 20 faculty represented the geographic and size range of institutions engaged in the preparation of doctoral graduates in mathematics education. The questions we asked in the survey included the following:

> Please indicate up to three technology-related experiences, understandings, or skills that a mathematics education doctoral student should have.

> Describe the types of extra-course technology-related experiences in which your doctoral students in mathematics education typically engage (specify uses of technology for data-gathering and data-processing, uses of technology for presentations, uses of technology for teaching demonstrations, and so on).

> Do your doctoral students in mathematics education complete a course (or courses) focused on technology? If yes, identify the course(s) and indicate which (if any) focus specifically on mathematics education.

> Do the courses that you identified have a major focus on research on technology and education? If yes, describe that focus (e.g., students read research studies, students conduct a literature review, students design and conduct a research study).

Results of the 20 survey respondents were compiled and shared with participants at the conference session.

To begin the conference session, we engaged participants in a discussion of various ways in which technology is used in mathematics classrooms. We seeded this discussion with the scenarios shown in Figure 1. Participants discussed the use of technology as a learning or teaching tool in each context. They were also asked to identify interesting research questions that we would want doctoral students to ask concerning issues in each context.

Using the results of the survey and our initial discussions stemming from Figure 1, participants formed groups and were asked to generate responses to the following questions:

---

Scenarios to Consider:

North Penn High School has a large mathematics department that is well-equipped with a variety of computing and handheld technologies. As we peer into the halls and classrooms of North Penn we get a glimpse of the following activities:

- A group of students are in the hallways using a motion detector and graphing calculator to capture distance and time data as they engage in a Match that Graph activity. The students are discussing the ways in which their physical motion needs to be adjusted to collect data that better matches a particular distance vs. time graph.
- Mr. Alpha has a class of Algebra students in a computer lab using an intelligent tutoring tool that can help prepare them for an end-of-course exam.
- Mrs. Beta has students using a dynamic geometry software application to follow directions to construct various quadrilaterals and then to compare the properties of each that remain invariant under various dragging actions.
- Mrs. Delta has her students working on a problem in her Calculus class. As she circulates throughout the room, she uses an application in her handheld palm device to keep track of students work and make notes about their mathematical thinking. She uses these notes to help decide which students to ask to share their work and to later have a record that she can use to trace students' ideas throughout the unit of study.
- Mr. Lambda has his Trigonometry class in the library where they are using the internet to find examples of applications of a sine function in business, weather, geology, etc.
- A group of students are gathered in the cafeteria using their graphing calculators that include a computer algebra system (CAS) to solve a problem assigned in their Algebra II class. The teacher had instructed students to solve the problem using whatever methods and tools they desired and that they would be expected to share their solution approaches in class the next day.
- Mrs. Omega is showing a video that illustrates a proof of the Pythagorean Theorem and discusses some of the history of the development of this theorem and examples of applications of the theorem in the various careers.

---

*What researchable questions specific to the teaching and learning of mathematics might doctoral students in mathematics education ask about uses of technology tools in each of these contexts within North Penn High School?*

---

FIGURE 1. Sample of ways in which technology is used in mathematics classrooms.

What should doctoral students in mathematics education understand about ways to think about mathematical tools in teaching, learning, and research?

What are some examples and models for helping doctoral students develop these understandings?

The major aim of this paper is to discuss the understandings needed by doctoral students in mathematics education about the use of mathematical technology tools in mathematics education and the implications these understandings have for the design of doctoral programs. Our recommendations have emerged from the perspectives shared by the conference participants and survey respondents and from our own experiences and research.

## Core Knowledge

Session participants and survey respondents suggested that all doctoral students need a core set of 21st Century technology skills expected of one holding a research-intensive degree. These skills include fluency with a variety of technology tools used in scholarly work: professional productivity software (e.g., word processing, presentation software, database, spreadsheet); search engines, databases, and bibliographic software (e.g., EndNote, RefWorks); statistical packages (e.g., SPSS, SAS); text and video analysis software (e.g., NVivo, HyperResearch); online class organizers (e.g., Blackboard, WebCT), and capabilities with research data collection and preparation (e.g., digital video, audio, web-based surveys, large national databases (e.g., NCES), software to assist in transcription). Although facility with these tools is critical for educational scholarship in the 21st Century, this knowledge base does not address the specialized knowledge needed by doctoral graduates in mathematics education.

Doctoral graduates in mathematics education also need a basic understanding of how to use various technology tools commonly used in the context of mathematics education, technologies we consider to be *mathematical tools*. They need familiarity with and flexibility in using mathematical tools such as graphing calculators, computer algebra systems (e.g., TI-89, TI-92, Mathematica, Maple), spreadsheets, dynamical geometry software, and dynamical statistics software. A major aspect of their understanding of these tools is an understanding of the distinction between the mathematical object being represented and the inscription used for that representation (Heid & Zembat, 2007). Inherent in that understanding is representational fluency and connections among multiple representations of a mathematical object. Mathematics education doctoral students need to gain experiences with various mathematical tools in the context of their roles as: 1) *mathematics learners* before being able to explore the effects of use of the tool on learning, and 2) *mathematics teachers* before assisting others to learn to teach mathematics with technology. As teachers of mathematics teachers, they could also benefit from experience in designing technology-based environments.

Doctoral graduates in mathematics education need a level of understanding of learning mathematics with technology that transcends skilled use in their own learning of mathematics. They need an in-depth understanding of the theory and research specific to mathematics teaching and learning in technological environments (e.g. Blume & Heid, in press; Guin, Ruthven, & Trouche, 2005; Heid &

Blume, in press; Hoyles & Noss 2003; Kaput, 1992; Kieran & Yerushalmy, 2004; Zbiek, Heid, Blume, & Dick, 2007). This understanding should include:

- understanding of research related to the use of technology to support teaching and learning mathematics,
- knowledge of ways in which technology can be used to promote reflection about teaching and growth as professionals,
- understanding of different theoretical arguments about student learning and how technology use relates to general learning theory,
- understanding of the cognitive theory connected with technological tools, and
- broad awareness of the instability introduced by technology that influences what mathematics we should teach as well as how we can teach it.

The understandings described here will serve the teacher of mathematics teachers as well as underpin the work of those who intend to engage in development or conduct research on the use of technology in the teaching and learning of mathematics.

Doctoral graduates in mathematics education also need an understanding of the research and theory related to use of technology in the *teaching* of mathematics (e.g., Hollebrands & Zbiek, 2004; Lee, 2005; Zbiek & Hollebrands, in press), including:

- understanding of the research centering specifically on the use of mathematical technologies at the K-12 level so that they can support research-based technology practices with pre-service teachers,
- knowledge of the theoretical issues behind the use of technology in mathematics education,
- a general awareness of research surrounding existing technologies not situated in mathematics education but that can be used in the teaching of mathematics, and
- knowledge of foundational research in the area of technology and teacher education (e.g., Koehler & Mishra, 2005; Niess, 2005).

The construct of instrumental genesis also underpins our thinking about the technology-related knowledge and experiences these individuals need. Technology per se does not have the same effect or meaning across the range of individuals who use it. As the user gains experience with the tool, a two-way relationship develops between the user and the technological artifact, with the technology transforming the way the user thinks about the tool and the user transforming the tool uses for his or her purposes. This process of developing this tool-user relationship is called instrumental genesis (Guin, Ruthven, & Trouche, 2005). In order for mathematics educators to interact effectively with students regarding the use of technology, each must have developed a relationship with the technology being used. This relationship develops through intense experience using the tool for mathematics learning and teaching coupled with reflection on that experience.

We think about the impact of technology on the teaching and learning of mathematics as the impact of technology on factors involved in mathematics learning as well as on relationships among those factors. This position was developed in the research perspective presented by Zbiek and colleagues (2007) and is encapsulated by the diagram from that work shown in Figure 2. For example, not only can technology affect the teacher and the curriculum, but it also has the potential to impact the relationship between the teacher and the curriculum. Computer algebra systems

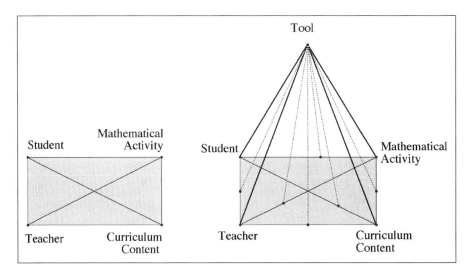

FIGURE 2. Technology mediates relationships among the student, the teacher, the mathematical activity, and the curriculum content in mathematics teaching and learning (Zbiek, Heid, Blume, & Dick, 2007, p. 1172).

can affect the mathematics curriculum by affording students the opportunity to offload execution of some routine algorithms, but it also can affect how the teacher thinks about the curriculum because it can call into question the traditional relationship between skills and concepts in school mathematics. Dynamical geometry tools can affect the mathematics curriculum by affording greater opportunity for mathematical investigations while affecting the relationship of students to the curriculum by accommodating a different view of mathematics. A doctoral graduate in mathematics education should understand these relationships and how they may affect different aspects of their job as researchers, teacher educators, curriculum developers, and so on.

Several additional important issues emerged during the participants' group sessions. We mention several additional important issues raised by conference participants here without elaboration:

- It is important for technology users to distinguish token from type and mathematical object from its external representation in the thinking they do based on technologically generated geometric sketches. Although this is also true in paper-and-pencil environments, the perceived precision of technologically generated geometric sketches entice users to think of the technologically generated images as the mathematical objects themselves.
- In order to be able to use technology to accomplish what the user wants it to do, the user is often called upon to access a deeper and more flexible knowledge of the mathematics underpinning the technology use. This suggests that technology users may need to know more rather than less mathematics. This includes the need to uncover the mathematics embedded in technology tools.

- There is new mathematics that emerges from technology uses, including the mathematics of gaming, the frontiers of visualization, and techniques of data mining. This may impact the mathematics background that is likely to be useful to graduates of mathematics education doctoral programs.

In general, then, graduates of mathematics education doctoral programs should be able to use technology to do mathematics and to teach mathematics. They should know the mathematics that specific mathematical tools can help promote, and be able to analyze new tools for their mathematical potential. They should also be able to analyze how tools can affect mathematical practices, including the sociomathematical norms (e.g., using a tool as part of an argument). Given a mathematical idea, they should know what tools are available and how the tools can be used to develop a conceptual understanding of that idea. They should understand, given a particular technology tool, how that technology can afford or constrain the learning of a particular mathematical idea, and what impact it is likely to have on instructional strategies. Finally, they should have an understanding of instrumental genesis (both how the tool affects the strategy and how the user affects the tool).

## Examples and Models in Mathematics Education Doctoral Programs

Addressing how a doctoral student in mathematics education develops the core knowledge discussed previously is not easy. Programs vary greatly across institutions and some programs have a higher concentration of faculty who are active in research in the teaching and learning with technology. We assume that most doctoral programs have embedded opportunities for doctoral students to learn the 21st Century skills we discussed above (e.g., presentation software, bibliographic software, statistical packages, video analysis tools). Thus, we will focus our comments on suggested examples for providing opportunities for doctoral students in mathematics education to develop the core knowledge set that is specific to our discipline.

Only a few participants and survey respondents reported that their institution had a specific graduate level course related to research in teaching and learning mathematics with technology (e.g., The Pennsylvania State University, North Carolina State University, University of Georgia, University of Missouri). Faculty teaching these courses could share their syllabi and perhaps explore ways that doctoral students from other universities could participate in such courses either through summer exchanges or distance education technologies. Whether or not a specific course is available, appropriate technology experiences can be included in various doctoral level mathematics education courses. For example:

- Within mathematics and statistics courses, embed appropriate technology for doctoral students to use in their own learning.
- Within a course on curriculum, engage doctoral students in a textbook analysis in which they critically examine the ways technology is used throughout a mathematics text, and identify untapped opportunities for including technology in the textbook that could enhance mathematics learning.

- Within a course on the learning and teaching of a specific content area (e.g., geometry, algebra, statistics), discuss how various technologies can afford or constrain the learning of certain concepts.
- Within a general educational technology course, create more individualized projects in which doctoral students read and write about the use of technology in mathematics.

There are several additional models that can be useful in facilitating the development of core knowledge for mathematics education doctoral students.

- Have a prerequisite skills test[1] that covers several of the basic types of mathematical tools (e.g., spreadsheets, graphing calculators, CAS, dynamical geometry software, dynamical statistical software). Doctoral students are expected to obtain the skill through self-study and experiences and pass the skills test early in the doctoral program.
- Engage doctoral students in research involving undergraduate preservice teachers who are learning to teach mathematics in technological environments.
- Engage doctoral students in teaching undergraduate mathematics or preservice methods courses in which mathematical technology tools are used.
- Provide K-12 school-based internships in which technology integration is expected. Such internships can lead to school-university partnerships and opportunities for research questions to emerge from doctoral students' experiences in classrooms.
- Provide opportunities for small scale research studies on issues of teaching and learning mathematics with technology, either embedded in coursework, or as part of research internships.
- Provide opportunities to interview learners in the course of technology-intensive task-based interviews.
- Expect a certain advanced level of skill and knowledge about theories and research about mathematical technology tools to be demonstrated through part of the comprehensive/qualifying/preliminary exam process.

Whether or not technology is a focus of a graduate program in mathematics education, individuals with doctoral graduates in mathematics education should have experience using technology as research assistants to carry out and implement research studies and using mathematics technology to conceptualize, plan, and carry out studies on mathematics teaching and learning. The level of this experience will vary but should prepare doctoral students to understand important research issues regarding the use of technology in the teaching and learning of mathematics.

## Conclusion

The Technology Principle set forth in the NCTM *Principles and Standards for School Mathematics* (2000) and the technology-related suggestions of the AMTE *Principles to Guide the Design and Implementation of Doctoral Programs in Mathematics Education* have thrown down the gauntlet for doctoral programs in mathematics education to prepare their graduates to lead their respective mathematics

---

[1]North Carolina State University has at times used a test designed for the end of its undergraduate-level technology-enhanced methods class for graduate students to take before enrolling in a graduate-level class on technology in mathematics education. Contact Hollylynne S. Lee for information on the test.

education communities to research, curriculum, and teaching that reflects current knowledge and practice regarding technology in mathematics teaching and learning. The suggestions that have emerged from the 2007 conference on Doctoral Programs in Mathematics Education should help provide programs with more specificity for what doctoral students should come to understand and possible ways that such understandings can be developed. Different programs will accept the challenge in different ways, but each program should take the challenge seriously.

*M. Kathleen Heid*
*The Pennsylvania State University*
*University Park, PA 16802*
*mkh2@email.psu.edu*

*Hollylynne Stohl Lee*
*North Carolina State University*
*Raleigh, NC 27695*
*hollylynne@ncsu.edu*

# Part 3

## Developing Stewards
## of the Discipline: Delivery Systems

CBMS Issues in Mathematics Education
Volume **15**, 2008

# Program Delivery Issues, Opportunities, and Challenges

## Denise S. Mewborn

The critical shortage of collegiate mathematics educators and the great variation in existing doctoral programs in mathematics education suggest that faculty
might consider ways to bridge institutional boundaries to enhance their students'
experiences. Much of the learning in a doctoral program, particularly for full-time
residential students, is intangible and transcends formal courses and assistantship
duties. Golde (this volume) described these intangibles as growing out of an "intellectual community" within the discipline. She described an intellectual community
as the bedrock of the discipline and characterized such a community as one in which
there are partnerships between students and faculty where all parties are able to
participate meaningfully in activities with full access to resources. She argued that
participating in this type of environment leads to a shared sense of responsibility for
shaping the future of the field. Although much of the language in documents from
the Carnegie Initiative on the Doctorate (e.g., Golde & Walker, 2006) focuses on
departments within institutions as the locus of intellectual communities, in this paper, I propose ways in which the mathematics education community at large might
cross institutional boundaries to provide and sustain broader intellectual communities for its doctoral students. I begin with a short overview of why we need to
create cross-institutional intellectual communities, followed by possible avenues for
creating such communities, and end with a brief description of challenges to the
creation of intellectual communities.

### The Issues

Doctoral students need at least three things in a doctoral program– interaction
with peers, interaction with "more knowledgeable others" (usually considered to
be faculty members), and access to resources. To some degree, each of these is a
challenge for most programs. In programs where there are few students or many
students attend on a part-time basis, there may not be a cadre of peers with whom
doctoral students can interact on a daily basis. Similarly, in small programs there
may be only one or two faculty members available to work with doctoral students,
and specific areas of expertise may not match the interests of students. In a related

I want to extend my thanks to the students and faculty members at the University of Georgia
who participated in the doctoral conference seminar in the fall of 2007 and provided extensive
input into this paper. I am also grateful to Andrew M. Tyminski of Purdue University for his
comments on an earlier draft of the paper.

vein, faculty members in smaller programs often do not have a local group of peers with whom to consult about program matters (such as appropriate readings for a course, a particularly challenging dissertation study design, a student who needs extra help with writing). The lack of a peer group, particularly for students, can occur in larger programs as well, especially if a student is interested in a topic that is a bit out of the mainstream for that institution. For instance, at my own institution, a candidate interested in student learning in higher level collegiate mathematics courses would find very few fellow students with a similar interest and no faculty member conducting research in this area. Similar situations occur with access to resources, such as data, teacher education materials, or historical curriculum documents. By creating an intellectual community (or multiple, smaller intellectual communities) across institutional boundaries, cooperating programs can provide peers, more knowledgeable others, and resources for doctoral students and faculty members to help all involved achieve their goals.

In the remainder of this paper, I describe opportunities for the field of mathematics education to develop and enhance existing intellectual communities for doctoral students. I will address ways that we can do this through modifications to current practices, through modifications to events outside of doctoral programs, and through replicating prototypes that have been tried in small and specific instances. I want to emphasize that although we generally default to thinking about ways to engage doctoral students in research, I intend these options to be viewed more broadly. For instance, we could build intellectual communities around issues of policy, teacher education, curriculum development, or technology in addition to research. Each option that I outline below is fraught with logistical, financial, and bureaucratic problems, making it easy to dismiss the idea as impossible without giving it a thorough vetting. Despite these challenges, I hope that we will consider what each of these options might mean for our own programs and our own students. Even if an idea cannot be fully implemented in the near future, it may be possible to take a kernel of that idea and spin it into something that is feasible with existing resources.

## The Opportunities

**Modifications to Existing Programs.** In this section I examine some existing, but perhaps underutilized, modifications to features of doctoral programs. First, students can be encouraged to utilize people external to their university at various points in their doctoral program. This has potential for making use of the expertise in the mathematics education community at large. Such involvement would need to be sustained and genuine–not simply reading the final dissertation product and providing "external validation" as is commonly done at some universities. Rather, an external person might be involved in suggesting readings on a particular topic for a student, in discussing major ideas in a subfield with the student, thinking through the development of a syllabus or the design of a professional development workshop, or participating in the design and development of the dissertation study. The benefits of such an arrangement to the student are fairly obvious, particularly when no one at the student's institution has the desired expertise. This could also be a means of tapping unused resources in the mathematics education community. There are many mathematics educators with a wealth of experience and knowledge on particular topics who are not at doctoral-granting institutions and who therefore miss the opportunity to engage with doctoral students. Such individuals may be at higher education institutions, professional organizations, or non-profit organizations (such as TERC and EDC). The rapidly growing cadre of emeritus faculty members in our field is another largely untapped resource. To effectively utilize the expertise of others, doctoral students would need guidance in identifying who in the field has the type of expertise that would be beneficial to them.

Several of the international panelists at the conference noted that their doctoral students commonly spend a portion of the doctoral program studying at another institution. This is an idea proposed by some of the Centers for Learning and Teaching but has not come to fruition in a substantial way. A doctoral student could spend a few weeks to a semester (or even a year) at another institution where faculty members or students with similar interests exist or visit at an institution that had resources (such as a data set) that would be useful to the doctoral student. Universities that are in close proximity to one another could exchange students during the summers relatively inexpensively. These exchanges need not be between similar institutions as students from research universities could learn a great deal from settings that are teaching-intensive and vice versa. Similarly, students from urban and rural campuses could broaden their horizons by switching places for a period of time. For several years the National Science Foundation and its equivalent in South Africa sponsored a student exchange program, whereby students from South Africa came to selected institutions in the U.S. for periods of three to six months, usually when they were at dissertation stage. These students were able to take advantage of print and electronic resources that were difficult to access in South Africa, and, more importantly, shared their dissertation studies with U.S. faculty members and graduate students. This was a two-way exchange in that the South African students received input and advice about their studies, references to consult, help in reanalyzing data, suggestions for organization of the dissertation, etc.-but, importantly, those of us in the US who were fortunate enough to work with them also gained insight into the research problems that were of interest to South African scholars and the context of teaching and learning mathematics in South Africa. In the area of equity, in particular, there was much to learn from these students and their research programs. The exchange program was intended to be a two-way exchange, but very few U.S. doctoral students took advantage of the opportunity to go to South Africa.

The growing availability of videoconferencing technology allows for the creation of shared experiences for doctoral students, ranging from one-time colloquia to full seminars or courses. Such experiences might be implemented as one student from University X sitting in on an existing event at University Y, or roughly equal numbers of students from two or more universities participating in the same event. An extended course or seminar might be taught by one faculty member or team-taught by faculty members from multiple institutions. Some of the Centers for Teaching and Learning have experimented with various models for full courses, and sample syllabi are available at http://www.CLTnet.org under the Resources link. All of the usual issues surrounding distance technology need to be addressed-such as how parties from distant locations, particularly single individuals at distant locations, participate meaningfully in the experience. One lesson learned by some of the Centers is that an initial face-to-face gathering of all parties seems to facilitate more meaningful dialogue later in the course.

Another venue for inducting doctoral students into the profession is to include them on departmental committees in meaningful roles. For instance, many of our graduates will be faced with the need to participate in a teacher education accreditation process at some point in their careers. By participating in the preparation of an accreditation report and the site visit as doctoral students, these future faculty members gain exposure to the goals of a teacher education program, observe the activities used to meet these goals, and evaluate the assessment system that enables the monitoring of these goals. It is important to note that in order to achieve maximum benefit from such a committee assignment, doctoral students need to be intellectually engaged with meaningful roles on the committee and not just be asked to do busy work.

**Modifications to Other Existing Events.** Many existing events, such as conferences, workshops, and institutes, have been or could be, structured to include a component for doctoral students. The National Council of Teachers of Mathematics Research Presession has included a brown bag lunch roundtable where doctoral students have an opportunity to meet for an hour with a distinguished mathematics education researcher. This tradition could be expanded to other conferences and topics other than research. For example, the Association of Mathematics Teacher Educators (AMTE) annual conference could include roundtables for doctoral students who are interested in either research about or the teaching of preservice and inservice teachers to spend time with experienced faculty members. These sessions could also be expanded beyond an hour to half-day sessions.

The North American Chapter of the International Group for the Psychology of Mathematics Education (PME-NA) has typically offered a single session that is for doctoral students only. These sessions sometimes feature new assistant professors providing advice on acquiring a position or getting published after becoming a faculty member and at other times feature senior doctoral students sharing information that is of interest to other doctoral students. Again, the topics of such sessions could be expanded to include other topics or changed to cover a longer duration. PME-NA is usually heavily attended by doctoral students, and the venue is often self-contained, making it an ideal place for doctoral students to engage with more senior scholars in the field.

The American Educational Research Association and the Association of Mathematics Teacher Educators typically hold pre-conference workshops and mini-courses of varying lengths. This is an idea that could be targeted to doctoral students and could cover a range of topics. Such sessions could be held in conjunction with major meetings or in conjunction with smaller conferences or institutes. An interesting idea that was piloted by the Center for the Study of Mathematics Curriculum was to hold a post-conference session for doctoral students who attended an international conference on mathematics curriculum. This format provided doctoral students an opportunity to discuss the ideas of the conference after experiencing it. Some of the major speakers from the conference participated as well, so the doctoral students had an opportunity to meet with them in a smaller and less-formal setting and to engage in substantive discussions about issues of interest to the doctoral students.

Different conferences capture different audiences. Thus, conferences such as those hosted by the Mathematical Association of America, the American Mathematical Society, the American Mathematical Association of Two-Year Colleges and the Research Council on Mathematics Learning should be considered as venues for doctoral student interaction as well. In states where there are multiple doctoral programs, state level conferences may provide opportunities for gathering doctoral students together.

Yet another possibility would be to hold a conference that is only for doctoral students. The purpose and goals of the conference would need to be carefully articulated so that the program could be designed accordingly, and a means of ensuring that all students have access to the conference would need to be devised. A variation on this idea would be a short "working conference" or retreat. The College of Education at the University of Georgia offers a "writing retreat" once a year for doctoral students and twice a year for faculty members. The session is limited to 15 participants and is hosted by a senior faculty member. The group meets off-campus for a three-day weekend, and each participant has a writing goal. Participants spend some time writing, some time exchanging text with peers, some time in whole group discussions about common issues, and some time working one-on-one with a senior colleague getting feedback on their writing. Such a model could focus on other topics of interest to doctoral students, such as crafting a syllabus and tasks for a teacher education course or writing grants.

**Prototypes to Replicate.** There are several prototypes of events designed to build a cross-institutional intellectual community that might be replicated or expanded to difference venues. For example, the Center for Proficiency in Teaching Mathematics (CPTM) held a multi-layered summer institute in the summer of 2004. The primary participants in the institute were mathematicians, mathematics educators, and school-based providers of professional development all having a primary interest in elementary school teacher learning. A number of doctoral students from both the University of Michigan and the University of Georgia participated in the institute in a variety of roles. Prior to the institute they were involved in designing the schedule and developing certain sessions. They were also involved in designing the research study that accompanied the institute. During the institute they functioned primarily as researchers, taking field notes, running video cameras, and conducting interviews with participants. However, they were also able to spend some time "off duty" as researchers and participate in the institute as learners. At other times (usually early in the morning or late in the evening), they met with CPTM faculty members to debrief the days' events, make modifications to the next days' events, review the research data that had been collected, and modify the research plan based on preliminary analyses of the data. The doctoral students arrived at the institute two days before the participants in order to finalize and coordinate research plans, and they spent a great deal of this time in a formal course that was co-taught by faculty members from each institution. The course continued after the institute when the doctoral students had returned to their home institutions. Some sessions were joint sessions facilitated by distance learning technology, and other sessions were held off-line at one institution. Cross-institutional teams of doctoral students were created, and these teams analyzed portions of the data from the institute and produced final reports. The design of this institute allowed the organizers to meet multiple goals at one time. They were able to provide professional development for the teacher educators, collect and analyze data about the institute, and provide a meaningful learning experience for doctoral students simultaneously. The relationships that were developed among the doctoral students across institutions and between the doctoral students and the conference participants have continued to this day.

Beginning in the 1950s and continuing through the post-Sputnik era, the National Science Foundation (NSF) sponsored many summer institutes, academic year institutes, inservice institutes, and fellowships for high school and college teachers of mathematics and science. Each of these programs had a distinct purpose, but most were aimed at some combination of strengthening content knowledge and enhancing pedagogical practices. Many of these programs provided opportunities for high school teachers to earn masters degrees through graduate study at institutions of higher education. Many current leaders in the field point to these NSF-funded activities as pivotal in their careers (Ferrini-Mundy, this volume). Today we find ourselves in a similar situation to the Sputnik era, with a shortage of mathematics teachers and mathematics educators and in a country that is losing ground to international competitors in the global economy. It would, therefore, be worthwhile for the field to take stock of what happened in the NSF institutes in the 50s and 60s to see what aspects of those activities might be replicated today, perhaps with NSF funding or with support from other sources.

Another idea comes from the South African Winter Research School that was jointly sponsored by the National Research Foundation in South Africa and the National Science Foundation in the U.S. for several years beginning in 2000. South Africa has very few full-time doctoral students, and their doctoral program is based on independent research rather than courses. Thus, the funding agencies provided an opportunity to bring together approximately 60 doctoral students in mathematics and science education from universities across the country for one week during their winter break in June. They also brought in two teams of scholars from around the world, including South African scholars, to work with the students. The research school consisted of two courses that each ran for five days. One ran in the mornings and one in the afternoons. Each day was structured as a combination of plenary sessions and smaller working sessions facilitated by individual instructors. In the late afternoon each instructor met individually with two or three students to discuss a piece of each student's writing, to help refine a research question, to develop a methodology, or to meet whatever need the student had. In the evenings, South African scholars (who were not instructors at the research school) came in to give presentations on contemporary research in mathematics or science education in the country. The South African Research School could be taken as a model for an intensive conference for doctoral students, but the topic need not be research.

Some of the Centers for Learning and Teaching have organized small annual conferences aimed primarily at doctoral students. The Mid-Atlantic Center, for instance, had held an annual conference in which faculty members, doctoral students, and practitioners from partner school districts convene to share ideas and work in progress. A portion of the conference is devoted to doctoral students who are at various stages of their dissertations presenting their ideas for critical feedback. Students who are in earlier stages of the dissertation, such as refining their questions, framework, or methods, present shorter sessions, while doctoral students who are further along in their data collection and analysis present longer sessions. All sessions have substantial time for feedback. For more information see the description of the activities at: http://www.education.umd.edu/macmtl/activities_misc.htm#conference.

In a similar vein, the Center for the Study of Mathematics Curriculum organized annual research conferences focusing on different issues, including Research on Mathematics Curricula, and Studying the Impact of Policy. Each conference involved doctoral students and faculty from CSMC institutions along with Doctoral Fellows from other institutions with a shared interest in mathematics curriculum issues. Keynote addresses helped inform and set the stage for small group discussions and the development of action plans.

Field trips involving students from multiple institutions could serve as opportunities to bring students together around a common interest. For example, a faculty member with expertise in policy might offer to take a group of students from multiple sites to Washington, DC for a multi-day seminar on policy. The students could visit the National Science Foundation to meet with program officers about current funding priorities, visit the National Council of Teachers of Mathematics to meet with the legislative liaison to learn about the Council's position on various issues, visit Capitol Hill with the liaison to meet with their legislators to discuss current legislation, and perhaps meet with staff associated with bills affecting mathematics education policy.

Modern technology could be used in a variety of ways to support and sustain communities of learners among doctoral students. Hosted web conferencing, discussion boards, and academic course management software could all be used to support groups of students interested in engaging in sustained dialogue on particular topics. Such groups could function as electronic special interest groups. For example, the National Science Digital Library (http://nsdl.org) could be a place to add a pathway for doctoral students to share resources on particular topics. Much thought and care would need to be put into designing these environments so that they did not simply replicate existing listservs or web sites. Someone would need to have a vision and provide some leadership for each community, at least at the outset.

## The Challenges

A central challenge is how to provide these intangible experiences for all doctoral students, especially those who are not on assistantship, are not enrolled full-time, or are at an institution with a small number of doctoral students.

There will be several challenges to this type of work. Obvious challenges include time, money, human capital, the innate bureaucracy of higher education, and the need to overcome institutional inertia. A larger challenge will be leadership. One of the characteristics of an intellectual community is that it is deliberately tended (Golde & Walker, 2006). What individuals, institutions, professional organizations, or agencies will step up and take on this responsibility? It is not necessary for everything to be highly coordinated, but there should be a standard mechanism for letting people know of opportunities and a mechanism for sharing what we learn as we try various configurations of these and other ideas. There also needs to be some coordination so that we do not have a rash of ten different opportunities in the next three years and then nothing after that. Local, state, and regional efforts may be an inexpensive starting place and may help us build models for how to create intellectual communities of students and faculty members across institutions. The issues that I outlined at the beginning of this paper will not diminish in importance in the coming years, so it is imperative that we devote time and effort to the development and sustenance of intellectual communities so that our field will continue to flourish.

*Denise Mewborn*
*University of Georgia*
*Athens, GA 30602-7124*
*dmewborn@uga.edu*

# Breakout Sessions

# Doctoral Preparation of Researchers

## James A. Middleton and Barbara Dougherty

Discussions during the first National Conference on Doctoral Programs in Mathematics Education revealed that the very nature of mathematics education doctoral study varied widely across institutions, and, "in particular, the nature of the research preparation doctoral students receive differs dramatically from university to university" (Lester & Carpenter, 2001). Conference participants suggested that this diversity resulted, in part, from the fact that as the study of mathematics teaching and learning, policy and practice becomes increasingly complex, doctoral programs must change accordingly. The diversity in programs observed reflects attempts of programs to generate new models of preparation and initiation into the field.

Additional dilemmas emerged at the 2007 conference, often prompted by the way the field of mathematics education exists in a nether world between reflection and action, between science and engineering, between scholarship and professional practice, and between the content of mathematics and the field of education. Some programs have the responsibility of producing teacher educators, others mathematics faculty. Some programs have a significant professional development, curriculum or technology focus. Still others, a significant proportion, see their role as flexibly attempting to meet the needs and aspirations of the different students who apply to their program across a variety of focus areas. In essence, doctoral programs in mathematics education try to locate themselves in some fruitful position in the space defined by these continua. As the American Statistical Association (2007) notes, as social and cognitive behavior is seen as increasingly complex, progress in the field requires a blend of many perspectives from a variety of fields to make heads or tails of it all. How does one fruitfully define the field so that programs can meaningfully locate themselves in a collective, progressive discipline?

Niss (1999) provides a concise description of what research in mathematics education is and how it is differentiated from work in mathematics proper, the other social sciences or education fields. In that description, he lists four key areas that define a common ground in the field. It is an expansive vision, but it is inclusive and clearly intent on delineating *mathematics education research* from research that utilizes mathematics merely as an area of context or application of general theory. We paraphrased his depiction as a prompt to orient breakout participants and to stimulate their development of shared goals for preparation of students as mathematics education researchers.

**Subject:** The scientific and scholarly field of research and development which aims at *identifying, characterizing,* and *understanding* phenomena and processes actually or potentially involved in the *teaching* and *learning* of *mathematics* at *any educational level.*

**Endeavor:** Attempts to uncover and clarify *causal relationships* and *mechanisms* are the focus.

**Approaches:** Addresses *all matters* that are pertinent to the teaching and learning of mathematics, irrespective of which scientific, ideological, political, societal or other spheres this may involve. The field makes use of considerations, methods and results from *other fields and disciplines* whenever this is deemed relevant.

**Activities:** Comprises different kinds of activities, ranging from theoretical or empirical *fundamental research,* through *applied research* and *development* to *systematic, reflective, practice.*

The task of the breakout sessions was to solicit participants' thoughts and practices on how to meaningfully prepare individuals acculturated in mathematics education research and, equipped with the knowledge, skills, and dispositions to programmatically enhance the collective knowledge base on teaching, learning, policy and practice in mathematics education. In addition, the role of practitioners and knowledge-users was addressed as this represents a large proportion of doctoral graduates' career choices.

This paper summarizes the collective goals and creative ideas for moving the field forward by focusing on the development of researchers. The conversation in the 2007 conference differed from that in the 1999 conference in that participants changed focus from that of *research preparation of doctoral candidates* to the *preparation of researchers*: a shift from subject to object. This shift is significant in that it marks a collective goal to situate our graduates in a range of contexts, while recognizing the multiplicity of roles research plays in the grander education enterprise.

## Discussion of Program Goals and Innovations

**Signature Practices of Current Programs.** Participants agreed that it is a general goal of programs in mathematics education to prepare doctoral candidates who are both consumers of research and producers of new knowledge, but it became clear that the vision of what that preparation looks like, what specific goals programs have for their candidates, what signature practices define program graduates (or what niche graduates fill in the field) varies widely (see Table 1). Of the 72 participants in the two breakout sessions, no single set of goals identify the field, even though all the programs were described as "mathematics education." Moreover, it is apparent that even within the primary interests of the faculty representing a major proportion of doctoral programs participating in the conference (generic curriculum and instruction and equity/diversity), there are varying practices and sub-foci. This highlights the lack of uniformity across the field, and points out that within our reasonably large community, smaller sub-communities are developing. In part, it may be due to the fact that many mathematics educators come to the field from programs in psychology, cognitive science, teacher education, and technology. Fully one-quarter of the participants in the workshop received their own doctorates from programs other than mathematics education proper.

TABLE 1. Signature practices (or market niche) of current doctoral programs as expressed by breakout session participants.

| Focus of Program | Number of Participants |
|---|---|
| **Generic PhD in Curriculum and Instruction**<br>No focus<br>Variety of options to fit needs of student<br>Interdisciplinary | 11 |
| **Equity/Diversity**<br>Latinos, second language; Urban equity/diversity<br>Equity, race, social justice | 11 |
| **Collegiate mathematics education**<br>Research in undergraduate mathematics education<br>Teaching undergraduate mathematics | 10 |
| **Teacher education**<br>Undergraduate teacher education<br>Learning and teaching<br>Preservice teachers in mathematics education | 8 |
| **Professional development**<br>Studying K-12 teaching<br>Reflective teachers and researcher<br>Building teacher leaders | 5 |
| **Cognitive, developmental and learning sciences/STEM**<br>Cognition/learning<br>Learning with technology tools<br>STEM Ed with focus in mathematics education | 5 |
| **Mathematics curriculum trends, design and analysis** | 2 |
| **Policy** | 1 |
| **Rural mathematics education** | 1 |
| **Distributed doctoral program** | 1 |
| **Total** | 55 |

Three major factors related to program identity were found across groups. First, there is a critical difference in the preparation of candidates whose career goals are primarily to become researchers in universities and think-tanks versus those who aspire to become practitioners in school systems, government agencies and the like. The research experiences, coursework and dissertation options for candidates should be a factor in the preparation for their future professional work. Moreover, funding opportunities, candidates' time investment (part-time versus full-time students), and mobility of applicants and graduates dictate that programs for "researchers" versus "practitioners" be designed differently or have some flexibility.

Second, another major factor reflected in the breakout sessions concerned matching faculty expertise with student research interests. Given that many programs represented at the conference have fewer than three mathematics education faculty members, and few had more than 15, it is impossible to meet the particular research needs of all students. Some mechanism for either placing students in the most appropriate programs (requiring some cooperative recruitment and placement practices across universities), or for allowing faculty from different universities to serve in some mentoring capacities is absolutely critical.

Third, there is the larger need of creating a supportive community for the preparation and induction of researchers that includes all members of the field. The discussion begun by Barbro Grevholm stimulated faculty to think of ways in which externships and study opportunities could be structured so that students would be able to interact in a variety of communities and work with a variety of colleagues, both graduate students and faculty.

## Desired Characteristics of Our Graduates

While the 1999 conference focused on the creation of researchers who would ply their skills in a variety of occupational roles as opposed to focusing on the research preparation of doctoral candidates, the overarching conversation in 2007 focused on creating experiences that enable students to develop an identity as researchers and for them to take ownership over the research enterprise. In particular, the development of a disposition of inquiry by which important theoretical and practical problems are contemplated and solutions to those problems generated was seen as the key aesthetic of program graduates. This requires creating environments in which doctoral students are stimulated to be critical of the current status of the field and to improve the field by connecting research to existing intellectual conversations and projecting new, transformative innovations. In short, a primary goal of our programs is to develop a theoretical, programmatic sense of self-in-the-field within each doctoral student.

**Research, Early and Often.** In 2001, the Carnegie Initiative on the Doctorate proffered the following goals for developing researchers in doctoral programs: Generation of new knowledge, conservation of the history and systems of the field, and transformation of the field by communicating research to others in the field and to the community of practitioners. They termed the designed set of experiences leading to these skills and dispositions the *pedagogy of research*. Rather than merely immersing students in research experiences, students need to be involved in *the whole gamut* of knowledge generation beginning when they enter their doctoral training. This implies the *guarantee* that students work on research projects, learning to undertake research from start to finish, *but* that such research experiences are not merely simulations, but the real thing, ranging from small projects students might do themselves to collaborative research conducted by groups of students to more formal projects led by faculty.

These opportunities must allow the student to gain an understanding of context, ranging from teacher education or mathematics courses at the university to field-based studies of practices to larger policy-related studies. What is critical here, however, is that these experiences not be haphazard, but organized along some developmental trajectory for the student so that their knowledge of and about research develops, and their ability to conduct research is successively enhanced. Breakout participants felt specific experiences should be required, even to the extent that presentations at professional meetings and publication of professional products be required prior to advancing to the dissertation stage or at least prior to graduating.

**Engagement with Community of Faculty and Students.** Perhaps the most emphasized set of goals conference participants proffered revolved around developing a sense of local community within programs. The generally accepted metaphor for learning in these discussions was that of a community of practice (e.g., Lave & Wenger, 1991; Wenger, 1998). In such a community, professors provide mentorship into our culture as students become involved in the key practices that define the professoriate: Work in, on, and around research.

There was some expressed tension in how to design programs that provide both close individual mentorship in the research area of a faculty mentor, and experience in more than one type of research project. One suggested innovation is to create fluid groups of faculty and students organized around research issues, wherein a variety of projects could reside. Research meetings, therefore, would serve a functional role in moving the project forward, and address the larger intellectual purpose of blending learnings across projects, methods and interpretive frames (American Statistical Association, 2007).

Underlying these discussions was the unresolved problem of resources, both human and fiscal. While there was general agreement that programs need a critical mass of faculty and cohorts of mostly full-time students and the financial support necessary for such, many of the current programs in the field consist of one or two faculty in mathematics education, usually situated within a larger Curriculum and Instruction or Mathematics department (see Table 1). The call for innovative means by which to collaborate across institutions, faculty groups, and research themes was expressed. The field appears ready for creative solutions to bring together the broader community of faculty and other resources with doctoral students to provide opportunities for research experiences.

**Coursework.** There was general consistency among participants' views of their programs that academic coursework does not always fit the needs of students' research experiences. Part of the problem involves the timing of prerequisites and course content. Research projects often require students to develop skills ad hoc, in response to a particular issue of theory or method. These just-in-time learning opportunities are not planned and are, therefore, unlikely to dovetail with what might be expected in a theoretical (academic) perspective. That is, students are often taught a particular template to follow in designing, and implementing research studies. However, in the real world of research, this rigidity may appear much more elastic because of the context in which the research is being conducted or other constraints. Moreover, faculty were concerned that students gain extensive knowledge and skills in both qualitative and quantitative methods, especially with regard to the design of research. This, coupled with the fact that such methodological courses are typically taught in educational psychology departments or by faculty other than those in the mathematics education "program," creates a real concern regarding both the quality of students' experiences and their applicability to the mathematics education enterprise.

To put these concerns into context, and to bridge some (but not all) of the gaps inherent to such (dis)organization, participants made suggestions of necessary courses or other planned experiences that students need to develop the knowledge, skills and dispositions that would enable them to move the field forward in both an intellectual and a pragmatic capacity.

*Introduction to the PhD.* Many students are thrust into doctoral programs with little knowledge of what is expected, what the timeline and expectations are for them, and the extent to which their program is not driven by courses and sequences, but by self-directed or community-directed learning and research. Students need such an introduction and orientation to the goals of their program to enable them to project their own path through the system.

*Thinking about research.* Sierpenska (2003) wrote that the field of mathematics education needs to engage in reflective practice in a fashion similar to the way we expect our pre- and in-service teachers to do so. She suggested that we should engage in more debate, more critique, and more "hard analytic thinking about the phenomena we study and about the validity of our claims about them" (p. 32). In addition to a good grounding in mathematics education literature, participants felt that not enough emphasis is placed on thinking about research areas in mathematics education. Historical perspectives, systemic and systematic issues, and seminal papers were mentioned as core knowledge that students must acquire to enable them to gain a sense of identity with the field and to project their own place in that field. Participants from a variety of capacities mentioned that the ability to give and receive constructive criticism was a key component of doctoral studies. Above all, the collection of these skills and dispositions needed to be developed and formed through a carefully designed set of opportunities situated in a psychologically safe environment.

*Research design and methods.* There was consensus that both quantitative and qualitative expertise is critical for all doctoral candidates in order that they are able to read papers in the field and to develop the ability to ask critical questions, operationalize those questions, and conduct original research. One area on which participants felt the field did not place enough emphasis was the design of research, spanning the range from experimental design and causal modeling to design research and its variants. The complexity of the field is growing and mathematics education research programs must prepare students to deal with the often bewildering variety of techniques, tools, and models for thinking about scholarly inquiry. One of the keys to bringing this knowledge together is to develop explicit courses and other structured experiences focused directly on mathematics education problems, questions, and traditions. One group suggested developing a course devoted to critiquing research as one way of accomplishing this goal. Standards for judging research (e.g., Schoenfeld, 1999) such as descriptive and explanatory power, scope and predictive power, rigor and specificity, falsifiability, replicability/transportability and triangulation would be central topics of discussion and exemplars from research would be required reading.

*Courses oriented towards students' research projects.* Often students need extensive help formulating and writing their own research. Many students need opportunities to address specific skills such as formulating their investigative question(s), matching methods to questions (and not vice versa), designing and handling the logistics of carrying out a study, and even technical writing assistance. Participants felt that such opportunities should be present in any doctoral program, to the extent that in some programs, a course directly addressing students' research might be developed. One example presented was a doctoral writing seminar held as a week-long retreat, where students bring research reports or dissertations in various stages of development, and engage in communal reporting, critique, and revision. This example also addresses issues of building community as it engages students in the presentation of one's original research, making it public to teach others and to receive critiques so the paper and the overall research program can improve.

*Other disciplinary traditions.* While the community felt that students need methodological training in mathematics education specifically, participants also acknowledged that mathematics education derives its methods and theoretical traditions primarily from psychology, sociology and anthropology as well as history, political science and economics. Understanding one or more of these traditions is important as candidates develop an epistemological stance on one or more research areas around which they organize their professional work. However, there was no consensus on what courses, what level of emphasis should be placed on each, or what extent other departments or scholars needed to be involved in the delivery of this disciplinary knowledge.

*Experience with policy.* Some participants suggested that the field does not engage students enough in the study of policy and its implications. Faculty members often enter the policy arena as experts called upon to develop standards, review policies and practices at schools, districts, and state departments, and provide other consultative assistance. Knowledge of policy research, how implications from research are interpreted and utilized, and how the education system works was suggested as critical knowledge.

Again, each of these suggestions begs the question: To what extent do doctoral programs have the expertise and/or fiscal resources to offer specialized/advanced courses in each of these areas? In particular, it is unlikely that any program can do it all, particularly as the niche markets for programs vary greatly. Some larger organization of faculty and programs is necessary to make these learning opportunities available to all of our students, regardless of the location and size of their program.

**Develop 'Virtual' Community Across Institutions.** Throughout the conference, the notion of a larger set of connections among and between doctoral programs took root. Many of the conversations focused on providing "externships" by which doctoral candidates at one university might be given the opportunity to work on a research project at another university. The metaphor tossed about was that of a research "field experience," similar to student teaching field experiences, where the student would work with a faculty member at another institution in a mentored fashion.

These experiences might take a variety of forms. Short visits would provide particular training. Semester-long experiences would allow students to enroll in on-site courses and engage fully in a research program. To enable these exchanges, some kind of student travel support funds would have to be generated. On the other hand, distance learning would allow universities to share courses or develop mutual research projects and be less encumbered with the financial and time-related expenses of physical travel to and from collaborating sites. Distance technologies have the distinct advantage of allowing a large number of students and faculty members to engage with each other simultaneously, providing opportunities to network around research ideas and published research. Several CLTs have pioneered online meetings, courses and forums that might be fruitfully expanded to other collaborative arrangements across universities.

## Closing Comments

The field of mathematics education has made significant gains with respect to the quality and diversity of models of doctoral preparation of researchers. Namely, programs have capitalized on the recommendations made by Lester & Carpenter (2001) regarding the immersion of students in research-related experiences and the development of communities of researchers. CLTs and other ground-breaking projects have afforded a new set of models for how programs, faculty, and students across universities can create a larger mathematics education community fostering the research capabilities of young professionals.

However, there are still many concerns that are relatively unchanged. The task of finding the right mix of research methods with actual research experiences at the right time in students' doctoral programs is still a tough problem to solve. Moreover, the notion of core knowledge still has problems associated with integrating all the areas of application that mathematics education purports to inform. In particular, the increase in focus on undergraduate mathematics education, teacher development and the huge policy arena has opened new focal points that do not easily dovetail with the disciplinary needs of the mathematics education field and the traditions of research on teaching and learning in K-12 education

It is clear that a vibrant mathematics education community feels the need for innovative and creative solutions to address the struggles with purpose and audience of doctoral programs. As the conference ended, there appeared to be a new synergy among the represented institutions and individual faculty members that may spur needed actions to bring focused and substantive research experiences into our programs.

*James A. Middleton*
*Arizona State University*
*Tempe, AZ 85287-1011*
*JAMES.MIDDLETON@asu.edu*

*Barbara Dougherty*
*The University of Mississippi*
*University, MS 38677*
*bdougher@olemiss.edu*

# Key Components of Mathematics Education Doctoral Programs in the United States: Current Practices and Suggestions for Improvement

## William S. Bush and Enrique Galindo

Doctoral programs in mathematics education across the United States have undergone significant changes during the past 25 years. According to Reys and Kilpatrick (2001), "these programs have taken many forms, as the focus of preparation varies greatly from one institution to another. While one program may consist of a large component of mathematical content together with selected graduate courses in education, another program may offer a more balanced set of courses in mathematics and mathematics education." (p. 20). Their analyses of these programs also revealed considerable diversity with respect to the number and background of faculty, number of students, number and types of courses and learning experiences, examinations, dissertations, and entrance and exit requirements (Reys, Glasgow, Ragan & Simms, 2001). Specialized programs in mathematics education have evolved from only a few programs in the early 1960s to over 100 in 2007 (Reys, Glasgow, Teuscher & Nevels, 2007). In recent years, largely as the result of increased specializations in colleges of education, shortages of mathematics educators with doctorates, and the emergence of mathematics education as a field of study, doctoral programs have increased significantly across the country (Reys, 2000).

This paper reports the discussions on components of mathematics education doctoral programs. Specifically, we will (1) describe both common and unique practices and components of current mathematics education doctoral programs across the United States, (2) compare these results to previous discussions at the first National Conference on Doctoral Programs in Mathematics Education in 1999; and (3) share insights and suggestions from conference participants for improving mathematics education doctoral programs in the U. S. We extracted summarized information from discussions of 42 faculty and graduate students who were divided into 11 groups of four or five during the sessions. Participants responded to a list of questions about the practices and components of their doctoral programs. They also were asked to describe current limitations or problems with their own doctoral programs and to reflect on changes or promising practices that might improve their programs. The questions were:

- What are your current practices?
- Are they working?

- Why or why not?
- What strategies are you using to address those practices not working?
- What suggestions do you have for improvement of your program?

The session was divided into four 20-minute intervals so that groups had the opportunity to discuss each of four doctoral components: Collaboration, Coursework, Examinations, and Dissertations. The following sections summarize the information gathered from these discussions. When a list of topics is provided, we have placed them in order according to frequency. That is, the first topics were identified and discussed most often by participants.

## Collaboration Within and Across Mathematics Education Doctoral Programs

The issue of collaboration has been an important one since the first National Conference on Doctoral Programs in 1999. At that time the 48 institutions that responded to a survey had a mean of 5 faculty members and a small number of new doctoral students were admitted each year (Reys, et al., 2001). One of the main challenges faced by small doctoral programs in mathematics education identified then was the ability to offer high-quality programs with limited faculty expertise and small numbers of students (Fey, 2001). Collaboration was seen as one way to surmount these challenges. Fey remarked, "this situation cries out for inter-institutional collaboration, making the best of each university's faculty and programmatic resources available beyond its usual enrollment boundaries" (p. 59). By 2007, the 70 institutions surveyed had a range of 2 to 19 faculty members with a mode of 4 (Reys, et al., 2007), indicating that the faculty resources are still constrained for most programs.

We sought to learn from conference participants the extent to which collaboration, within and across mathematics education doctoral programs, were either a common practice at their institutions or being considered as an option in the future. Conference participants identified a variety of activities in which different groups collaborated in conducting their doctoral program in mathematics education. The most common purpose for collaboration among faculty involved designing and teaching graduate courses. Faculty also collaborated in conducting research, serving on doctoral committees, making presentations or conducting professional development, involvement in field experiences, conducting funded projects, and improving programs.

Participants indicated that the most common type of collaborations within doctoral programs were between mathematics educators and mathematicians. To a lesser extent, mathematics educators also collaborated with educational psychologists, sociologists/experts in culture, statisticians/research methodologists, science educators, education leadership faculty, and technology experts.

When asked the motivations for collaboration among faculty associated with their doctoral programs, participants reported: (1) setting program goals and planning program activities; (2) establishing dissertation committees with varied expertise; and (3) building intellectual communities. Participants indicated that collaborations resulted in several positive outcomes in their programs: they allowed departments to share positions, connected doctoral programs to local schools and districts, and improved local school districts. Finally, participants suggested that doctoral programs could improve through collaborations by using doctoral students more purposefully to build stronger collaborations and by encouraging faculty and administrators to work more deliberately and harder in building collaborations among various groups on and off campus.

At the first National Conference on Doctoral Programs in 1999, Lesh, Crider, and Gummer (2001) describe a collaborative doctoral program in mathematics education among four Indiana universities and the challenges, benefits, and shortcomings of such a partnership. At our session at the second conference, these types of collaborations were more prevalent across universities, largely as the result of the Centers for Learning and Teaching funded by the National Science Foundation over the past six years. In particular, the collaborative doctoral program established among the five universities in the Appalachian Collaborative Center for Learning, Assessment, and Instruction in Mathematics (ACCLAIM) was prominent in the discussions.

## Coursework in Mathematics Education Doctoral Programs

For the first National Conference on Doctoral Programs, participants reported seven main areas of emphasis within mathematics education programs. These areas included general foundations, research in mathematics education, research methods, technology, teaching and learning mathematics, mathematics curriculum, and mathematics content. Participants reported that the areas receiving more emphasis were research in mathematics education, and teaching and learning mathematics. Areas that received little emphasis were technology and general foundations (Reys, et al., 2001). In addition to considering coursework as an effective way for acquisition of many kinds of knowledge, courses can take many forms so that the professional goals of doctoral students of diverse backgrounds and experiences can be met. For example, field experiences, internships with professional development and curriculum development projects, internships in policy-making roles, and research internships were some of the suggestions of coursework possibilities that were seen as useful in the preparation of mathematics education doctorates.

At the 2007 conference we wanted to determine required coursework, participants' perceptions of its effectiveness, and future coursework under consideration. We asked participants to share required coursework currently found in their respective doctoral programs. Their responses revealed a wide range of courses that included research methodology, mathematics education, mathematics, general learning theories/psychology; conducting professional development, technology, and history of mathematics. We then asked them to discuss the extent to which these courses were effective and what changes might be necessary to improve them. Our discussion will center on the three most common courses mentioned above.

**Research Methodology Courses.** Research methodology courses were identified as critical courses for a doctorate in mathematics education. At the first National Conference on Doctoral Programs, several groups of participants discussed the coursework required of mathematics education doctoral students. In summarizing the discussions about the research preparation of doctoral students Lester and Carpenter (2001) identified "the development of knowledge in three areas: (a) "core" knowledge for all students, (b) knowledge in the student's own area of specialization, and (c) knowledge related to the specific topic/question of a student's dissertation." (p. 63). Citing an article by Walbesser and Eisenberg (1971), they raised the issue of whether a "smattering of generic quantitative and qualitative courses" prepares students sufficiently as perhaps "a thoughtfully considered set of courses that helps them learn about the full range of activities which active researchers engage" (p. 64). Lester and Carpenter summarized their discussion by making a strong case for getting doctoral students actively engaged in research prior to their dissertation, preferably through engagement in what Schoenfeld (1999) previously described as *research communities.*

In our session at the 2007 conference, the recommendations and changes suggested by participants were similar. They recommended deeper research apprenticeships for doctoral students and more opportunities for students to apply and engage in research prior to the dissertation. Participants also suggested that doctoral students needed courses highlighting mixed methods research and assessment, and evaluation strategies. Finally, some participants recommended offering parallel seminars on research in mathematics education that would help students make connections between research methods studied in inquiry courses and application of research methods in mathematics education. These suggestions appeared to reflect changes and expansion of research methodologies over the past eight years.

**Mathematics Education Courses.** As expected, participants recognized the importance of mathematics education courses in the doctorate. They identified a number of important mathematics education courses focusing on such topics as curriculum, teaching/pedagogy, learning, assessment, teacher education, technology, research, and history. By comparison, this list represents greater variety than the list of important mathematics education topics (mathematics learning, teaching and teacher education, and mathematics curriculum) offered by Presmeg and Wagner (2001) at the first National Conference on Doctoral Programs. When asked about issues or concerns with regard to mathematics education courses, participants in our sessions identified (1) the need for a greater variety of mathematics education courses in their programs, (2) courses that provide better connections with local school districts, (3) the need for better resources to support mathematics education courses, and (4) mathematics education courses that focused on mathematics teacher development.

**Mathematics Courses.** As indicated above, mathematics courses were identified third most often by participants as an important component of a mathematics education doctoral program. Furthermore, mathematics courses were mentioned most often as an area of concern or need in building a quality doctoral program in mathematics education. In their summary of discussions about mathematics requirements for mathematics education doctoral students at the first National Conference on Doctoral Programs, Dossey and Lappan (2001) described (1) the set of mathematics processes involved in "doing mathematics," (2) a formula for the level of mathematics needed by mathematics education doctoral students based on their grade span interest, and (3) a list of courses based on students' grade span interest. These guidelines provided a reasonably detailed description of the kinds of mathematics courses and experiences that would benefit mathematics education doctoral students.

We solicited from participants specific concerns with regard to the mathematics portion of their mathematics education doctoral programs. The issues and concerns about the mathematics preparation of mathematics educational doctoral students raised in our session were more pragmatic and less theoretical than those offered by

Dossey and Lappan (2001). Our participants indicated that (1) the mathematics courses offered by mathematics departments were not appropriate for mathematics education doctoral students, (2) their doctoral students needed more options with regard to the mathematics courses offered, (3) mathematics courses needed to focus more on exploration and problem solving, and (4) collaboration among mathematics educators and mathematicians was limited or nonexistent.

**Format of Courses.** In addition to course content, we asked participants to share the format of the coursework in their doctoral programs. They reported that course format included traditional face-to-face courses, distance learning courses, shorter seminars, and independent study.

In summary, while the main categories of courses that are part of doctoral programs remain the same as those reported in 1999, the courses mentioned by participants in our sessions vary greatly across doctoral programs, and faculty indicated that their programs would benefit from a variety of new and different courses. In particular, faculty representing smaller doctoral program felt the need for a greater variety of courses perhaps to be shared across institutions or through distance learning. The value of non-course experiences was part of the discussions in 1999 (Blume, 2001). Participants of the 2007 conference also emphasized the great contributions that non-course experiences provide to doctoral programs in mathematics education.

## Qualifying Examinations in Mathematics Education Doctoral Programs

In the survey conducted for the first National Conference on Doctoral Programs 96 percent of institutions reported that they required comprehensive exams (Reys, et al., 2001). In a recent survey that percentage was 89 percent (Reys et al, 2007). Also at the conference, participants indicated that comprehensive examinations were the primary means to assess a mathematics educator's repertoire of skills and dispositions. However, Fey (2001) raised several issues about the nature and purpose of qualifying examinations. He expressed concerns about the authenticity, predictive nature, and repetitiveness of such examinations while pointing out that "there are things about our field that anyone earning a doctorate should know" and "students should be able to organize their ideas into coherent presentations" (p. 60).

At the 2007 conference we attempted to ascertain the format and purpose of comprehensive examinations, as well as the extent to which participants feel that examinations meet their goals. Participants revealed a variety of formats and purposes of examinations in their respective doctoral programs. For example, the majority of doctoral programs require oral examinations, written examinations, or both, in ether take-home and/or sit-down format. Several participants indicated that qualifying examinations included literature reviews, or projects, dissertation proposals, or portfolios. Some participants mentioned non-traditional products included in qualifying examinations such as concept papers, videotape analysis, and course development.

In reflecting on their current qualifying examination practices, participants echoed some of the comments by Fey (2001) and recommended the following changes or improvements: (1) examinations should better reflect what mathematics educators do in their work and (2) examinations should be connected to students' dissertations. Other more technical recommendations included: (1) identifying clear criteria and purposes for their examinations; (2) using common qualifying examination formats; (3) reflecting a better balance between mathematics and mathematics education; and (4) include proposal defense as a required component of the qualifying examination..

In summary, although traditional assessments are still common as qualifying examinations in many mathematics education doctoral programs, some committees have implemented or are experimenting with non-traditional work-based products like portfolios, concept papers, videotape analysis, and course development. In addition, some faculties are seeking ways to improve the predictability, quality, and relevance of their examinations.

## Dissertations in Mathematics Education Doctoral Programs

For the first National Conference on Doctoral Programs in 1999 Lester and Carpenter noted that "the role and importance of the dissertation in the research preparation of doctoral students vary from institution to institution" and that "at some institutions the dissertation is the sole research experience in which students engage" (2001, p. 65). Dissertations are seen as an important part of the preparation of mathematics educators because they provide opportunities to synthesize information and integrate the results into an overall framework that helps advance the mathematics education knowledge base (Stiff, 2001). During the 1999 Conference of Doctoral Programs those doctoral programs that emphasize the preparation of researchers regarded the dissertation as a culminating research activity following three or more years of research-related activities (Lester & Carpenter, 2001). However, alternative ways to demonstrate research competencies have been part of the discussions at the two conferences. Fey (2001) discussed advantages of alternatives to the traditional five-chapter dissertation. Citing recommendations by Duke and Beck (1999) and Krathwohl (1994), he suggested that doctoral committees consider a dissertation format that included a series articles ready for publication. This recommendation was also echoed by Stiff (2001) in his chapter from the 1999 conference.

Our goal in this portion of the session was to determine the extent that participants encouraged alternative forms of dissertations in their programs and to solicit recommendations about alternative forms of dissertations. Most participants indicated that they continued to use the traditional five-chapter format. Other participants, however, shared that they had experimented with more non-traditional formats such as the series of research-oriented articles suggested by Duke and Beck (1999), Krathwohl (1994), and Fey (2001). A few participants indicated that they had used extensive literature/research reviews or practitioner-based articles as a substitute or portion for traditional dissertations. Participants also reported that much greater variety existed among formats for dissertation proposals. For example, dissertation proposals in their programs might report a previous smaller project, include the first three chapters of the dissertation, end-of-course examinations, reports of a pilot study, or shortened literature reviews.

Participants offered a variety of suggestions for making dissertations more relevant and practical for doctoral students. These suggestions included: (1) dissertations as a series of articles; (2) a product representing the collaborative work of several doctoral students; (3) a report connected to larger on larger research projects; or (4) a pilot study for a larger study.

Participants also strongly recommended that the dissertation process emphasize publication of research as a primary goal and dissertation committees clearly identify the purpose of the literature review and other components of the dissertation.

## What We Learned from the Breakout Sessions

Our findings represent a typical "bad news/good news" scenario. The bad news is that eight years after the first National Conference on Mathematics Doctoral Programs, faculties are still struggling with the same programmatic issues raised then. Some still struggle with collaboration with key components; appropriate courses in research methodology, mathematics and mathematics education; examinations that measure relevant skills and processes; and dissertations that prepare students for their subsequent work as researchers. On the good new side, however, faculties seem to be forging new and fruitful collaborations within and across programs, designing new and updated courses in research methodology, mathematics, and mathematics education, and experimenting with alternative examination and dissertation formats.

Clearly change is on the minds of many who direct doctoral programs and mentor doctoral students. While these two conferences have helped to identify issues and posit some solutions to those issues; it is clear that more collaborative and purposeful support is needed to help faculties who wish to change their program. In our minds, a logical next step in improving the quality of doctoral programs in mathematics education in the United States would be to convene special topic conferences and workshops to assist those faculties who wish to build meaningful collaborations, develop and offer a greater variety of courses, and explore different models for examinations and dissertations.

*William S. Bush*
*University of Louisville*
*Louisville, KY 40292*
*bill.bush@louisville.edu*

*Enrique Galindo*
*Indiana University*
*Bloomington, IN 47405*
*egalindo@indiana.edu*

CBMS Issues in Mathematics Education
Volume **15**, 2008

# On-line Delivery of Graduate Courses in Mathematics Education

## Maurice Burke and Vena M. Long

The critical shortage of mathematics teachers in K-12 education has been cited repeatedly in the literature and the press (Ingersoll, 2007). Another shortage exists for doctorates in mathematics education (Reys, Glasgow, Ragan & Simms, 2001). Reys (2002) brought to light the issue about the difficulty institutions of higher education have in filling positions in mathematics education. In fact, the shortage of mathematics educators is expected to grow as these individuals retire. (Reys 2006, Reys, Glasgow, Teuscher, & Nevels 2007)

Given that most mathematics education programs focus on individual learning within the context of classroom teaching and mathematics curriculum, it is easy to support the assumption made by many, if not most, doctoral programs in mathematics education that teaching experience in the K-12 system is a very important prerequisite for their students. (Reys, et al., 2007) It is further assumed that these students' grasp of the contexts of learning mathematics and their first-hand experiences in observing children learning mathematics, along with their grasp of the educational process as it plays out in schools provide a needed backdrop for conducting as well as utilizing mathematics education research.

But herein lays a fundamental quandary for doctoral programs in mathematics education. The certification process is time consuming and, in the case of four-year, undergraduate programs, places severe limits on the amount of time spent studying mathematics. Five year programs require a degree in mathematics but add to the cost, which in the context of poor starting salaries translates into large debts that fledgling teachers must pay before even considering a doctoral program. Furthermore, after several years in the teaching profession, young teachers often find themselves place-bound due to many factors including family, mortgages, and economic necessity. As if these factors were not enough, young teachers' curiosity about the teaching/learning process is often diminished by the realities of schooling that often lead teachers into a survival mode. Even if they can survive this Charybdis with their curiosity intact they must still overcome the Scylla which is the rapid fading of their understanding of undergraduate mathematics into the "you didn't use it so you lose it" bin. Teachers are often unwilling to reestablish the necessary mathematical foundation needed for success in mathematics education doctoral programs requiring a significant amount of advanced graduate mathematics courses.

While the need is felt nationally, some locations face greater complications in trying to create and nurture future mathematics educators. Rural areas, with their geographic isolation, make pursuing an advanced degree even more problematic. With the nearest universities often four or more hours away by car, the costs and time demands make continuing one's education almost beyond the grasp of most rural teachers. Although distance education has made inroads in some of these locations, the residency requirement of most doctoral programs puts a halt to many teachers' thoughts of entering a doctoral program. Creativity, flexibility and new technology may help reach this untapped pool of potential mathematics education leadership.

Doctoral programs in mathematics education can adapt to the environment of place-bound teachers in order to attract them to the rigors of doctoral work. We will share our experience of two such adaptations that include online coursework in lieu of traditional classroom course delivery and web-mediated internships in lieu of residency. These adaptations have provided ramps enabling some students to pursue doctoral work. However, we want to make it clear that both of our doctoral programs still involve many of the traditional face-to-face components.

A variety of software exists to support web-based instruction in both the asynchronous and synchronous modes. *Blackboard* and *WebCT* are two commercial class management systems. *Moodle* is open source software that provides the same kinds of tools: drop boxes for assignments, discussion boards, posting of announcements and assignments, grade books, etc. *Centra*, *E-luminate* and *Adobe Connect* are frequently used tools for synchronous communication. These tools allow for real-time discussions, shared applications, small group discussions, etc. Students can use icons to raise their hand, applaud, laugh, cry, and answer questions. The instructor can give students the "microphone," give them control of an application such as a spreadsheet or a dynamic geometry tool or send them to a particular website. Video is also possible through mini-cams.

## Online Courses - Asynchronous Mode

The Center for Teaching and Learning in the West (CLTW) offers a number of online courses in asynchronous mode. (For complete listing see the CLTW website at http://www.cltw.org/) Montana State University (MSU) faculty are responsible for several of these courses. From a strictly technological point of view, online coursework in the mode practiced by the mathematics education faculty at MSU can be viewed as a sophisticated e-mail system. The asynchronous communications of the participants and instructor are organized into topic folders that everyone can read. Simultaneous communication via chat rooms is sometimes used, but with circumstances like those at MSU they have been found to be somewhat inefficient. This is due to the fact that our students are scattered all over the globe and finding the time to "chat" together is like trying to schedule an impromptu faculty meeting.

We generally have between 12 and 20 graduate students in our online masters and doctoral courses at MSU. They consist of teachers in the field, on-campus graduate teaching assistants, and sometimes individuals in the private sector working part time toward their degrees. Students work independently and/or in small groups on the tasks designed for the course. In fact, the curriculum plan of an online graduate course engages students in the same kinds of inquiry activities often found in face-to-face doctoral courses in mathematics education. More specifically, students:

- are exposed to the phenomena under study using readings or direct experiences or other means;
- identify questions or problems related to their understanding of the phenomena and conduct an organized investigation of the phenomena to address these questions or problem;
- summarize and present the results of their investigations to other students and the professor;
- engage in critical reflection on their work including feedback from others and self-assessment.

The examples provided below are not meant to be templates for online instruction. To a large extent the format of the activity depends on the particular content being studied and the objective of the activity. However, the examples do illustrate the potential of online instruction to engage doctoral students in inquiry activities.

### Investigate/Summarize/Discuss/Revise Tasks.

a. ERMO Summaries

In this activity, students are assigned to read an article or set of articles and write an "Earn the Right to My Opinion" summary of the readings. The ERMO summary must accurately summarize the major points made by the article(s) in order to earn the right to an opinion - and conclude with a focused paragraph stating the reaction or opinion of the student about those major points. To facilitate the critical reflection activity, students are assigned to a discussion group with three or four other students. They read each other's ERMO summaries and write a paragraph or two on things they learned from their peer's summaries. This critical reflection requires self-assessment and provides a way to motivate the careful reading of each other's summaries. If they feel their peers misinterpreted some aspect of the reading(s), they are urged to bring this up in the discussion of the opinions voiced in the ERMO summaries. Incidentally, there is usually a dramatic jump in the quality of the ERMO summaries after the first iteration of this process as the graduate students reach for the high bar set by other students in the class.

b. Research Papers and Paper Conferences

In this activity each student is asked to write a research paper for a course, similar to what is done in the face-to-face delivery of courses. On a specified date they post their research papers in a folder set aside for their group. They are then assigned to write and post a one-page critique of the other research papers submitted by their discussion group. Once the critiques are posted, a group discussion is held. This session is moderated by the professor. In the end, recommendations are made to the author for revising the paper. After revisions, their final papers are submitted to the professor.

**Living Laboratory/Action Research Tasks.** One of the significant advantages of working with place-bound teachers in the online environment is access to the living laboratory of their classrooms. This enables the on-campus graduate students and individuals in the private sector taking the course to indirectly access real classrooms and collaborate with practicing teachers to jointly investigate issues.

a. Role Playing

   In a recently offered assessment course, the class got into a lively discussion of the *MontCAS* test (Montana's high-stakes CRT), which was about to be given to students in Montana. One teacher in each group volunteered their mathematics class to be the target school. The group then created, administered and scored a "standardized" test. As this process unfolded, the group members used the group discussion folder to raise issues and concerns that occurred to them from the vantage point of their roles in the testing process. The experience drove home the significance of the issues being raised in the research articles they were reading in the course, including alignment, English as a second language, reliability of scoring rubrics, and the politics of terminology (such as the meaning of "proficient" and AYP).

b. Lesson Study

   On occasion, students in our online courses are divided into small groups to conduct mini-lesson studies in the class of one of the practicing teachers in the group.

c. Reality Curriculum

   The online environment and its incredible tool space of e-journals and other resources provide a variety of opportunities for online classes to explore current issues and bring current phenomena into their work in the course. Professors increasingly put short readings from books on e-reserves. This allows them to use many sources in a course. The coupling of these with up-to-the-minute web resources produces a sense of reality in our curriculum. This sense is further strengthened when the online, asynchronous discussion format allows us to bring in outside experts as discussants.

**Joint Productive Activity or Development Tasks.** Sometimes "inquiry" takes on forms not captured by our previous categories of tasks. In the online environment, with its shared text spaces that students can contribute to asynchronously, there are many opportunities for joint activities that build resources for the entire class to access. Professors set the task and its boundaries and contribute start-up resources. Students and the professor contribute to and monitor the development of the resources.

a. Creating a Shared Work Product

In a recently offered assessment course, each group of students was challenged to produce a "glossary of assessment strategies." There had to be 25 strategies and each needed to be described in a paragraph and illustrated with an example or vignette. The groups quickly produced 10-15 strategies but then had to dig deeply to complete the task. Other examples of shared work products developed in online courses include, a joint review of literature on a particular topic in mathematics education, and a shared survey of pedagogically inspired websites for the teaching of geometry.

b. Problem Solving

Many of our courses focus on mathematical topics. We typically start a problem solving unit with an exploration of some phenomena the students can relate to and then pose deep problems that challenge everyone in the class. In their groups they engage in dialogues and shared strategies. They look to each other for insights and eavesdrop frequently on the discussions of other groups. Each student is required to write up and submit the solutions on their own, and in their own words. The group support structure allows novice problem solvers a chance to keep pace with the experts in their groups. Once again, the online and public nature of the group discussions allows intensive eavesdropping that is difficult to accomplish in face-to-face settings.

c. Creating Their Own Blog of Great Insights and Works and Interactions from the Course.

Most class management systems have a feature that allows the professor to set up a workspace for individual students that essentially gives them control of a shell within the overall course shell that the professor controls. In courses where discussions are rich and numerous (over 2000 postings counts as numerous) one of the difficulties students have is keeping track of all the new ideas or questions posed. By creating their own blog of interesting ideas and quotes from the discussions, as well as offering their peers a space to interact with them, each student not only creates a written journal that organizes what they learned in the class but they also have created a space for critical reflection. This personal resource is extremely useful to the students when writing summative essays.

## Online Courses - Synchronous Mode

In the Appalachian Collaborative Center for Learning, Assessment and Instruction in Mathematics (ACCLAIM) delivery of courses to a targeted rural population, the use of a distance learning model was essential. ACCLAIM experimented with a variety of delivery modes but felt it was most successful with a combination of an asynchronous component managed by *Blackboard* or *Moodle* and a synchronous component mediated by *Centra*.

ACCLAIM deems the synchronous component to be absolutely necessary for a variety of reasons. To create a virtual classroom, discussion and interaction between students and instructor and between students is vital for promoting deep thinking and the sharing of ideas in real time. Required meeting times help students involved in work and family to stay on task and on a reasonable timeline. For a cohort model to succeed all students must progress in the same time frame. [ See www.acclaim-math.org for a full description of the program of study.] In addition, students may teach various segments of the courses, lead a discussion on an article, or demonstrate a selected piece of software. Mathematics can be done "on the fly" using one of various peripherals, and student-created work can be shared either via a document camera or through student generated work in real time.

Courses in mathematics, mathematics education, research and rural education have been successfully delivered via the web. This mechanism has allowed all of our students to benefit from all of the professors in mathematics education at the five partnering institutions and has allowed them access to leaders in the field but not necessarily at any of our collaborating universities. For example, Paul Theobald, who holds an endowed chair in rural education at Buffalo State in New York, taught a course on the history of rural education in America to each cohort.

The traditional residency requirement in doctoral work is designed to ensure that each student has at least one year of in-depth work in an academic setting with professors actively engaged in research, teaching and service. In lieu of a traditional residency requirement (usually technically defined as 2-3 semesters of full-time enrollment), ACCLAIM has negotiated an innovative residency which includes two summers of 9 semester hours of coursework each, along with the academic year in between. During this intervening academic year, students are enrolled in 6 semester hours of coursework including 3 hours of internship each semester.

The internship is based on the *Principles to Guide the Design and Implementation of Doctoral Programs in Mathematics Education* (AMTE, 2003). Each student negotiates an individual contract outlining specific activities selected to add to their knowledge in the areas of K-16 teaching, supervising student teachers, designing and implementing a research study, designing and/or facilitating professional development activities, preparing grant proposals, and writing for publication. For example with respect to K-16 teaching, a high school teacher would be charged with observing for several consecutive days in a primary classroom and a middle school classroom and perhaps working with a college professor to re-design a syllabus. For professional development, if a student had never presented at a professional meeting, they would be charged with getting on the program at a state meeting. If they had presented at a state meeting, the charge might be getting on the program of an NCTM regional.

The internship students from across ACCLAIM meet on-line every two weeks to discuss their activities and share thoughts with respect to a paper addressing one of the areas of study. *Blackboard* was used for students to submit their completed activities and track their progress through their contract.

**A Course Guide for Professors.** Not everyone wants to teach in this mode and not everyone who wants to, does it well. Just as students underestimate the commitment an online course requires, some professors also fail to realize the nature of the task. When reflecting on the activities outlined above, several observations should be made.

    1. The professor can become a 24/7 teacher. For asynchronous courses students will be working at odd hours and on weekends. When they encounter

problems, they often expect an instant response to an email. Some professors log in frequently and daily to keep up with the discussions and the
needs of the course. At the very least, the professor must indicate when
s/hc will be available and the rate of response students can expect i.e. at
least once within 24 hours.

2. Because of the potential increase in student writing, peer and self-assessment
   must be fostered. This can be addressed in task design as in the above
   examples. Students (and the professor) must understand that the professor cannot respond to or give feedback individually on every posting in
   the course.

3. The course must be prepared in its entirety from the beginning. Students
   working on-line must be able to organize their work and time in order to
   be successful. Sudden changes, new assignments, and surprise vacations
   are not acceptable. When circumstances do require changes, these should
   be discussed as early as possible with students and necessary accommodations made.

4. Good online discussions whether through discussion boards or micro-
   phones need spark and purpose. Sometimes to get a spark you invoke
   devices such as caricature. For example, a fictional character might be
   invited into your class as an outside observer or expert. The students
   don't have to know the name on their screen does not belong to a real
   person. Even if they know it is a fictional character it allows you a safe
   way to address sensitive subjects and challenge beliefs. For example, a
   pesky sixth grader challenges the teachers to convince him that their way
   of adding fractions is better than his way, which is to add numerators and
   add denominators. Or, Howard Curmudgeon, a math teacher of 35 years,
   challenges their beliefs that all students can learn mathematics.

5. Topics that require mathematical problem solving must be carefully thought
   out in terms of what is expected of students. Technology requirements,
   both hardware and software, must be communicated clearly in advance of
   the course. Not every platform or budget can or should be accommodated.

## Summary

The power of technology should not be over estimated. This power can be
accessed to help mitigate but perhaps not solve some problems in education. Geographically isolated, disabled, and place-bound populations can be reached with
high quality educational opportunities. Shortages in critical areas can be alleviated
or at least addressed.

There are also disclaimers that need to be made. First, other adaptations can
be made to address the shortage of doctoral faculty in mathematics education. For
example, traditional doctoral programs can recruit young doctoral students who
are just completing Masters Degrees in pure or applied mathematics, and build in
certification and teaching experience into their doctoral work. The downside of this
strategy is that it has the potential to greatly lengthen the time needed to earn

the doctorate. Second, reaching out to place-bound teachers with doctoral course-work and internships sometimes creates new sets of issues. University policies and practices can create huge barriers. Incompletes can quickly become failing grades hindering progression or re-entry. Third, not only do online opportunities greatly increase the number of potential graduate students, but they also greatly increase the number of potential ABD experiences with students only remotely involved in the faculty advisor's research interests. These are but three disclaimers out of many that could be made. Needless to say, there are no easy fixes for doctoral programs seeking to increase the pool of graduate students in mathematics education. However, creativity, flexibility, and technology provide a viable option.

*Maurice J. Burke*
*Montana State University*
*Bozeman, MT 59717-2400*
*burke@math.montana.edu*

*Vena Long*
*University of Tennessee*
*Knoxville, TN 37996*
*vlong@utk.edu*

CBMS Issues in Mathematics Education
Volume **15**, 2008

# Mathematics Education Doctoral Programs: Approaches to Part-Time Students

Gladis Kersaint and Gerald A. Goldin

This paper addresses issues specific to part-time doctoral students in mathematics education, and offers some methods for supporting these students in the completion of their programs. We consider the following questions:

- What are the important characteristics and associated needs of part-time doctoral students? Are there similarities in these across various mathematics education doctoral programs?
- What are the issues and challenges that are associated with the preparation of part-time doctoral students?
- What strategies have been shown to be effective in mathematics education doctoral programs that serve part-time students? What new suggestions can be offered?
- What possibilities and opportunities do part-time students provide for the enrichment of doctoral programs?

In addressing these questions, we first describe some characteristics of the mathematics education and teacher education faculty members whose views are reflected in our summary.

## Characteristics of Educators Contributing to the Discussion

The discussion about part-time mathematics education doctoral students attracted two distinct sets of participants. The first set included mathematics educators in active doctoral programs, who had a significant number of part-time doctoral students enrolled in their program. These faculty members wanted to learn from and share strategies addressing programmatic and other issues related to part-time doctoral students. The other set of participants included individuals in the process of developing doctoral programs, who were anticipating enrollment of part-time students. These faculty members were seeking guidance in the development of their doctoral programs, and wanted to learn from the experiences of those who had addressed problems and incorporated effective strategies as part of their program.

**Faculty Experiences As Doctoral Students.** We surveyed faculty participants regarding their own histories as doctoral students. A significant majority had themselves been exclusively full-time students: among 30 faculty participants in two different sessions, only 8 had studied part-time for any portion of their doctoral work, and for most of these participants the part-time study had been only in their first year, as part of a transition into doctoral study. Thus they had been typically part-time for a year or less, followed by full-time study for the remainder of their doctoral program. Of course, not all the participants had received their doctorates in mathematics education - a diverse set of fields were represented (including mathematics, physics, psychology, curriculum and instruction, and others).

**Status of Currently-Enrolled Mathematics Education Doctoral Students.** We also surveyed participants regarding their estimates of the numbers of doctoral students in their active programs who are currently full-time, or currently part-time. With the exception of the universities who were part of currently-funded centers, the majority of participants reported that only a few of the students enrolled in their programs were full-time students. Overall, the current number of full-time students in participants' programs was estimated around 150 and the current number of part-time students about 235. The latter includes students working full time, but enrolled in dissertation study.

These data suggest that many mathematics educators may not understand from their own personal histories the nature of the educational experiences of the majority of their doctoral students. It is therefore important for doctoral faculty to assess those experiences as they are occurring. Perhaps it is also the case that students who receive their doctorates after part-time study are less likely to join the professoriate than those who are full time throughout. One explanation for this phenomenon is that part-time students are working in another job, and upon completion of their doctorate they remain with the same employer.

## Characteristics of Part-Time Doctoral Students

There appeared to be a substantial consensus across different mathematics education doctoral programs as to the characteristics of part-time students. Typically part-time students were described as individuals sharing many of the following characteristics:

- They did not receive funding either through teaching or research assistantships or through fellowships, and as a result did not regularly enroll in a full load of courses (usually defined to be at least 9 credit hours per semester).
- They are typically accomplished professionals in their current jobs (e.g., college or community college instructor in mathematics, teacher of mathematics or elementary school teacher, district level content specialist), and are likely to be fully engaged in their current work as they seek an advanced degree. Some may have major family commitments (e.g., caring for young children) that keep them from full-time study.
- They bring to their doctoral programs a wealth of experiences. Many of them have been active in local, regional, or sometimes national mathematics education contexts. Some embody extraordinary levels of practical knowledge (e.g. in urban education, or in educational work with minority or disadvantaged students).

- Typically they either do not intend to leave their current jobs, or else plan to seek career advancement within their current employment contexts (e.g., increases in pay, or promotions to positions of greater leadership).
- They typically attend evening classes, and may travel across great distances or over significant commuting times to do so.

We also discovered that there may be a need to broaden our understanding of what is meant by "part time." University policies and where applicable, residency requirements, typically define a student's enrollment status based on the number of credit hours the student takes in any given semester, so that a graduate student taking fewer than 9 credit hours is considered a part-time student. However, several participants suggested that this interpretation of "part-time student" needs to be broadened and defined by the student's experiences in the program, rather than the number of hours the student is enrolled in courses or dissertation study. For example, a student might be enrolled in 9 credit hours of coursework to fulfill a mandatory residency requirement, but may nevertheless be working full-time, planning to finish outstanding assignments and remove "incomplete" grades during the summer. Such a student may face the same challenges as other students who are "officially" considered part-time. The needs of part-time doctoral students in mathematics education are best addressed by considering the challenges they are likely to face.

### Issues and Challenges in Preparing Part-Time Doctoral Students

**Career Paths for Part-Time Doctoral Students.** Participants discussed the many options available to those earning doctoral degrees with an emphasis in mathematics education. But part time students, whether or not they are "officially" part time, may not have the opportunities to share in the rich variety of experiences typically afforded to full-time doctoral students. These include working on faculty research projects, attending seminars and colloquia, teaching or assisting in methods courses, assisting with the organization of locally-sponsored workshops and conferences, serving on departmental or university committees, and participating fully in student life. Because they typically maintain high current levels of responsibilities, there is little, if any, time to participate in other professional activities. They typically have limited contact with university faculty or with their peers in doctoral programs, outside of attending class sessions. Thus part-time students may acquire a less complete understanding of the range of activities in which faculty members engage.

In addition, there is the obvious fact that part time students are likely to take years longer than full time students to complete the requirements of their doctorates.

For these reasons, part-time students are likely to be less inclined and/or less able than full-time students to explore all of the professional leadership options available to those who complete mathematics education doctorates.

In our discussion groups, participants agreed that many part-time students' goals tend to remain localized to leadership roles in their current professional contexts. Only rarely do they consider becoming researchers. Some enroll in doctoral programs as a condition for continued employment (e.g., some community college faculty), so that earning a doctoral degree serves a specific, predefined purpose. For others, career options are limited because they are regionally bound due to family

or financial commitments. Doctoral students who are accomplished and profession-
ally advanced in their fields may find it financially prohibitive to change careers
paths; not only a cut in salary but also some loss of retirement benefits may be a
consequence of changing jobs.

On the other hand, some students who enter doctoral programs with fixed career plans (e.g., to remain in their current positions) do learn enough about other
options to seriously consider them. Several participants asked whether current
mathematics education faculty represented our profession to doctoral students sufficiently well, truly functioning as stewards of our field and encouraging students
to pursue the professoriate through our words and actions.

Thus one challenge regarding part-time students is to open up their understandings and perceptions of the variety of career paths available to them in mathematics
education, including academic research, and to portray these paths in an attractive
and richly-textured way.

**Building a Sense of Community Among Part-Time Students.** Full-
time doctoral students are typically provided with a variety of opportunities to
participate with faculty and peers as members of the mathematics education community. They benefit directly from faculty mentorship, work with faculty (e.g., in
coauthoring articles or in research), and participate in some of the functions of university mathematics educators (e.g., in developing and teaching methods courses).
They interact with other doctoral students who share common interests, engaging
in many "unstructured" activities, casual conversations, and personal interactions
outside of coursework. In short, they become part of a "community of scholars."
But students who come to campus only to take classes do not have the same opportunities for such engagement.

Thus another challenge is to find ways to integrate part-time students into a
more extended learning community.

**Learning from the Experience Base of Part-Time Students.** For the
reasons discussed, it is often the case that the "voices" of part-time doctoral students are subordinated to those of full-time students in discussions of issues, in
seminars, and in the formulation of research projects. Yet it is often the case that
part-time students, as a result of their professional experiences, bring hard-won
expertise in the "front line" issues of concern to mathematics educators.

Thus a third challenge, related to that of creating a more extended learning
community, is to bring into the foreground the professional understandings that
part-time students have, in a way that is of benefit to the entire mathematics
education program.

**Programmatic or Organizational Issues.** Part-time students may have
difficulty meeting certain program requirements - for example, courses in mathematics, statistics, or psychology that may be important to their doctoral work are
sometimes offered only during daytime hours. Thus another challenge is to find
ways in which part-time students have access to course offerings so they can meet
their academic needs under existing constraints.

## Suggestions for Effective Strategies

Several participants shared approaches they used successfully to build a community among doctoral students in general, and among part-time students in particular. Some reported that they require doctoral students to complete mandatory non-coursework experiences. For example, students may be required (and/or incentives may be provided) to:

- attend seminars on Saturdays or other nights of the week,
- participate in all-day research symposia,
- attend monthly social gatherings to share and exchange ideas, or
- collaborate on joint projects with peers.

All of these strategies are intended to encourage part-time students to interact with faculty and other doctoral students.

Other participants reported their doctoral programs require students to enroll as members of a cohort or a modified cohort (e.g., taking all their mathematics education doctoral courses together), in order to build a sense of community. Students who enroll as members of such a cohort tend to connect with their peers by sharing common experiences. In fact, several reported that peers helped to motivate each other to complete the program.

In addition, ideas were offered concerning the use of web-based media, such as course or seminar bulletin boards, to foster ongoing discussions that include both part-time and full-time students, and partnering on-and off-campus students around the fulfillment of assignments or projects.

Another suggestion is to provide structured ways for (at least some) part-time students to share the professional expertise they have acquired through consideration of the problems they are currently addressing in mathematics education (e.g., in public school or community college classrooms, or in school district policy issues). These topics are then introduced as concrete domains of inquiry for research or for academic discussions.

Financial support can be provided to enable part-time students to travel to professional meetings and conferences and participate in research presentations.

Additional suggestions included special summer workshops and institutes, internship courses, increased uses of various distance learning technologies, and pairing full-time and part-time students in research.

To ensure continued advancement by part-time students, an annual write-up addressing each student's progress toward the doctoral degree can be an important and helpful tool.

Some participants wondered whether it might be beneficial to develop mathematics education doctoral programs specifically for part-time students. As one participant asked, "What is the purpose of the doctoral program? Should we prepare all students the same, or should we differentiate between programs for full- and part-time students?" Differentiated programs could have different goals, expectations, requirements, and outcomes. Programs might address the needs of specific target populations, as indeed some do now (e.g., developing practitioner experts who will work in urban environments). Such programs can be more focused, and address the career-goals of those enrolled. Some participants debated the value of preparing all students as if they were to become researchers, when our informal survey suggests that the majority do not have this goal.

A related issue is the variable way that distinctions are drawn between different doctoral degrees (e.g., Ed.D. and Ph.D. degrees, with the former sometimes placing greater emphasis on educational practice, and the latter sometimes placing greater emphasis on academic research). It was remarked that sometimes institutional prestige issues related to the type of degree that is offered bear no relationship to the type of preparation with which students are actually provided. In drawing distinctions when "targeted" programs are designed, it is important to avoid an unintended "caste system" that might effectively limit the prospects of part time students.

## Opportunities Provided by Part-Time Students in Mathematics Education

Discussions confirmed that participants regarded part-time students as offering a rich resource. For example at the MetroMath Center, (based at Rutgers University, the City University of New York Graduate Center, and the University of Pennslyvania), part-time students embody an important source of expertise on the day-to-day issues affecting mathematics education in urban schools. In general, their presence helps doctoral programs to be self-sustaining, and allows courses to be offered that might not otherwise have sufficient enrollments. They are typically energetic and skilled professionals, adept at juggling many different responsibilities.

The process of addressing their needs may offer partnership opportunities at our universities, including partnerships across departments (e.g., designing mathematics course sections to meet part-time students' needs) and external partnerships (e.g., partnerships with school districts to facilitate their employees' participation in doctoral programs or in site-based research).

Thus, as doctoral programs in mathematics education and related areas successfully implement strategies that address part-time students' needs, we would expect these programs to be enriched with expertise, energy, a wider sense of community, and new, vibrant partnership possibilities.

## Conclusions

To sum up, participants entertained a broad range of issues related to preparing part-time mathematics education doctoral students. Far from being a liability, significant involvement by these students provides an important opportunity to enhance and strengthen the pool of mathematics educators available in the field. With many positions to be filled, not just in higher education, but in the broader mathematics education community, part-time students in significant numbers are essential.

*Gerald A. Goldin*
*Rutgers - The State University of New Jersey*
*Piscataway, NJ 08854-8019*
*geraldgoldin@dimacs.rutgers.edu*

*Gladis Kersaint*
*University of South Florida*
*Tampa, FL 33620-5650*
*kersaint@coedu.usf.edu*

CBMS Issues in Mathematics Education
Volume 15, 2008

# Induction of Doctoral Graduates in Mathematics Education into the Profession

Barbara J. Reys, Gwendolyn M. Lloyd, Karen Marrongelle,
and Matthew S. Winsor

This report documents the ideas and issues on the induction of new graduates into their professional careers at institutions of higher education. Mathematicians and mathematics educators were asked to consider the following questions:

> What strategies are useful in supporting the induction of new doctoral graduates of mathematics education into the profession? In particular, what ideas and activities are useful in supporting recent graduates in their roles in higher education (e.g., establishing a research agenda and identifying research partners; developing as a college teacher; taking on active service roles)? How can the community of mathematics educators facilitate ongoing learning opportunities in key areas (e.g., policy issues, technological advances, evolving research/statistical techniques) for new faculty assuming major responsibilities in mathematics education areas of teaching, research and service?

Our view of induction focuses on the processes by which new faculty members, holding recently awarded doctoral degrees in mathematics education, are introduced to and supported in their new positions in higher education. Induction includes a range of activities and opportunities that support new faculty members in making a smooth transition from life as a doctoral student to the new professional roles and responsibilities of an assistant professor of mathematics education. Induction is the joint responsibility of hiring institutions and the mathematics education community at large. Existing induction strategies include programs provided by higher education institutions and by professional organizations (e.g., NCTM, MAA, AMTE, AERA). To provide further support for new faculty members, we need to expand some existing successful induction opportunities and create new opportunities.

## Induction Opportunities Provided by the Hiring Institution

Hiring institutions use a variety of strategies to support induction of new faculty. For example, most universities sponsor workshops/seminars related to teaching and grant-writing for new faculty. Within departments or disciplinary groups, research seminars and committee work also create occasions for new faculty to benefit from interactions with more experienced colleagues. However, the most prominent and potentially worthwhile induction program sponsored by institutions involves mentoring of new faculty by assigned senior faculty.

Although mentoring opportunities exist in most academic departments and/or universities, a good deal of variance in the formality and productivity of mentor-mentee relationships exists. The effectiveness of unstructured mentoring programs depends on many things, including the nature of the match between mentor-mentee (e.g., In mathematics departments, new mathematics education faculty members are often mentored by mathematicians), the purpose of the relationship (to provide support or to direct the new faculty member's research agenda), and the time available and/or reward for mentoring. The strategies can be classified as *personnel mentoring strategies* and *activity-based mentoring strategies.*

**Personnel Mentoring Strategies.** These strategies focus on mentoring of junior faculty by senior faculty or teams of senior faculty (both discipline specific and cross-discipline), as well as peer-mentoring strategies. Currently available and suggested strategies include:

- Establish mentoring teams – rather than a single mentor – for new faculty. The mentoring team can meet regularly with the new hire and provide guidance regarding the direction of the faculty member's research, teaching, and service efforts as well as learn about institution-specific policies and practices. Various members of the team can take on different advising roles, thereby distributing the responsibility and focusing the interaction.
- Invite emeritus faculty to mentor new faculty. Emeritus members of the faculty bring knowledge of departmental and institutional history, as well as departmental politics, to provide unique mentoring experiences for new faculty.
- Invite new faculty to co-advise doctoral student research with senior faculty or with faculty from other institutions as a means of helping ease new faculty into the important work of doctoral advising.
- Consider specialized mentoring opportunities for specific populations (e.g, new female faculty or the first faculty member from an underrepresented group).
- Design opportunities for peer-mentoring. For example, establish a means for junior faculty across disciplines at an institution to meet regularly in informal support groups.

**Activity-Based Mentoring Strategies.** Opportunities exist for developing new faculty knowledge and expertise outside a direct mentoring relationship. Current and suggested strategies include:

- Develop opportunities and events that allow new faculty to return to their 'home' institutions for a period of time to review research, discuss opportunities for collaboration, and exchange ideas.
- Encourage new faculty to attend grant-writing workshops and regional grants conferences sponsored by local, regional, or national funding agencies.
- Sponsor writing seminars and retreats for new faculty. These might take the form of intra- or inter-institutional (regional) retreats.
- Develop seminars in which faculty regularly meet to share research ideas.

Even when new faculty have supportive mentors and opportunities to participate fully in the academic community, adjustment to a new professorship is very challenging (Tyminski this volume). Professional organizations provide important opportunities to support personnel growth, development, and assimilation into the broader community of mathematics education.

### Induction Opportunities Provided by Professional Communities

Professional organizations and other cross-institutional communities in mathematics education play an important role in the induction of new faculty. These groups sponsor special sessions and/or pre-sessions for new faculty to share their research and teaching activities. Funding agencies often sponsor grant-writing workshops that target young researchers. Special workshops and programs, hosted by professional organizations, funded projects, or other groups, may offer additional opportunities for initiation into the profession and professional development. In particular, we examine three examples of the work of various professional communities supporting the development of new faculty: Centers for Learning and Teaching (CLTs), Association of Mathematics Teacher Educators (AMTE) Mentoring Task Force, and the Mathematical Association of America (MAA) Project NExT program.

**Centers for Learning and Teaching.** Seven CLTs funded since 2000 by the National Science Foundation (NSF) have a primary focus on mathematics education. Several have provided extensive opportunities for advanced doctoral students and young researchers to take part in collaborative research activities and networking with more experienced researchers who share the new faculty member's research interest. For example, the Center for Proficiency in Teacher Education has organized and facilitated summer workshops for teacher educators and mathematicians to explore and gain expertise in teacher preparation in mathematics. The Center for the Study of Mathematics Curriculum holds an annual research conference focused on mathematics curriculum and invites new and mid-career researchers from other institutions to contribute to and benefit from the network of faculty and doctoral students focused on this common research area. Other CLTs offer similar opportunities for new faculty development (see CLTNet.org for information on the work of each CLT). However, since NSF is no longer supporting CLTs, new ways of continuing these opportunities will need to be created.

**AMTE Mentoring Task Force.** The Task Force was charged, "to seek ways to mentor new faculty and doctoral students in teaching, scholarship, and professional responsibilities while networking with other mathematics teacher educators." Given that the academic home of mathematics teacher education varies by institution – education departments or mathematics departments – the Task Force acknowledged that the support and challenges may vary depending on the departmental home of faculty and programs. Thus, they suggest different strategies, depending on who teaches future teachers (mathematicians teaching preservice education courses and/or mathematics content courses for teachers, adjunct or short term faculty hired to teach or support field-based experiences, mathematics educators in either education or mathematics departments). The Task Force recommends that AMTE pursue the following actions:

- Support the development of policy documents and other resources. For example, language is needed to describe the important and valued role of faculty with regard to training future teachers. Additionally, materials are needed that provide ideas, resources, and references for teaching mathematics education courses.
- Establish an AMTE Committee on Mentoring to generate interest, raise awareness, and establish networks focused on teacher education (offer short courses at conferences, sponsor listservs, etc.).
- Establish an AMTE-sponsored Mentor Program, matching new members with a group of experienced faculty who can meet at AMTE meetings.

**MAA Project NExT.** Project NExT (New Experiences in Teaching) is a professional development program for new or recent PhDs in the mathematical sciences developed by the Mathematical Association of America. In particular,

> [Project NExT] addresses all aspects of an academic career: improving the teaching and learning of mathematics, engaging in research and scholarship, and participating in professional activities. It also provides the participants with a network of peers and mentors as they assume these responsibilities (for more information, see: http://archives.math.utk.edu/projnext/)

Since its inception in 1994, Project NExT has supported 1000 Fellows from universities and colleges in the United States and Canada. NExT Fellows hold a PhD in a field related to the mathematical sciences (pure and applied mathematics, mathematics education, or statistical sciences), are in their first or second year of post PhD teaching, and are housed in a Mathematics or Statistics Department (mathematics educators teaching in a College of Education are not eligible to participate). The home department of the Fellow must commit resources to send NExT Fellows to three conferences sponsored by the American Mathematical Society and the Mathematical Association of America.

Upon becoming a Project NExT Fellow, participants attend three meetings (two MAA Mathfest meetings held in consecutive summers and one joint meeting of the AMS and MAA held annually in January). At the meetings, NExT Fellows attend a variety of workshops exclusively for NExT fellows, given by veterans in the field of mathematical sciences, which address the following topics:

- Innovative approaches to a variety of introductory and advanced courses;
- Using writing to help students learn mathematics;
- Involving undergraduates in mathematical research;
- Alternative methods of assessing student learning;
- Preparing future K-12 teachers of mathematics;
- Writing grant proposals; and
- Balancing teaching and research.

In addition to attending workshops, NExT Fellows are assigned a mentor from the field. The mentor serves as a guide for NExT Fellows as they start working in their department. The mentor usually has research interests similar to those of the NExT Fellow. Mentors also serve as a point of contact between the NExT Fellow and other researchers in the field.

Project NExT also sponsors a listserv that is exclusive to Fellows. The listserv is an avenue for Fellows to collaborate. Topics from the listserv include, but are not limited to, choice of textbooks, how to generate interest in mathematics among undergraduates, help with creating new classes for specific groups (such as liberal arts students or future teachers), and effective assessment methods. One thread of the Project NExT listserv is dedicated to the topic of educating future teachers.

Anecdotal evidence suggests that being a NExT Fellow has several benefits. One NExT Fellow noted, "One of the greatest benefits of being a Fellow is being able to share ideas about teaching and career issues with a community of scholars who are at similar points in their careers." Another NExT Fellow noted that through networking, Fellows receive the encouragement needed to succeed in the field of mathematical sciences. Project NExT also introduces Fellows to professional activities provided by the Mathematical Association of America.

## Future Directions

More can and should be done to support new faculty in mathematics education. Within the setting of existing conferences sponsored by professional organizations (e.g., NCTM, AMTE, PME-NA, AERA and SIG-RME), a variety of activities should be explored with conference organizers. Some of these activities exist and others need to be initiated or expanded. Current and proposed activities include:

- Facilitate mentoring sessions for new faculty on topics of interest (teaching, research).
- Identify new mathematics education faculty members at national conferences (via some indicator on the badge) with encouragement to veteran faculty to meet and interact with new faculty.
- Create a listserv for new faculty in mathematics education (not limited to Project NExT Fellows).
- Host research catalyst conferences (as separate conferences or as a pre- or post-session to an existing conference) at which new and experienced faculty and advanced doctoral students can come together to discuss and collaborate on research of mutual interest.
- Establish mentoring networks focused on particular research foci. The networks should include mathematics educators at all stages of their careers. The networks should reach outside the departments of a local institution to include other institutions in the region, in order to include isolated faculty (i.e., faculty who are the only mathematics educators at their site) in the process.
- Create a listserv for research issues in mathematics education. Participants would include faculty from all points of the career continuum as mentors as well as new faculty.
- Design specific conference sessions for new faculty and advanced doctoral students at AMTE, NCTM, and PME-NA conferences (e.g., hold NCATE workshops for new faculty at national meetings).
- Create regional groups in which (isolated) junior faculty learn from experienced mathematics education faculty in the region.

In addition to these ideas, we wish to draw attention to the success of Project NExT as a formal, organized structure for providing ongoing support for new faculty. It may be possible for Project NExT to be expanded to include more mathematics education faculty. Alternatively, a "sister" project could be developed with collaboration of MAA, NCTM, and AMTE focused on new mathematics education faculty, regardless of their home department.

Our field faces an urgent need to develop activities and programs to support faculty new to academic mathematics education positions. Given the shortage of doctorates in mathematics education, it is critical that we retain those prepared to enter the profession. Likewise, it is critical to develop programs that support those doing the work of mathematics education (research, service, teaching) regardless of their academic training.

*Barbara J. Reys*
*University of Missouri*
*Columbia, MO 65211*
*reysb@missouri.edu*

*Gwendolyn M. Lloyd*
*Virginia Tech*
*Blacksburg VA 24061-0123*
*lloyd@vt.edu*

*Karen Marrongelle*
*Portland State University*
*Portland, OR 97207*
*karenmar@pdx.edu*

*Matthew S. Winsor*
*University of Texas-El Paso*
*El Paso, TX 79968-0514*
*mwinsor@utep.edu*

Part 4


Doctoral Programs in Mathematics Education:
Some International Perspectives

CBMS Issues in Mathematics Education
Volume **15**, 2008

# Doctoral Programs in Mathematics Education:
# An International Perspective

## Jeremy Kilpatrick

The study of any phenomenon is enhanced by attention to the various habitats in which it can be situated, and that is certainly true of doctoral programs as educational phenomena. Doctoral programs in mathematics education take strikingly different forms as they are institutionalized across the country (Reys & Kilpatrick, 2001), and they differ even more when one looks abroad. The panel session entitled "Doctoral Programs in Mathematics Education: An International Perspective" gave conference attendees a glimpse of dimensions on which such programs can differ as well as common features they might share.

Several months before the conference, the panelists were asked to: (a) prepare a brief paper highlighting key elements of the doctoral program or programs in mathematics education with which they were most familiar, (b) be prepared to share ideas and approaches to the preparation of doctoral students in mathematics education that characterize that program or those programs, (c) identify unique or particularly strong features of the program or programs that they thought would be of interest to conference attendees and perhaps even be transportable to other programs, and (d) revise their paper to reflect discussions, interactions, and insights they gained at the conference. To focus discussion following their presentations, panelists were asked to think about five questions:

(1) What criteria do prospective students have to meet to be admitted to the doctoral program?
(2) What variations are there in the program beyond the master's degree, and how are those variations taken into account?
(3) How is the doctoral dissertation evaluated?
(4) What is your experience with cross-institutional, as opposed to single-institutional, programs?
(5) How is your doctoral program evaluated?

At the session, there was time to discuss only the last question before audience members began to ask questions of their own. Their questions concerned the doctoral students' share of program costs; the male/female ratio of students and faculty in the programs; and key elements of the programs that might, or might not, enhance U.S. doctoral programs. Additional questions dealt with the following topics: teaching experience as a doctoral program requirement; the nature of bachelor's degree programs, and how they related to the completion time for doctoral programs; the relation between mathematics education research and the society of research mathematicians in each country; the importance in the doctoral program of a knowledge of mathematics; the importance in the program of a knowledge of technology; the transferability of a Ph.D. in mathematics education to and from each country; how U.S. programs affect their doctoral programs; and what makes a dissertation in their programs "good enough."

Clearly, these questions covered many more topics than could be addressed adequately in a single paper, so it is not surprising that in revising their papers, the panelists were not able to deal with all of them. Nevertheless, these questions did help the panelists see what was on the minds of people concerned with U.S. doctoral programs in mathematics education.

Beatriz D'Ambrosio addresses Brazilian doctoral programs from the perspective of one who has been both a student and a faculty member in the United States and a faculty member in Brazil. Features of the Brazilian programs that appear to be unique, or at least very different from those of U.S. programs, are the system by which Brazilian programs are accredited and given a quality score, the alignment between faculty research interests and programs of study, the requirement of a preliminary dissertation proposal for admission to the program and of a pilot study and refined dissertation proposal for the qualifying examination, and the emphasis on doctoral students from different institutions participating in a common intellectual community. Particularly striking about the Brazilian situation are the rapidity with which programs have appeared and grown, and the productive way in which programs have used the cross-national and cross-institutional experience of faculty members and students.

Barbro Grevholm directs the Nordic Graduate School in Mathematics Education and has been a faculty member in Sweden and Norway. She gives an overview of Nordic doctoral programs in mathematics education, pointing out-like D'Ambrosio-how relatively new the programs are. Unusual features of Nordic programs include the public defense of the thesis in a disputation against one or more opponents, and sometimes other examiners and the public; the national graduate schools, cross-national workshops, and cross-national summer schools; the seminars for supervisors of doctoral studies; and the seminars organized when 90 percent of the thesis is completed (some U.S. universities have similar seminars). As Grevholm observes, special problems arise in the Nordic countries owing to the small size of the programs and the need for a critical mass of researchers.

Masataka Koyama discusses the four mathematics education doctoral programs in Japan. He points out the differences between the two more-established programs located in single institutions and the two newer programs conducted jointly across institutions. He also notes that there are course doctorates and thesis doctorates, with the latter being the more common route. An unusual feature of the Japanese programs is the way in which they have been refocused recently so that graduates unable to find university positions will be prepared for other employment opportunities. The newer programs, both with a strong emphasis on practice, were designed especially to prepare professionals for schools and districts.

Luis Rico and his colleagues discuss graduate studies in mathematics education at the University of Granada, which has one of Spain's oldest, largest, and most highly ranked doctoral programs in mathematics education. As in Brazil, a preliminary thesis proposal is required for admission to the doctoral program, and the proposal is refined during an extended research workshop. An unusual feature of graduate studies at Granada is that the courses and seminars are all in the master's program, and the doctoral program is entirely devoted to the doctoral thesis. Whereas at other Spanish universities and in other fields, the great majority of doctoral students fail to complete the thesis, the attrition rate for the mathematics education program in Granada is much lower although nonetheless of concern to the faculty. The recent availability of the European doctorate as an alternative program appears to be a promising innovation.

In all of the countries represented on the panel, the doctoral programs in mathematics education are relatively new, and most are relatively small. They have many of the same characteristics as U.S. programs, but they appear to include more cross-institutional and cross-national collaboration and exchange activities than are typical of U.S. programs. Each program discussed in the papers that follow has features that U.S. supervisors of doctoral students might consider adopting or adapting. Collectively, the programs show us how mathematics education is developing as an academic field, how far it has come, and where it might be going.

*Jeremy Kilpatrick*
*University of Georgia*
*Athens, GA 30602*
*jkilpat@uga.edu*

CBMS Issues in Mathematics Education
Volume **15**, 2008

# Doctoral Studies in Mathematics Education: Unique Features of Brazilian Programs

## Beatriz S. D'Ambrosio

## Introduction

Doctoral programs in mathematics education in Brazil are a recent phenomenon. Up until the late 1980s Brazilian doctoral candidates in mathematics education were tied to a very generalist program in education or a very specific program in mathematics. Course work was taken in mathematics or in education, then the focus of their dissertation could be on an issue in mathematics education when the host unit (school of education or department of mathematics) allowed for this type of deviation from the norm. However, little in the coursework was specific to mathematics education. Furthermore, the advisors would not have had specific training, or even interest, in research in mathematics education. The closest faculty to mathematics education were those with interest in research in mathematical modeling and curriculum development, or research in the learning of mathematics (area of educational psychology), or research in college teaching. Of course, an alternative was to pursue the degree in other countries. Hence, many of the early Brazilian PhDs in mathematics education were obtained at universities in the U.S. and Europe during the 1980s and 1990s.

The lack of human resources, i.e., individuals with PhDs in mathematics education, delayed the institutionalization of doctoral programs in Brazil. As one of the first PhDs in mathematics education obtained in the U.S., I returned to Brazil in 1987, at a time when many institutions were conceptualizing a doctoral program in mathematics education. UNICAMP (University at Campinas) had a vibrant doctoral program in education and established mathematics education as one of its areas of study. Their doctoral program in mathematics education was accredited in 2004. The State University of São Paulo in Rio Claro (UNESP) had an exciting master's program in mathematics education in the mathematics department and became the first institution to be accredited as a mathematics education doctoral program in 1994. Other institutions, including Catholic University at São Paulo (PUCSP) and the University of São Paulo (USP) were among many institutions seeking the establishment and accreditation of new doctoral programs in mathematics education. All of the young PhDs in mathematics education in Brazil were summoned to contribute to the creation of these exciting new programs. Fortunately, all of these institutions had strong master's programs. This provided a solid foundation for extending their curricula to include the new doctoral programs in mathematics education.

In this document I will describe some of the qualities of these Brazilian PhD programs, focusing primarily on the first institutions to conceptualize and institutionalize their programs. The focus will be on unique programmatic features that are characteristic of all Brazilian doctoral programs. For this work I studied a small set of programs representing institutions of different types (federal, state, and private) and housed in different units (education versus mathematics). While this work is not a comprehensive profile, it does provide a framework for viewing doctoral programs in mathematics education in Brazil.

There are a few characteristics of Brazilian doctoral programs that cut across all programs. Those include the accreditation process for Doctoral programs, the entrance examination for the programs, the experiences of students in the programs, and the opportunities for "sandwich" experience in any program. In the background of the doctoral granting process lie the federal agencies such as CAPES[1] and CNPQ[2]. Both agencies provide funding for students pursuing graduate degrees, faculty research, conferences, faculty development, and international faculty exchange. Hence these agencies play a fundamental role in sustaining the high quality of the graduate programs across the country.

## The Role of Federal Agencies in the Doctoral Process

CAPES is a governmental agency responsible for the education and professional development of faculty for higher education. In that capacity CAPES makes several major contributions to Brazilian doctoral programs. In particular, it contributes to programs by accrediting graduate programs, providing student scholarships and faculty scholarships, and supporting the institutions with external visitors.

**Accreditation.** One of the major roles that CAPES plays in higher education in Brazil is the accreditation and scoring of graduate programs in mathematics education (as well as all other graduate programs in the country). The scores of each program are posted and widely available. When students apply for scholarships they are encouraged to apply to schools with the highest ranking programs in their field. The accreditation process is used by students to select programs, by institutions to evaluate their programs, and by CAPES to oversee the quality of programs around the country. Only programs that score three or higher on a seven point scale are included in the data banks available to potential students seeking scholarships. In other words, a program requires a score of three or higher out of seven in order to be considered accredited. Currently there are only 39 graduate programs in education that have been accredited, and of these only nine are listed as offering accredited doctoral degrees in Mathematics or Science Education (in Brazil it is not unusual to consider mathematics as part of a science education program).

The institutions offering doctoral programs and wishing to be accredited are responsible for creating portfolios to document the quality of their programs and graduates. Portfolios include the qualifications of its faculty members, as well as their productivity, including the quality and impact of the work of each of its full

---

[1]*Coordenação de Aperfeiçoamento de Pessoal de Nível Superior* - Agency for the Improvement of Human Resources in Higher Education

[2]*Conselho Nacional de Desenvolvimento Científico e Tecnológico* - National Council of Scientific and Technological Development

time faculty members, and its adjunct faculty. Criteria for evaluating candidates for entry into the program as well as criteria for evaluating students in the qualifying process and their final thesis are part of the portfolio examined by CAPES.

The level of excellence of a program is determined by a committee of examiners (a group of mathematics educators from around the country appointed by CAPES). These examiners scrutinize program documents assessing each of the following indicators of excellence:

a. Faculty

The committee examines the qualifications of the faculty, exploring whether all faculty members involved in the doctoral program have doctorates themselves (and that these were mostly acquired at different institutions from the one in which they are employed). Other indicators of qualification include the faculty members' participation in research projects, conferences, edited books, national and international service. Examiners are also looking at participation of national and international researchers in the program, exchange programs with other institutions of high quality, and capacity of faculty for securing outside funding.

b. Research, development and service activities

The committee examines whether the faculty is organized around research programs and research groups which are aligned with course offerings; there is an adequate proportion of research projects to the number of faculty members; student activity and productivity is tied to the research groups and research programs of the faculty; faculty are involved in dissemination of knowledge through publications and in-service activity.

c. Program structure

The committee examines whether the activities of students in the doctoral program (course work, seminars, and research) are aligned to the faculties' research programs and related research groups; syllabi and bibliography of courses are current and of international quality; faculty are involved in both graduate and undergraduate education.

d. Intellectual productivity

The committee verifies that there is a correlation between the research programs and the dissertations produced, resulting in publications in journals of national and international circulation and of the highest quality; students have publications, or manuscripts accepted for publication, prior to defending their dissertation; faculty produce an average of two publications per faculty member per year (peer reviewed articles of international or national caliber, full papers in conference proceedings, academic books, or chapters in books) considered as excellent in the field, where one of them at least must be in an international journal ranked "Qualis A."[3]

e. Infrastructure

It is also important for programs to document that they have adequate facilities such as classrooms, faculty and student offices; the library is current and has a good collection of books, journals and reference materials related to the research programs and groups; the institution has a plan

_____

[3]Qualis A criteria for journals requires that articles be refereed, journal be periodic and regular, editorial board be highly qualified and representative of the field, and the journal should be highly recognized in the field.

for continued growth and updating of library materials; there is internet
capability and access to large data banks by students and faculty; there
are adequate laboratories for science programs.

f. Student body
Programs must document that the average time for completion of the program is 48 months for doctoral students. The thesis and dissertations are
of high quality, resulting necessarily in publications in nationally or internationally recognized venues; the studies have the potential of impact
in the educational system; the doctoral dissertation examination committees engage faculty members from outside of the institution; and the
doctoral students are involved in instruction, advising, or supervision of
undergraduates at the institution.

g. Visibility
The program is well known nationally and internationally as assessed by
the following indicators: the program regularly engages students, post-
doctorates, and researchers from other national or international research
centers; the faculty are invited to contribute to academic activities at well
known institutions nationally and internationally; the intellectual products are referenced by others nationally and internationally.

The existing doctoral programs in mathematics education range in scores from 3
to 6. With only one program scoring 6 points on the 7 point scale.

CAPES also provides the nation with a data bank of all accredited graduate
programs, including their evaluations. Students seeking entry into graduate education can match their research interests to the research programs and research
groups of the various institutions nationwide. The scores are used to determine the
number of scholarships, funding for research, funding for travel to conferences and
funding for visitors. Higher scoring institutions have greater success in securing
funds for sustaining their high quality activities.


**Scholarships.** Through the activities of the two agencies CAPES and CNPQ,
the government is heavily involved in the production of Brazilian doctorates. These
agencies fund many doctoral students (and some master's students) with scholarships. Doctoral students with funding make a full-time commitment as students
and receive a monthly salary from one of the agencies. This funding is sufficient
for students to lead a modest life and to not have outside work. Unlike graduate students in the U.S., it is unlikely that Brazilian graduate students will be
fully responsible for teaching a course at the university level. In general, doctoral
students' engagement with undergraduates occurs through an undergraduate research activity. It is not unusual for graduate students to mentor undergraduate
students conducting undergraduate research activities tied to a research project.
There are not professional development programs for college teaching offered to
graduate assistants as occurs in the U.S. Yet, with their master's degrees, many
doctoral students have already held positions at institutions of higher education,
either private colleges or as adjuncts at the state or federal institutions. With the
growing number of institutions of higher education in Brazil, it is still possible to
hold a faculty position with only a master's degree.

Likewise, students will not be paid to participate in funded grants or projects.
Instead, there is an expectation that all students will participate in the projects

of their major professors. In fact, such participation is often built into students' programs as a credited part of their study.

In order to support the faculty and potential doctoral students, CAPES and CNPQ, offer scholarships for graduate studies, for post-doctoral studies, for faculty improvement, and for international visitors. The most unique scholarship is the one associated with what are known as "sandwich programs." Students who begin their studies at one institution and are interested in the work of a scholar at a different institution can apply for a sandwich scholarship. Sandwich scholarship recipients spend one to two years at a different institution than the one granting their degree. Typically the student does the research project elsewhere and returns to defend the dissertation at the degree granting institution. Other students might develop their theoretical framework or analyze their data while visiting the host institution.

When the participating institutions are organized in an official collaboration the sandwich programs have the greatest success. In these cases, both faculties have negotiated the credit in advance to be attributed to each participating faculty member in the student's work. Ad hoc collaborations can sometimes lead to unnecessary stress for the student for several reasons. For example, there is not always agreement on which faculty member will take the lead on the dissertation work. Sometimes it is unclear whether or not there is agreement on whether the student will enroll in courses or seminars at the host institution. Another point of potential misunderstanding deals with whether the student and the major professor from the home institution will both be co-authors on any publications that result from the exchange experience. Some cultural issues also arise that are uncomfortable for the faculty at the host institutions or for the student coming from a very different professional culture.

### Entrance Requirements for Doctoral Programs in Brazil

Programs each admit a limited number of students. The number of available spaces in a program is directly related to the number of students that each faculty member can advise. As students graduate, spaces become available to work with specific faculty. Upon applying to a program a student must decide with which faculty member he or she wishes to work, based on common research interests. While the entrance requirements to doctoral programs vary slightly from one program to another, they share the requirement that students present a preliminary proposal for their doctoral thesis. Since most students will have completed a master's degree with a thesis requirement, they have had experience writing research proposals.

The research proposals submitted are 15-20 pages in length and include the rationale, the research question(s), a literature base, a theoretical framework and a methodology. Students must identify the research program to which their study would be aligned and in their entrance interviews they will be asked to describe the contributions they believe they can make to the research group.

Every program requires proficiency in a foreign language. Several programs require a written examination based on an issue in mathematics education to be written 'on the spot' and at one university (UNESP) the students must pass a three hour mathematics qualifying examination in a content area of their choice (picked from Calculus, Linear Algebra, or Euclidean Geometry).

## Programs of Study for Mathematics Education Doctoral Students at Brazilian Institutions

There are several characteristics of the Brazilian doctoral programs that differ from those in the U.S. For one, the programs are structured around the research interests of the faculty. The notion of "core knowledge" varies greatly from one program to another. Institutions are encouraged by the accreditation system to align the courses offered in a program and the structure of the program to the research interests of their faculty. Programs closely aligned to faculty research interests score higher than others in the accreditation process.

Students are required to present a paper at a conference, to publish an article in a refereed journal before completing their thesis, to present their research at colloquia, and to offer workshops to teachers. All of these activities are built into their programs for credit, and are listed as "supporting activities." The actual core courses required at each institution tend to constitute only about 15% of the credits in a student's program of studies. The rest of the credits are earned through work on research, approximately 15% for work with the research group to which the student becomes affiliated and 60% for work on the student's dissertation. In one case, where the doctoral program is offered by the mathematics department, students are required to take more classes than in other programs and these include at least three mathematics classes. None of the programs in schools of education (the majority of existing doctoral programs) require mathematics classes in the doctoral studies.

The qualifying process is also unique in Brazilian doctoral programs. Throughout the course of study, students have developed, modified, and improved their proposals. For the qualifying examination, students have typically done a pilot study for their dissertation study and presented the results of the pilot and a refinement of the proposal. Students defend their work to a committee of examiners, including one external examiner, i.e. a faculty from a different institution. This same group of examiners will participate in the student's final dissertation defense.

## Graduate Student Conference

Since 1997 graduate students in mathematics education have organized and participated in an annual conference on research in mathematics education. The goal of the conference is to create spaces for "researchers in training" to discuss their studies. The objectives of the conference are for students to participate by presenting their studies in progress and to help students refine the methodology or theoretical framework of their studies before they are completed. It is a three-day conference focused on the discussion and improvement of students' work in progress.

Students with similar research interests are organized in small study groups with participants from different institutions. The number of faculty invited as mentors depends on the number of student papers submitted. All studies submitted to a particular group are discussed by all of the groups' participants and by the faculty mentor(s). These groups are small and sufficient time is scheduled to discuss all of the studies in great detail. Some students have questions about their methodologies, others about the theoretical framework, and others about the analysis of the data. As the students in the focus groups are at different phases of their research work, their varying levels of experience provide for a natural mentoring environment, where all members of the group, whether novice or more experienced, fully contribute to the group deliberations.

## Conclusion

In essence the most unique feature of the doctoral programs in Brazil is the emphasis on the intellectual community in which students participate. The organization of the faculty around research groups and the program of study aligned to these groups offer students a unique experience as a research apprentice. The regular meetings of the groups, the group investment in the research studies, and the collaborative experiences of designing studies, collecting data, and analyzing data provide for students membership in an intellectual community. Students participate in the work as colleagues and collaborators. Throughout the duration of their program graduate students contribute to and learn from and with this group.

Numerous conferences and visitors provide cross-fertilization among the intellectual communities around the country. Graduate students are always actively participating in the activities of their groups, be it in hosting conferences and visitors, be it in presenting papers at national or international conferences, or be it as co-authors of publications and organization of edited books.

The accreditation system validates, supports, and sustains this organization around research groups and intellectual communities. While additional time could have been spent critiquing the system of scoring and accreditation, the goal has been to report on the system in place and leave the speculations of the pros and cons of such a system as a discussion item for our community of mathematics educators.

*Beatriz D'Ambrosio*
*Miami University*
*Oxford, OH 45056*
*dambrobs@muohio.edu*

CBMS Issues in Mathematics Education
Volume **15**, 2008

# Nordic Doctoral Programs in Didactics of Mathematics

## Barbro Grevholm

## Introduction

**A Short Historical Background of Doctoral Programmes in Didactics of Mathematics.** In Sweden the academic subject pedagogy (or general education) developed in the beginning of the $20^{th}$ century and doctoral studies in mathematics education evolved, but it was not until the mid-1990 that separate doctoral programs in mathematics education were constructed. The development in the other Nordic countries was similar to the Swedish experience.

In 2000 the Swedish Bank Centennial Foundation decided to offer 45 million Swedish crowns for a National Graduate School in mathematics with didactical direction. This led to the development of seven new doctoral programs in Swedish universities (Leder, Brandell & Grevholm, 2004).

**About terminology.** In Sweden and the Nordic countries mathematics education is called 'matematikdidaktik' (or similar words in the different languages), didactics of mathematics, thereby following the German and French tradition rather than the Anglo-Saxon. In Sweden, mathematics education is translated to 'matematikutbildning', which means education in mathematics, including school level and other levels. Thus there is a risk of misinterpretations when using the word mathematics education. Often these notions are used interchangeably.

## The Structure of Doctoral Programs in the Different Countries

This section will offer short descriptions of some features of the doctoral programs in didactics of mathematics in several Nordic countries.

**Denmark.** In Denmark, doctoral education lasts for three years and there is no compulsory course part. The doctoral student can have one or several supervisors. The research leads to a thesis that will be examined by three examiners, including two external examiners. The examiners read the thesis and produce a written document, where they classify the work as acceptable or not. After the acceptance

Thanks to Kirsti Kislenko, Madis Lepik, Jonina Vala Kristinsdottir and Ann Sofi Röj-Lindberg for assistance with information about the Baltic, Icelandic and Finnish situations for doctoral students. The work presented here is partly financed from NordForsk (project number 90969 at University of Agder) for which we are grateful. An extended version of this paper is available at www.nogsme.no.

the doctoral student is allowed to defend the thesis in a public viva (disputation). This allows external persons to criticise and discuss the content. The thesis is normally not published.

**Finland.** Following national and rather general guidelines, doctoral education in Finland is designed in ways decided at each university. Models exist where different disciplines are integrated into the same program and there are also separated models. Finnish doctoral education is normally four years of full time studies and builds on a master's degree. No university in Finland offers a separate doctoral program in didactics of mathematics.

**Iceland.** There is no special doctoral program in mathematics education in Iceland. Students interested in mathematics education enroll in a program for Educational Studies - Philosophy of Education.

**Norway.** In Norway the doctoral education is a three year study with course work and research leading to a written thesis. The prerequisites for study are a master's degree in mathematics or mathematics education and teaching experience. The examination is similar to the one in Denmark. The University of Agder is at the moment the only university that offers doctoral courses in mathematics education on a regular basis in the Nordic countries. Doctoral students get at least two supervisors (a main supervisor and a co-supervisor) and an individual study plan is made on a yearly basis. Two courses are compulsory, Theory of Science from a didactics of mathematics perspective (5 study points) and Research Methodology in Mathematics Education course (15 study points).

**Sweden.** The doctoral education in Sweden is a four-year full-time program of courses and research that build on a bachelor or master's degree. Programs in Sweden are situated within mathematics departments. It is recommended that students take half of their coursework in mathematics but courses in general pedagogy or mathematics education dominate. One or two supervisors work with the students and individual study plans are created each year.

**The Baltic Countries, Estonia, Latvia and Lithuania.** At the moment there is not a separate doctoral program in mathematics education in Estonia. Mathematics education is considered as one specialisation within the doctoral program in general pedagogy. The situation in other Baltic states, in Latvia and Lithuania, is similar.

### The Nordic Graduate School in Mathematics Education

Small research areas with only one or two students and one or two faculty are vulnerable and encourage institutions to consider collaborative programs. In 2004, the Nordic Graduate School in Mathematics Education (NoGSME) was founded with funding from the Nordic Research Academy (NordForsk). The NoGSME is a network of about 40 Nordic and Baltic research environments with graduate education in mathematics didactics. Around 115 supervisors and 86 doctoral students are part of the network. It is a five-year collaborative activity to establish an infrastructure that will eventually be supported by participating institutions.

### The Aim of a Nordic Graduate School in Mathematics Education (NoGSME) is to

- support and develop the education of researchers in mathematics education in the Nordic and Baltic countries,
- create constructive cooperation in order to raise the scientific quality of research in mathematics education,
- give all doctoral students in mathematics education access to the activities of the Graduate School
- create cooperation among a greater group of doctoral students and supervisors in order to share experiences and opportunities to improve the education of researchers.

The utmost aim is to create a network of cooperating partners, who can continue to collaborate after their five years of involvement with the Graduate School (Grevholm, 2004a).

The activities in the NoGSME can be summarised in the following points (Grevholm, 2004b, 2005a):

- Common courses are created with contributions from all researchers in the Nordic countries and international partners (Grevholm, 2004c).
- Seminar-series in specific research areas are offered as a complement to local series and workshops on subjects or issues of main importance (Grevholm, 2005b).
- Competence development for supervisors and exchange of experience is offered.
- Partnerships and collaboration with distinguished international scholars are built.
- A database for ongoing work, theses and greater development work in mathematics education has been created.
- Mobility stipends and special financial support for doctoral students are given.

In addition to developing a range of courses, the Nordic Graduate School has initiated special summer programs, seminars for supervisors and workshops that involve both faculty and doctoral students (Grevholm, 2006a, 2006b). The NoGSME is controlled by a board consisting of the director, one member from each of the five Nordic countries and a representative for the Baltic countries. The board meets about three times a year in connection with other NoGSME activities. The board is responsible for the initiatives and work and has to report to The Nordic Research Academy once a year.

**Cooperation with Nomad.** NoGSME has close cooperation with the journal *Nomad, Nordic Studies in Mathematics Education*. Doctoral students and supervisors are invited to publish in Nomad and in each issue of Nomad a few pages are devoted to the NoGSME program and activities (Grevholm, 2006c). The *Nordic Studies in Mathematics Education* is the natural choice for the first publications of the students. Contributors may publish in *Nomad* in their Scandinavian mother tongue or in English.

## Some Features Designed to Strengthen the Quality of Researcher Education

**Ninety Percent Seminars.** A number of initiatives have been taken in order to raise the quality of research. For example, ninety percent seminars have been introduced. When students and the supervisors agree that there is a manuscript comprising about 90 % of the final thesis a seminar is organised. An international expert in the area of study is invited to read the manuscript and gives constructive and creative feedback during the seminar. This information is used to strengthen the final phase of writing and it helps the doctoral student become aware of possible criticism.

**International Studies.** Another feature of importance for quality is international collaboration and studies abroad. There is an expectation for the students to spend one semester at another university, thus learning about a different academic institution and meeting other mentors and supervisors.

**Models for Supervision.** Supervision is a crucial part of the doctoral education. Joint supervision and other forms for organising supervision must be considered. For example, in order to ensure good and continuous quality in supervision the University of Agder has at least two supervisors for a doctoral student. Supervisors move, get sick or retire and it is important that students are not left in an unstable situation. At Luleå University of Technology an apprenticeship model of supervision has proven successful and seems to be embraced by many of the supervisors (Grevholm, Persson & Wall, 2005).

**Public Defence of the Dissertation.** A public defence of the dissertation and invited international opponents is typical for Nordic doctoral education. Once completed, publication of the thesis is expected as this makes the dissertation more widely available.

## Critical Issues for Mathematics Education Doctoral Programs in the Nordic Countries

**Supervision in a New Research Field.** Trying to build up and expand a new research field is not an easy task. There have been few experienced researchers to serve as supervisors. In Sweden, for example, many mathematicians serve as supervisors and realized they could only be of help for general matters in the education. Someone else had to do the actual mathematics education supervision. Over the years it has been necessary to find new supervisors, often by using an international scholar as additional supervisor. This is difficult when not many choices are available, so some supervisors have been over used.

**Intersubject Collaboration.** Collaboration between researchers in mathematics, mathematics education and general education has been tried in all the Nordic countries with varied success.

**Issues of Format in Theses.** The tradition from pedagogy is to write a monograph and from mathematics it is a selection of published papers with a preamble. Most students have been situated in mathematics departments so they have been strongly influenced to write a selection of papers. This raises a question as to how many papers must be published in journals before the dissertation is acceptable for a defence. In mathematics there has been a trend towards accepting theses where none of the papers are published. There has also been a similar shifting of traditions in mathematics education.

**Issues of Language in Theses.** A critical question relates to the language for the dissertation – mother tongue or English? It is difficult for the non-native English speaking writer to express fine nuances in English. But it is also clear that writing in English allows for more international readers. Avoiding use of the mother tongue may lead to a poor scientific language. It may also result in publications that will not be read by teachers in school. There are pros and cons to consider before the language used for the dissertation is finalized. In the end the decision is made by the student and the supervisor and reflects the intended use of the final product.

**Financing During and After the Dissertation.** The sources for financing doctoral studies differ from one place to another. In the Nordic countries academic studies are free; no costs are paid by students as all costs are covered by tax-money. Thus the salary of a doctoral student can be used entirely for the student's private needs. In Sweden and Norway the student must have guaranteed financing for the studies before he or she can be accepted into a doctoral program.

Upon completion of the dissertation there is a lack of post doctoral positions in didactics of mathematics. This creates problems for those who want to go on after the dissertation and qualify themselves to become a docent. In Sweden and Finland this is an academic title for which one must qualify through research and publications after the doctoral degree (the same as Habilitation in Germany). The normal rule of thumb is to publish as much as a second thesis.

**Vulnerability of Small Research Environments.** Many research environments in mathematics education in the Nordic countries are small with only one or two faculty and one or two students. It is difficult to solve the supervisor problem and to create a vivid and inspiring work situation in a community of researchers. The NoGSME was founded to address this problem.

## Some Observations Resulting from the Conference on Doctoral Programs

Some issues and questions discussed during this conference are also crucial in the Nordic countries, such as the structure and content of a program and challenges and opportunities of the delivery of the program, prerequisites, recruitment and monitoring student progress. The role of mathematics in a didactics of mathematics program is important also to us. The eternal question of when is a thesis good enough is international.

The question of accreditation is not one we have discussed, probably because of different academic traditions and culture. The issue of how a program can supply teaching experience is also not one we would raise. The doctoral education in the Nordic countries is seen as an education to become a researcher. The education to become a teacher must be given as a separate option (and is normally of equal length as the doctoral education). All academic teachers must take a course in university didactics or pedagogy.

Another aspect that became more transparent during the conference is the uniqueness and value of the cooperation between programs in the Nordic countries. That is one feature the US-programs could learn from our work. This was observed by Alan Bishop in the first conference on doctoral programs when he wrote: "To me this situation cries out for inter-institutional collaboration, making the best of each university's faculty and programmatic resources available beyond its usual enrollment boundaries." (Bishop, 2001, p 59)

Aspects of quality have obviously been of interest also to the community in US (Lester & Lambdin, 2003; Schoenfeld, 1999) and the Centers for Learning and Teaching in the USA. In the Nordic community we have profited from earlier discussions and experiences that were built up by the US-colleagues in the field.

*Barbro Grevholm*
*University of Agder*
*Kristiansand, Norway*
*Barbro.grevholm@uia.no*

CBMS Issues in Mathematics Education
Volume 15, 2008

# Japanese Doctoral Programs in Mathematics Education: Academic or Professional

Masataka Koyama

## Introduction

This paper will provide information about Japanese doctoral programs and the process for completing a doctorate in mathematics education in Japan. I hope the information will be helpful in learning about similarities/differences between our programs and yours (Reys & Kilpatrick, 2001). It may also provide ideas to improve and strengthen existing doctoral programs in mathematics education in both Japan and the United States.

## Four Doctoral Programs in Japan

Only a few Japanese institutions offer doctoral programs with a major area in mathematics education. Hiroshima University and the University of Tsukuba have the longest established doctoral programs in mathematics education. Here are the current Japanese institutions with doctoral programs in mathematics education:

- Doctoral Program at Hiroshima University established in 1966 (five-year program including two- year Master's program)
- Doctoral Program at University of Tsukuba established in 1975 (five-year program including two- year Master's program)
- United Doctoral Program at Tokyo Gakugei University with Saitama University, Chiba University and Yokohama National University established in 1996 (three-year program)
- Joint Doctoral Program at Hyogo University of Teacher Education with Joetsu University of Education, Naruto University of Education and Okayama University established in 1996 (three- year program)

**Doctoral Program at Hiroshima University.** Hiroshima University has a long history in teacher training and research in the field of education. Hiroshima Higher Normal School is a predecessor of the faculty of education at Hiroshima University.

The doctoral program in mathematics education at Hiroshima University is in the Graduate School of Education. Almost all students in the five-year doctoral program first graduate from a two-year master's program. Other students who have already completed a master's program at other universities can enter the final three-year portion of the Ph. D. program after successfully completing the examinations on general education, mathematics, mathematics education and one foreign language, and the research plan for a Ph. D. dissertation based on their master's dissertation (Hiroshima University, 2007).

**Doctoral Program at University of Tsukuba.** The University of Tsukuba also has a long history in teacher training and educational research. Tokyo Higher Normal School is a predecessor of the faculty of human sciences at University of Tsukuba.

The doctoral program in mathematics education at the University of Tsukuba is in the Graduate School of (Comprehensive) Human Sciences. A few of the students who pass their examinations and the research plan based on their master's dissertation are allowed to study for five years to complete a Ph. D. program in mathematics education. Like at Hiroshima University, students transferring from a different university can enter the final three-year portion of the Ph.D. program at Tsukuba upon successful completion of their examinations and the development of an approved research plan (University of Tsukuba, 2007).

**United Doctoral Program at Tokyo Gakugei University with Other Three Universities.** Tokyo Gakugei University is a teacher training university that had a master's program in mathematics education. In 1996 Tokyo Gakugei University along with Saitama University, Chiba University and Yokohama National University established the United Graduate School (Ph. D. program) in Sciences of School Education (Tokyo Gakugei University, 2007).

The doctoral program in mathematics education at the United Graduate School is a new three-year Ph. D. program. A few students who graduated with a master's program at any universities/institutions can be allowed to enter the three-year Ph. D. program under the examinations and the research plan based on their master's dissertation. Each student admitted to the program does research in mathematics education mainly at the one of four cooperating universities to which his/her chief supervisor belongs.

**Joint Doctoral Program at Hyogo University of Teacher Education with Other Three Universities.** In 1996 Hyogo University of Teacher Education along with Joetsu University of Education, Naruto University of Education, and Okayama University established the Joint Graduate School (Ph. D. program) in Sciences of School Education (Hyogo University of Teacher Education, 2007).

The doctoral program in mathematics education at the Joint Graduate School is a new three-year Ph. D. program. A few students who completed their master's program at any universities/institutions can be allowed to enter the three-year Ph. D. program assuming they pass the mathematics and mathematics education examinations and have a satisfactory research plan developed. Like at the United Doctoral Program at Tokyo Gakugei University, the students' research takes place mainly within the program to which his/her supervisor belongs.


In sum, there are four doctoral programs in mathematics education at national universities in Japan. They are classified into two different types: the individual university program and the collaborative or joint university program. In the next section, characteristics of these programs are briefly described.

## Characteristics of Doctoral Programs in Japan

**Purpose of Doctoral Programs and Positioning of Doctorates.** Doctoral programs in Japan have changed from a "goal" to a "starting point". The new vision of the doctorate in mathematics education is that it prepares a person not only to be a mathematics educator and researcher at universities/institutions but also to be professional classroom mathematics teacher and curriculum developer in schools or regional districts.

There are two types of doctorates. One is a "course doctorate" where students take courses, do their research autonomously, write articles for submission to journals of mathematics education, and prepare for jobs as mathematics educators at universities through an apprenticeship model. This is labor intensive and few students complete the doctoral programs in mathematics education with a course doctorate Ph.D. degree in Japan. The other doctorate is a "thesis doctorate" where applicants submit their doctoral thesis to a professor with a Ph. D. degree at a university which has the doctoral program in mathematics education. If the applicant has passed the examinations on mathematics education and one foreign language and has a successful defense of his/her doctoral thesis, then he/she can receive the "thesis doctorate" rather than the "course doctorate" in mathematics education. The culminating product for a "thesis doctorate" is a book which compiles all academic research works in the field of mathematics education done by the applicant.

The main purpose of two collaborative (united/joint) doctoral programs in mathematics education established in 1996 is recognized as the need for preparing doctoral students to be the professionals in schools and districts. Although any teaching experience of school mathematics is not explicitly prerequisite for program entry, the focus on "practice" and "school education" are key elements of these programs.

**Prerequisites for Program Entry.** The prerequisite for Japan doctoral programs (the latter three-year programs) in mathematics education is master's degree in any research area. The teaching experience is not explicitly needed for the program entry. Individuals have to pass both the written examinations on general education topics, mathematics, mathematics education and one foreign language, and the oral examinations on master's dissertation and a research plan for three years in the program. Each doctoral program has a special system for those who have jobs (usually as teachers in schools/colleges) so that part-time doctoral students are able to study in night courses or during the summer and winter vacations. As of academic year 2007 the doctoral student is required to pay the admission fee of about 2,500 USD for the first year and the tuition fee of about 4,700 USD per year in the case of doctoral program at Hiroshima University. Almost all doctoral students if they want are given a student loan from a national agency.

**Elements of Doctoral Programs.** Although the elements of doctoral program vary from one program to another in Japan, we identify three general areas as common among four doctoral programs in mathematics education: course work, examinations and the dissertation (Hiroshima University, 2007; University of Tsukuba, 2007; Tokyo Gakugei University, 2007; Hyogo University of Teacher Education, 2007).

## Course Work

- *Doctoral Program at Hiroshima University (five-year program)*
  - (a) Lectures on science, technology and society education; mathematics education; methodology in mathematics education; content-based studies of mathematics (algebra, geometry, analysis, statistics/probability and computer science).
  - (b) Studies of mathematics education; methodology in mathematics education; design in mathematics education; evaluation in mathematics education; content-based studies of mathematics (algebra, geometry, analysis, statistics/probability and computer science).
  - (c) Seminars on mathematics education; methodology in mathematics education; content-based studies of mathematics (algebra, geometry, analysis, statistics/probability and computer science).
  - (d) Practical studies of mathematics education; mathematics contents development (algebra, geometry, analysis, statistics/probability and computer science).
  - (e) Guided studies of mathematics education; contents of mathematics.
  - (f) Special studies of mathematics education.

- *Doctoral Program at the University of Tsukuba (five-year program)*
  - (a) Introductions to curriculum and teaching methods; curriculum and subjects.
  - (b) Study of mathematics education.
  - (c) Series of sequential seminars: Mathematics Education I, II, and III.
  - (d) Methodologies of science and mathematics education; additional mathematics education.

- *United Doctoral Program at Tokyo Gakugei University (three-year program)*
  - (a) Studies of mathematics education (principles, aims and methods, curriculum, and methodology).
  - (b) Special studies of mathematics education.

- *Joint Doctoral Program at Hyogo University of Teacher Education (three-year program)*
  - (a) Lectures on school education in modern society; modern culture and teaching contents; new scientific literacy.
  - (b) Studies of mathematics education; mathematics lessons; teaching materials of mathematics; mathematical structures; education of mathematical sciences; nature of mathematics and mathematics education.
  - (c) Special studies of mathematics education.

## Examinations

Doctoral students have to pass examinations on general education topics and mathematics education according to the requirements for completing a doctorate in mathematics education at their university. The examinations involve both written and oral segments.

## Dissertation

The final, but most important, element of doctoral programs is the preparation of a dissertation in mathematics education. The oral defense of the dissertation before a panel of faculty is the final step for the doctorate.

**Non-course Experiences in Doctoral Programs.** The non-course experiences for doctoral students often include formal and informal activities. For example, in the case of full-time doctoral students in mathematics education at Hiroshima University, the formal activities for them include preparing articles for submission to professional journals in mathematics education or in curriculum and instruction, teaching courses in an undergraduate or master's program as a teaching assistant, and learning about research while working as a graduate assistant for a research project selected by a chief supervisor in the department of mathematics education. On the other hand, the informal activities include editing an information magazine of international journals in the area of mathematics education, attending national and international meetings on mathematics education, participating in organizing a national meeting of mathematics education, observing the lesson studies of mathematics in schools, or teaching mathematics in schools/colleges as a part-time teacher.

**Process for Completing Doctoral Programs.** In Japan the process for completing doctoral programs (the latter three-year programs) is outlined in each program. For example, in the case of the doctoral program at Hiroshima University, the process for three years is as follows (Hiroshima University, 2007).

- *First Year*
  (1) Doctoral student asks a chief supervisor to form a group of three or four supervisors including qualified professors in different research areas, and submits his/her research theme (title of dissertation) through the chief supervisor to the dean of the graduate school of education.
  (2) The student pursues his/her research plan for three years under the chief supervisor, and then prepares a written research plan of 2000 to 4000 Japanese words including all figures.
  (3) The student has to take and pass the first examination on the research plan before the group of supervisors.
- *Second Year*
  (4) The student passes the examination and continues on the research plan and prepares at least two articles for submission to professional journals in the area of mathematics education in which all articles are strictly refereed by professional reviewers.
- *Third Year*
  (5) The student qualifies by preparing two articles (at least one published article) in journals and takes the second examination on his/her research results in a meeting open to faculties and students. The student prepares the paper for about a one-hour presentation, including, the list of articles, and a set of reprints of qualified articles published/accepted in the journals.
  (6) The student passes the examination, writes and submits the draft of doctoral dissertation to the group of supervisors.

(7) The student modifies/rewrites the draft and produces a final version of the doctoral dissertation. The student prepares the summary of dissertation in 4000 to 8000 Japanese words. Then the student submits the doctoral dissertation and its summary to the group of supervisors for their review.

(8) The student passes the review by his/her supervisors and submits the following to the dean of the graduate school of education.
   − Three hardcover copies of dissertation
   − List of articles
   − Personal history
   − 120 copies of abstract of the dissertation including the curriculum vitae and the list of articles

(9) The student after having his submission accepted by a faculty meeting of all professors then has to take and pass the final oral examination on the dissertation and the related area in mathematics education before an examination committee.

(10) The student, after passing the final examination and the judgment by the faculty meeting of all professors, is awarded a Ph. D. degree in mathematics education.

It is not an easy task for either the students or their chief supervisors to see that all of the program requirements are completed within three years according to the process. In fact some students need four or five years to complete the program because of the publication demands of the second examination which requires two articles (at least one published article) in the national/international journals in the area of mathematics education.

**Careers Pursued by Program Graduates.** In Japan almost all doctoral program graduates become mathematics educators and researchers in universities/colleges. However, a few doctoral graduates teach mathematics in K-12 schools. Currently there are 50 national universities which have a department/division of mathematics education, and there are about 100 professors who are identified as mathematics educators/researchers. Therefore, in Japan there are not many opportunities for doctoral graduates in mathematics education in national universities. Even though there are many teachers with master's degree in schools, it is not common for doctoral graduates to teach school mathematics as K-12 classroom teachers in Japan.

This situation has resulted in a repositioning of the focus of the Ph.D. programs in Japan. Today, in Japan the purpose of Ph.D. studies has shifted from a goal to a starting point. There seems to be a political decision/support by the Ministry of Education in Japan to prepare doctoral students not only to be mathematics educators and researchers at universities/institutions but also to be professional classroom mathematics teachers, school leaders, and curriculum developers in schools or regional districts. In the near future, I hope the employment opportunities for doctoral graduates will increase. To make this happen, we need to rethink the nature and elements of Japanese doctoral programs in mathematics education with regard to both the needs of doctoral students and the political decisions of governments.

## Summary

There are clear differences between the program structure, goals, and opportunities associated with doctoral studies in mathematics education in Japan and the U.S. For example, the U.S. has many more doctoral programs in mathematics education and candidates/students, even including international students, than Japan. There are many more employment opportunities for doctoral graduates in the U.S. than in Japan. Moreover in Japan, while I think we have been doing rich research activities and reflect good practices of teaching school mathematics, we have never had any national conference on doctoral programs in mathematics education.

I believe the key issue of Japanese doctoral programs in mathematics education is the need to rethink the nature and elements of doctoral programs in mathematics education from the academic and/or the professional perspectives in due consideration of both the needs of doctoral students and the political decisions of governments. We have no doubt that there are educational, cultural, and political differences among countries. However, we can share ideas about the issues as we strive to improve and strengthen existing doctoral programs in mathematics education through participating in this National Conference on Doctoral Programs in Mathematics Education. The most important thing what I have learned by participating in the conference is how we need to keep the quality of the Ph. D. degree high, while we extend and improve the doctoral programs in mathematics education.

*Masataka Koyama*
*Department of Mathematics Education*
*Graduate School of Education*
*Hiroshima University*
*1-1-1, Kagamiyama, Higashi-Hiroshima,*
*739-8524 Japan*
*mkoyama@hiroshima-u.ac.jp*

CBMS Issues in Mathematics Education
Volume 15, 2008

# Post-Graduate Study Program in Mathematics Education at the University of Granada (Spain)

Luis Rico, Antonio Fernández-Cano, Encarnación Castro
and Manuel Torralbo

## Historical Context of Spanish Graduate Studies in Mathematics Education

In the 1960s, interest in mathematics grew considerably in Spain. During this time, new faculties were created to promote the study of mathematics throughout the country. This expansion reached beyond the well-established, traditional centres at the Universities of Barcelona, Madrid and Zaragoza. Subsequently, in the early 1970s, due to changes in the statutes founding these faculties, the new Institutes of Educational Science spurred research on education in the university. Spanish universities integrated the study of the Didactics of Mathematics into their curricula in the 1970s. The 1983 Organic Law of University Reform allowed Spanish universities to undergo academic and administrative restructuring. This promoted the study of Didactics of Mathematics in Spanish universities and from this date on, mathematics education was established as an area of knowledge in Spain (Kilpatrick, Rico and Sierra, 1994).

## Developing Departments of Didactics of Mathematics

The Law of University Reform (LRU) resulted in the organization of Departments, each specializing in a specific area of knowledge, or in several related ones. In some Spanish universities (Granada, Complutense of Madrid, Valencia and Sevilla), separate Departments of the Didactics of Mathematics were formed. In other universities, specialists in the Didactics of Mathematics were integrated into mixed Education Departments with faculty representing other specialized fields of education or integrated into Departments of Mathematics with other mathematics specialists. These groupings grew according to the local traditions and prior relations between colleagues in other subject matters. The current university departments that include the study of the Didactics of Mathematics have among their goals to:

- define and promote a disciplinary field and knowledge area of the Didactics of Mathematics.
- organize and develop research and teaching specific to the area of Didactics of Mathematics at each University.

- provide a legal framework and administrative structure for the group of university professors and researchers involved in mathematics education.
- perform the initial training in the Didactics of Mathematics for teachers of preschool, primary education and secondary education.
- initiate and sustain the training of researchers in the Didactics of Mathematics through a doctoral program.

## Graduate and Doctoral Study in Mathematics Education

The Masters program provides specialized training in the second cycle and gives students recognized knowledge through a specific degree. Once students have obtained a minimum of 60 credits in official programs or the official degree of Master, they are able to apply for admission to the PhD program. Doctoral courses in the Didactics of Mathematics last for two years. The doctorate requires advanced training in the techniques and methods of research. This training results in developing and defending the doctoral thesis, which is an original work of research in the related disciplinary field. In their official graduate programs, universities assign a specific number of credits to each subject and training activity included in the program. In addition, universities establish each doctoral programs lines of research, the listing of professors and researchers responsible for directing PhD theses, the maximum number of students they can advise, the admission and selection criteria, and requirements for methodological and scientific training.

## Didactics of Mathematics Doctoral Study at the University of Granada

The University of Granada officially established post-graduate programs in the Didactics of Mathematics. They consist of a Masters in the Didactics of Mathematics and a PhD in the Didactics of Mathematics. These programs have received favourable evaluation from the National Agency for Evaluation of Quality and Accreditation, through verification that the programs fulfil the criteria and achieve the indicators and standards of quality required for accreditation. The University of Granada's PhD program in the Didactics of Mathematics has these objectives:

- to begin research on topics fundamental to the Didactics of Mathematics;
- to develop the capacity to define problems relevant to the teaching and learning of mathematics and to perform an exhaustive and systematic study of the same, which allows students to conduct applied research;
- to encourage the deeper understanding of specific areas of mathematical content (numerical thinking, mathematical analysis, problem solving, algebra, geometry, statistics, and probability) within mathematics education;
- to establish and maintain a forum for critique, debate and communication of the current state and recent development of research in the Didactics of Mathematics, as well as its theoretical and methodological advances;
- to stimulate the production of new theoretical and instrumental elements in the area, with contributions in each line of research, and to apply them to training students in research and integrating their new work.

**Admission Criteria.** The evaluation of applicants is based on three criteria:

- the quality of their previous academic curriculum (60%);

- the listing of courses, conferences and seminars taken related to the Didactics of Mathematics (15%);
- publications and other scientific or professional merits they have produced related to the Didactics of Mathematics (25%).

Students who apply for admission to the Masters in the Didactics of Mathematics usually hold a Bachelors degree in Mathematics.

**Structure of the Curriculum.** The regulating guidelines establish that programs should include:

- courses or workshops on the fundamental content of the scientific, technical or artistic field to which the graduate program is dedicated;
- courses or seminars on methodology and training in research techniques;
- directed research projects;
- courses or seminars on fields related to the program and of interest for research projects.

The Program is organized into five modules, which structure the courses and the required training activities:

Module I: Research methodology courses, which direct the student in general training for educational research as applied to mathematics education. The courses offered in this module are:

- *Research in Mathematics Education. Methodological Advances.* 4 credits.
- *Research Design in Mathematics Education.* 3 credits.

Module II: Cross-cutting courses, oriented to presenting a clear view of mathematics education as a research field. The courses offered in this module are:

- *Theory of Mathematics Education.* 3 credits.
- *Design, Development, and Assessment of the Mathematics Curriculum.* 3 credits.
- *Ethnomathematics, Teacher Training, and Curricular Innovation.* 3 credits.
- *Mathematics Teachers' Professional Knowledge and Development.* 4 credits.

Module III: Specialized courses that address topics in mathematics, such as numerical and algebraic thinking, mathematical analysis, problem solving, statistics, probability, and geometry. The courses offered in this module are:

- *Numerical and Algebraic Thinking I.* 4 credits.
- *Numerical and Algebraic Thinking II.* 4 credits.
- *Foundations of Statistical Education.* 3 credits.
- *Didactics of Probability and Combinatorics.* 4credits.
- *Epistemology and the Didactics of Statistics.* 3 credits.
- *Didactics of Geometry.* 3 credits.

Module IV: Research Workshop where complementary subjects are analysed and lectures and short courses offered by researchers and outside experts. 4 credits

Module V: Research project for the Masters degree, developed in one of the existing lines of research and supervised by an advisor from the Department, 20 credits. This work is presented in a public departmental workshop for debate and approval.

**Recognized Lines of Research.** The initial training of researchers offered within the Didactics of Mathematics program is structured by five research lines:

- *Didactics of Mathematics: Numerical Thinking*
- *Didactics of Probability and Statistics*
- *Mathematics Curriculum Design, Development, and Assessment*
- *Training of Mathematics Teachers*
- *Theory and Methods of Research in Mathematics Education*

The lines of research in Numerical Thinking and Didactics of Probability and Statistics indicate priorities in the area of research on curricular innovation. The topics studied in the Didactics of Mathematics of the University of Granada are, first, Arithmetic, Algebra and Analysis, and, second, Statistics and Probability, with emphasis on numerical structures in the former.The research line Training of Mathematics Teachers focuses on the area of professional knowledge and development of the mathematics teacher. The research lines Mathematics Curriculum Design, Development, and Assessment and Theory and Methods of Research in Mathematics Education focus on the areas of theoretical grounding and development of the Didactics of Mathematics. Each research line is grounded in its own theoretical framework and methodology, but the criterion for its determination is the area in which research is being performed.

## Learning Expectations for Doctoral Studies in Mathematics EducationMethodological Courses

The course *Mathematics Education Research: Methodological Advances* addresses three core groups of problems:

- i.) logical stages of research in mathematics education, with the definition of the research problem, the literature review and nature of the empirical data;
- ii.) different methods of research in mathematics education, considering: methods that focus respectively on the material, on teaching, on learning, on the educational collective, and on integrated methods;
- iii.) evaluation of research in Mathematics Education.

The general capacities that this course seeks to develop are:

- capacity to evaluate critically reports and projects that prepare the PhD candidate to be a user of research in mathematics education;
- methodological knowledge and skills that enable the PhD candidate to do research in mathematics education; that is, to produce research;
- capacity to understand and interpret the role of research in improving practice in mathematics education and its genesis and development.

The course *Research Design in Mathematics Education* complements the previous course but is more technical in its coverage. The goal here is to develop in the student a repertoire of knowledge and skills for the design of research projects that enable the student to carry out studies in the Didactics of Mathematics. More specifically, students should develop capacities to:

- understand the concept of design and the role that it plays in the design of a research project;
- detect and characterize research design in mathematics education;
- design their own research in mathematics education;

- evaluate the design of a research project in mathematics education.

**Cross-cutting Courses.** These courses constitute a basic central content and establish the specific character of the program. *Research Design in Mathematics Education* is dedicated to the foundations of the Didactics of Mathematics, its problems, information sources, theoretical frameworks, epistemological grounding, research paradigms and schools of thought. This course provides tools for a research program in the teaching and learning of mathematics that seeks to integrate diverse theoretical approaches and schools of thought. *Design, Development, and Assessment of the Mathematics Curriculum* tackles the foundations of curricular theory and the problems that derive in the Didactics of Mathematics from the need to consider the complexity of training plans implemented in educational institutions. The course proposes a framework for general action relative to the design, development and evaluation of the mathematics curriculum through the so-called *mathematics curriculum organizers* and, from these tools, develops a method specific to the didactic analysis of curricular topics in mathematics. In this course, the student learns to handle the curriculum organizers as research instruments for improving the teaching and learning of school mathematics. *Mathematics Teachers' Professional Knowledge and Development* analyses the teaching functions and reflects on the teaching of mathematics; it thus focuses on:

- establishing dimensions that characterize the mathematics teacher;
- establishing familiarity with some lines of research and work methods in training mathematics teachers;
- initiating an investigation of beliefs concerning mathematics and its teaching and learning;
- practicing analyzing professional problems
- becoming aware of professional development as a teacher.

*Ethnomathematics, Teacher Training, and Curricular Innovation* reiterates, from a different perspective, the subjects addressed in the three previous courses. It emphasizes that mathematics is not only a formal science but also, primarily, a fundamental part of all cultures present throughout our multicultural society.

**Specialized Courses.** The lines of research offer specialized courses in which the doctoral candidate is shown the state of the art in specific fields of the Didactics of Mathematics. Specific research problems and priorities are presented in lines such as Numerical Thinking, the Didactics of Statistics and Probability, Arithmetic Problems and Problem-solving Strategies, Didactics of Algebra, Didactics of Analysis, and the Didactics of Geometry. Visiting professors participate in these courses, and their contributions foster the exchange of information with other research centres in mathematics education. The goal of this experience is to place the novice researcher in contact with different research groups; this goal takes specific form in the choice of the first research project for the masters student. To detect and identify a problem, the researcher in training begins to situate him- or herself in one of the areas of research activity in mathematics education, that is, tries to specify the problem he or she wishes to study, the subjects with which he or she plans to work, and the institution in which the study will be carried out. This choice is initially very general and responds to a concern that has emerged in the researchers' professional work in mathematics education. The researcher works gradually to define the question of interests with greater precision in the problematic area and then seeks to express first intuitions clearly and to define them. The choice of the area is an important decision for PhD candidates, as it will condition the students' work and involves integrating them into a research team. To make good decisions, it is necessary to know in some detail the degree of development of the Department's lines of research.

**Seminar and Research Project.** The Research Workshop is the natural place where the student in the program encounters research in progress and confronts the practical problems involved in beginning and developing research. The research work is presented in various sessions of the workshop program, in which its design, state of progress and subsequent development are debated and discussed in detail. At the end of the work, the student is required to make a final presentation to the workshop participants. The Research Workshop has among its goals the public presentation, discussion and evaluation of the production and results of the research performed by the students in the doctoral program in its various phases. The main learning expectation of both the workshop and the research study is to introduce the student in a practical way to the areas, theoretical frameworks, methods and techniques of research in mathematics education prior to work on the PhD thesis.

**PhD Thesis.** The thesis consists of an original, unpublished research project performed by the doctoral candidate under the supervision of the director on a subject matter related to the Didactics of Mathematics. The thesis is evaluated by the thesis director or directors and formally approved by the Department. Before the presentation and defense of a doctoral thesis or any other research project with academic validity, each of the members of the committee will evaluate the work and produce a report indicating specifically that the work submitted for consideration fulfills the basic requirements of scientific quality to be submitted for approval. In this prior report, the committee members may make whatever observations they consider relevant to improving and modifying the study. The work will not be presented for defense until it has reasonably satisfied the recommendations indicated. The jury members can also recommend that the presentation and defense of the work be postponed until it is improved significantly.

## Two Decades of Doctoral Study at the University of Granada

The Doctoral Program in the Didactics of Mathematics at the University of Granada has been in existence for two decades, and from 1994 to 2008 has awarded nearly 40 PhDs. This two-decade period of development was positively acknowledged in August of 2006 when the Spanish Secretary of the State of Universities and Research awarded its highest distinction of Quality Mention to the program. Doctoral programs that obtain the Quality Mention are positioned for:

- participation in national programs for competitive subsidies and aid to foster and promote higher education and scientific research, as well as the policies for training human resources in the above-mentioned areas;
- allocation of resources, both those of the institution itself and external aid, whether public or private ;
- cooperation with the entrepreneurial sector, as well as with other entities and institutions, both national and international.

The evaluation process for the Quality Mention focused on:

- justification of the proposal for projected training activities in the PhD program and general objectives;
- contents and structure of the PhD program;
- guarantee of quality control within the program;
- research record (refers to the last five years: 2001-2005, of professors and researchers who participate in the PhD program);
- record of PhD theses of students registered in the program and directed in the last five years (2001-2005), by the Doctors who participate in the doctoral program in the academic year 2006-2007;
- data related to the publication of research results related directly to the doctoral theses defended in the last five years (2001-2005), directed by professors and researchers who will participate in the doctoral program;
- record of doctoral candidates currently active in writing a doctoral thesis and who have entered candidacy in the last five years (2001-2005);
- number of students who have completed the advanced training phase in the last five academic years (2000-2001 to 2004-2005). Number of students registered for the first time in academic years (2000-2001 to 2004-2005);
- record of students who have participated in mobility programs while writing their doctoral thesis in the last five years (2001 to 2005).

**Some Evaluative Indicators About the Program.** With the aim for obtaining Quality Mention, the program was submitted to a general evaluation. Here are some evaluative indicators:

- The students are mostly Spanish nationals but in recent years an increasing number are from Latin America.
- The department receives funding from national and regional governments. It has also received a total of 300,000 € in funding from international competitions through the European Union.
- The success rate of the PhD program of the Department of Didactics of Mathematics at the University of Granada is 34% (38 theses defended/112 PhD candidates).
- Luis Rico is a major advisor having directed 16 PhD theses.
- There are currently more male PhD candidates and directors in this program (Fernández-Cano, Torralbo & Vallejo, 2007). However, efforts are being made to seek a gender balance.

### The Context of PhD Study in Europe

The multinationality of the European Union means that its different countries must combine models, traditions and normative and cultural guidelines that sometimes differ and even conflict. If we can gain anything from studying the doctorate in Europe, it is its plurality and high degree of differences, not only between different countries but also within each country. We need follow-up and prospective studies of this problem, like those performed periodically by the Carnegie Foundation (2006) in the U.S. Considerable efforts have been made to find a convergence in European PhD studies through successive conferences of the ministers responsible for it (*European University Association*, 2005). Political and structural changes in post-graduate studies under the auspices of the Bologna Declaration and following the implementation of the *European Credit Transfer System*, are leading to the restructuring of graduate and doctoral studies in each country. In general, the European Community directives are generic and seek primarily to make the education received more transparent, to make results more easily comparable and to enhance student mobility. In accordance with the proposal of the European Qualifications Framework, no specific number of either years or ECTS credits has been established for doctoral training (Ministerio de Educación y Ciencia, 2006). The first fruit of this interest in convergence is the so-called European Doctorate (*Doctor Europeus*). To receive this degree, the candidate must fulfil the following requirements:

- The student must complete his or her training in another European university through a mobility program. The research work must be completed, at least in part, in another European country, the candidate earning credit for a stay of at least three months spent developing activities related to the thesis.
- Two qualified experts outside the home PhD program should support the thesis. Neither of the professors who write these reports may be the director of the PhD thesis. The reports must be reasoned and must testify to the appropriateness of granting the degree of Doctor.
- One of the members of the thesis committee that will evaluate the doctoral thesis must belong to a higher education institution or research institute in another European country and this institution must be different than that of the professors who have made the earlier report on the dissertation study.
- Part of the doctoral thesis defence and an abstract must be completed in the official language of another European nation state, to be determined by the doctoral candidate.

## Looking to the Future

The graduate program in the Didactics of Mathematics Education of the University of Granada faces a number of challenges in its immediate future. In less than seven years, it faces the specific and internal problem of renewing its distinctly veteran team of professors. It also seeks the capacity to maintain and even increase program offerings to Latin American and North African students. New courses might be implemented concerning Information Technologies and Mathematics Education, and the Impact of Mathematics Educational Research on Policy and Practice. Other relevant questions include:

- How can we improve the dramatic failure rates of thesis completion?
- How can we improve evaluation of the thesis?
- How can we improve the impact of the thesis on teaching practice, educational policy and legal norms?
- How can we improve the PhD candidate-doctor relationship?

We need to make follow-up studies of the graduates to learn what they are doing and how the doctoral preparation they received might be improved. It would also be beneficial to consider seriously the creation of specific centres for the PhD (*doctoral schools*); such modes of study and institutions are already operating in Europe and the U.S but are not even being tested in Spain.

*Luis Rico*
*Universidad de Granada*
*Granada, España*
*lrico@ugr.es*

*Antonio Fernández-Cano*
*Universidad de Granada*
*Granada, España*
*afcano@ugr.es*

*Encarnación Castro*
*Universidad de Granada*
*Granada, España*
*encastro@ugr.es*

*Manuel Torralbo*
*Universidad de Córdoba*
*Córdoba, España*
*ma1torom@uco.es*

# Part 5

# Accreditation

# Accreditation of Doctoral Programs: A Lack of Consensus

Glenda Lappan, Jill Newton, and Dawn Teuscher

## Introduction

When surveyed about the need for national standards in mathematics education doctoral programs, 47% of conference participants agreed, 40% disagreed, and the remaining 13% declined to commit. That is, the debate regarding the need for national standards and/or accreditation for doctoral programs in the mathematics education community is far from settled. Dr. Glenda Lappan served as the moderator for this session and panel members included Drs. Jenny Bay-Williams, University of Louisville, Jere Confrey, North Carolina State University, Francis "Skip" Fennell, McDaniel College, and Mark Klespis, Sam Houston State University.

Dr. Lappan opened the session by referring to accreditation as "an issue that has been in the room with us since the beginning of the conference." She set the context for the accreditation discussion by highlighting the great diversity of mathematics education doctoral programs. She outlined ways in which doctoral programs vary, as described in *One Field, Many Paths: U.S. Doctoral Programs in Mathematics Education* (Reys & Kilpatrick, 2001), including: (1) organizational structure (e.g., department in which the program is located, (2) size (e.g., number of students), (3) prerequisite knowledge (e.g., mathematics background), (4) prerequisite experiences (e.g., teaching), and (5) program structure (e.g., course work).

Lappan then summarized recommendations of core knowledge and related experiences essential for doctoral programs in mathematics education as outlined in *Principles to Guide the Design and Implementation of Doctoral Programs in Mathematics Education*, (AMTE, 2003) including: (1) mathematics content, (2) research, (3) learning, (4) teaching and teacher education, (5) technology, (6) curriculum, (7) assessment, and (8) history of social, political, and economic context of mathematics education.

Lappan noted that some countries do have evaluation procedures for doctoral programs (D'Ambrosio, this volume). Finally, Arthur Levine's *Educating Researchers* (2007) was discussed. He proposed a nine-point template for judging the quality of researcher education programs, including the need for: (1) explicit purpose, (2) curricular coherence, (3) curricular balance, (4) faculty composition, (5) admission standards, (6) completion standards, (7) high quality research, (8) adequate finances, and (9) continuing assessment.

The overarching question for the panel was: Would it raise the caliber of doctoral student preparation to have a mechanism for evaluation and accreditation of programs, and if so how? Two sub-questions were presented to panel members for their response: (1) What are the advantages and disadvantages of an accreditation system for mathematics education doctoral programs? (2) What should we do to address marginal programs, planned or anticipated programs, and stagnant programs? Are guidelines enough? How do we avoid needless bureaucracy?

To give the reader a sense of the session, we summarize the advantages and disadvantages of accreditation of mathematics education doctoral programs as described by the panelists and conference participants. Then we pose questions for discussion.

## Advantages

Several major themes regarding the advantages of accreditation of mathematics education doctoral programs emerged during the discussion. These themes addressed the following questions: Would accreditation improve the *quality* of doctoral programs? Would accreditation improve the *status* of doctoral programs in mathematics education? Would an accreditation system facilitate the *development* of new programs? Would a common set of standards for accreditation help *define* what is meant by a doctorate in mathematics education?

The question regarding the possibility of accreditation improving the quality of mathematics education doctoral programs was probably most directly addressed by a participant who said, "There should be some regulations of the quality of ALL mathematics doctoral programs in education." A panelist suggested that external pressure may encourage more thoughtful discussions about doctoral programs in the same way that NCATE (National Council for Accreditation of Teacher Education) provides opportunities for discussions about undergraduate programs. Another conference participant added "If having, say, three mathematics education faculty who are productive is required for accreditation, this could help institutions prioritize mathematics education in hiring."

Several people proposed that accreditation could serve to increase the status of mathematics education as a field. One panelist used phrases such as "acceptance of the field," "acceptance of what we do," "taken more seriously as a profession," and "how we may be perceived in other fields" to describe the need for the consideration of accreditation in an effort to increase the status of mathematics education. Another participant asked: "How do you want the outside community to view your profession?" Two panel members addressed the perceived or actual lack of rigor in mathematics education doctoral programs. These comments addressed both the quality and status of doctoral programs.

A panelist and other conference participants suggested that accreditation standards or guidelines may be helpful for designing new programs. The panelist discussed his program's struggle to get up and running using only the guidelines produced by NCTM and AMTE in the joint position statement mentioned earlier. He suggested that something more definitive might have helped their program develop more quickly. Finally, it was suggested that an accreditation system or some form of standards may help to define what is meant by a doctoral degree in mathematics education. This led to questions about the mathematics education community. For example, "Can/Does the community share a definition of what constitutes a mathematics education researcher?" and "Is mathematics education a discipline? Is it an interdiscipline? Is it a multi-discipline?"

Additional comments were made addressing the advantages of an accreditation system for mathematics education doctoral programs: "The faculty at an institution would be more aware that they sink or swim together. This could also prompt cross-institution collaboration on programs." A panelist expressed support for an accreditation system as a way in which to validate the program's effectiveness to external sources, saying "My pressure comes from my department, my university, and the state. They want an external source to say that the program is high quality. Therefore there needs to be some accreditation by someone." Many participants expressed advantages of "guidelines" rather than a formal accreditation system. For example, one participant said, "Guidelines constructive, accreditation restrictive." Another participant suggested an "evaluation guide," saying "Perhaps a useful document would be an evaluation guide for doctoral programs. Something to help us shape formative and summative evaluation of individual programs."

This summary of the advantages of accreditation in mathematics education doctoral programs indicates that many in the field are calling for some version of guidelines, standards, or accreditation system. Now, we turn to the other side of the coin and summarize the disadvantages addressed by the conference participants.

## Disadvantages

Not everyone was willing to accept accreditation as an obvious step forward. In fact, numerous reasons were provided for why accreditation for doctoral programs in mathematics education would not be an advantageous step at this time. These reasons are grouped into four larger questions. First, *where* do we begin in the process of deciding what it means to allow a doctoral program to exist or not? Second, *who* will conduct the work related to designing and conducting the accreditation process? Third, *how* will the accreditation process be conducted and enforced? Fourth, *what* purpose will accreditation of the doctoral program in mathematics education have for a particular institution?

Where do we begin in the process of accreditation of doctoral programs in mathematics education? During the conference many discussions and talks focused on what core courses and skills doctoral students in mathematics education need prior to entering academia. Several key questions arose: "Is mathematics education a discipline? How can we set criteria for being judged if we do not know the boundaries?" The criteria set in an accreditation process are important because it could eliminate some programs that may be serving a different population of doctoral students than is typically seen in other programs. Another conference participant asked, "What are the goals of a doctoral program? Without an answer to this, questions of evaluation and accreditation have no frame." Two panel members suggested the need for more informal conversations about doctoral programs that will shape our thinking on what is important for doctoral students by moving past guidelines and having a process with teeth in it.

There was a general concern about who would develop, conduct and administer the accreditation process. One panelist said, "Review committees often lack the expertise to judge and review doctoral programs." A participant asked, "Who gets to decide what counts? Who is left out of this process? How might this effect the types of students attracted to the field?" The role of accreditation may fall into the hands of current faculty members in mathematics education; however, the current responsibilities of mathematics educators are numerous. Faculty members are often overburdened with committee work, both in and out of their own institution, teaching, and conducting research.

Participants identified external control and pressures as another reason for not wanting accreditation. One participant said, "We should vigorously resist external pressures that are motivated by economic or political concerns that have little to do with educational consideration." A panelist stated "my pressure comes from my department, my university, and the state. They want an external source to say that the program is high quality." This external pressure may encourage change in a stagnant system, but some felt decisions regarding doctoral programs should be left in the hands of those people who are knowledgeable about their own programs and students. One panel member added, "We develop the guidelines and evaluation tools. It is up to us to decide what is important."

Another area of concern was how the accreditation process would work. Some people felt the accreditation process was restrictive and would encourage conformity and limit creativity providing "cookie-cutter" doctoral programs as one participant stated. Currently doctoral programs in mathematics education are varied in many aspects, which were discussed during this session and others. Some students receive experiences related to teaching mathematics methods courses during their doctoral programs. Other students receive valuable experience working on multiple research projects. Still other students gain a deep understanding of mathematics and how it can be taught effectively. This variation brings diversity to doctoral students' knowledge and builds innovation and creativity in the field. A concern of some is evidenced by a participant who asked, "How exactly might such accreditation reviews be structured so that they would value the productive difference between programs rather than being an inappropriately homogenizing influence?"

The final concern was how an accreditation system would affect their doctoral program and students. Both panelists and participants mentioned that NCATE provided status to institutions that is absent within the mathematics education field. For example, one panelist described how some mathematicians work on their doctorates in mathematics education because it is not as rigorous. However, participants questioned whether NCATE really provides higher status. One conference participant stated, "Accreditation ... is perceived by many as an indicator of lower status." Another stated, "NCATE is too much work and does not give status. Students are unaware." This raises the question: What will accreditation of doctoral programs do for each of our institutions?

## Conclusion

After a lively discussion on the issue of accreditation of doctoral programs in mathematics education, some ideas are clearer. All doctoral programs in mathematics education are not the same, nor, in the opinions of most of the participants, should they be. What perhaps should be clearer to the field and to potential students is what a particular program prepares doctoral students to do or be. Participants argued that the needs in certain locations may be different. Some areas of the country may need graduates with more advanced training who are excellent preparers of future teachers. Others areas may need more researchers. A salient question is, "Are all doctoral programs to prepare users of research or producers of research or both?" Clearly four-year colleges and research universities do not have the same missions. However, this does not mean that colleges and universities do not have important work to do to support the productivity and quality of life in their area of the country. However, conditions in an area of the country change over time. PhD programs today are different from those in the USA 100 years ago. The fact that change is inevitable challenges us to figure out how to monitor our doctoral programs in a positive way.

The accreditation panel raised issues both positive and negative about externally imposed standards. What they and the audience seemed to accept was that we need ways to monitor, examine, and continually innovate in our programs. We do so in the spirit of building the most effective programs for producing educated teachers, researchers, leaders, and innovators for the future. The question the panel and audience discussion leaves us with is, "How do we as a community work together to create the structure and expertise through which to examine our doctoral programs in mathematics education with the goal of improving what they offer to our students and the Nation?"

*Glenda Lappan*
*Michigan State University*
*East Lansing, MI 48824*
*glappan@math.msu.edu*

*Jill Newton*
*Purdue University*
*West Lafayette, IN 47907*
*janewton@purdue.edu*

*Dawn Teuscher*
*Arizona State University Polytechnic Campus*
*Tempe, AZ 85287*
*dawn.teuscher@asu.edu*

# Part 6

# Reflections from Within

CBMS Issues in Mathematics Education
Volume 15, 2008

# Preparing the Next Generation of Mathematics Educators: An Assistant Professor's Experience

Andrew Tyminski

It is July 31 and I am in my office at a top-tier institution. I just finished meeting with one of my doctoral students in order to advise him on courses for the fall semester. I am staring at the mounds of paper stacked on my desk that I need to attend to. I am preparing a syllabus to teach a new doctoral course at my institution on research in mathematics education. I am also in the process of evaluating and revising the elementary mathematics methods course. I have two sets of doctoral comprehensive exams that I need to read, assess and offer comments. When I am finished reading those exams I need to prepare for the oral exams both of which will be held within the next 2 weeks. I serve as a co-chair on one of these committees, so I also need to coordinate the date, time and arrange for the room. To say I have a lot on my plate would be an understatement. At times it is more than a little overwhelming.

It is recognized that all of these tasks and countless more are certainly expectations of faculty members at research institutions, so it sounds like I am complaining a bit, right? Perhaps I should elaborate on my situation a bit more. I mentioned my first doctoral student; everything seems to be under control with him. But then again he is just starting his program this semester. My second student, whose committee I co-chair, has been "in my care" since April. In May, I was asked to comment on and contribute comprehensive exam questions for her. Because of geographic separation we have only recently spoken in person. The other committee I serve on is for a student I will not meet until I see her at her oral exam. It defies explanation until I mention that I defended my dissertation three weeks ago, moved here a few days ago, and still have not participated in my own commencement. In fact, my job and contract do not *officially* begin for another 2 weeks.

Of course my situation is a bit unusual in its extremes, but I posit that in many ways, it is not that different from what any first year faculty member experiences as they begin their career. The general sense may be summarized with a statement such as "I worked for 4 years to get to this point. Now, what am I supposed to be doing?" As we complete our doctoral programs and apply for jobs at various types of institutions we are told of our expected job responsibilities. Job announcements often include phrases such as teaching undergraduate and graduate courses; advising prospective mathematics teachers; supervising mathematics education master's and doctoral students' programs and research; supervising student teachers; providing service, outreach, and leadership to the University; establishing a research program; and last (but certainly not least) pursuing external funding is strongly encouraged.

All of the above expectations can be sorted into two main categories: tasks we do to further our students' careers and tasks we do to further our career. Some of these expectations are familiar; we may have even had some experience with them as a part of or prior to our own doctoral studies. Other expectations are a bit more ambiguous in what they encompass and how one engages in them. Beyond the notion of what each expectation involves, there are larger questions of how one engages in these activities in a successful manner. A small sample of the questions I faced in my first semester as a faculty member was: How do I develop a research program? What constitutes service and in what type of activities should I be engaging? How do I effectively advise a graduate student? Am I prepared to direct a quality research project at the master's or doctoral level? Where should I be looking for external funding? How do I write a competitive grant proposal? How do I craft a course from scratch? How should I assess my students' work?

Shouldn't my program have prepared me with answers to these questions; and if not, what could it have included that would have helped? These questions were two of the large topics of discussion at the National Conference on Doctoral Programs on Mathematics Education and will be addressed in the next section of this commentary. First, I offer examples from my own experiences and also incorporate some of the ideas raised within the small group discussions I engaged in during the conference.

## What Did My Program Prepare Me For?

In a direct manner, the many varied experiences I had as a student in my doctoral program definitely prepared me to take on some of these tasks. I was asked to read and critique my colleagues' written work and ideas, as well as published research in mathematics education. I reviewed submitted articles for a peer-reviewed journal. I taught four semesters in the elementary mathematics education program. Each semester I was assigned to a faculty member, who served as a mentor and sounding board for my ideas. During another year, I worked closely with secondary school student teachers and their cooperating teachers as a part of a project that focused on developing mentoring relationships and school based learning communities. I participated as a researcher in a large-scale research project with multiple faculty members and graduate students from both my home institution as well as other universities. I also served as the primary instructor for a yearlong professional development activity within a low socio-economic school district. Each of these activities is similar to the tasks in which a new faculty member may be expected to engage. And, as a result of my experiences with these particular tasks I feel as though I was prepared to engage in them and had a sense of how to do so successfully.

For other tasks my program had more of an indirect impact. I had experiences in a lot of the same types of activities when I was a student as I now do as a faculty member. I was advised-extremely well I might add. I took graduate courses in research, mathematics, learning, teaching and curriculum, wrote comprehensive exams, defended them orally, prepared a research proposal, conducted research, and wrote an acceptable dissertation. The difference is that I experienced each of these program components as a student and from a learner's point of view. I have an understanding of what it took for me to be successful in these tasks, but not what success looked like in a more general sense. I was a part of these experiences, but I did not facilitate them as I now must do. Nor was I necessarily privy to the thought processes of my instructors, mentors or committee members as they performed their duties. So although I have a sense of the role a faculty member plays in directing these activities, I did not develop an insider's perspective of how to do them effectively while in graduate school.

### How Could My Doctoral Program Have Been Different?

I learned much from my graduate program, but I also lacked some additional experiences which could have better prepared me. In some cases I lacked the insider's perspective from faculty members I alluded to earlier. Within my teaching experiences I was able to discuss issues such as creating a syllabus, planning, assessment, and field experiences with faculty mentors. There was a free exchange of ideas and I learned about both their decisions as well as the reasoning that went into them. In other aspects of my program however, specifically as it pertained to my comprehensive exams and defenses, it would have been helpful if my advisor and committee members were able to share some of their thought processes. I realize that in the beginning of a program, this type of access is probably not needed nor recommended. But as a student progresses it would be helpful to share some of what goes into making the decisions that are made. At some institutions for instance, students are a part of the comprehensive exam process and are asked to help create their own questions. Engaging in the process of crafting questions that challenge a student to analyze and defend ideas within their own area of research could be a beneficial experience and help prepare a doctoral student for their future roles.

The defense process offers another possibility for gaining an insider's perspective. Defenses are generally open to the public and students should be encouraged to attend them. Some institutions require that a student attend at least one defense prior to their own-usually so the student has a sense of what to expect. I submit though that observing a defense with the intent of learning from the committee members would offer a different experience. If one is not expected to answer the questions, he could learn much about how committees work by paying close attention to how and when faculty members pose questions and how they react to the responses. Including an opportunity to discuss the defense with the committee afterwards could also contribute to the doctoral student's knowledge of the defense process.

Beyond suggestions that address the insider's perspective are experiences that ask doctoral students to engage in activities during their program which will prepare them to further their emerging academic careers. For many doctoral students, this entails opportunities to engage in scholarly writing as well as experiences in competing for funding opportunities. I would have benefited from mentoring experiences with grant work. My program was supported by faculty members' grants, but I did not engage in the process of scouting, preparing and writing the proposals for these grants. To become a productive faculty member, junior faculty members need to know where to look for funding, how to write a competitive proposal, how to prepare a budget, and how to manage the research that is often a component of the grant, especially those that involve working with teachers or students. Engaging in this process alongside experienced faculty members would have been very beneficial to my future grant seeking endeavors. Faculty members receiving assistance from doctoral students in background research and writing could also benefit from this type of partnership.

From a publishing standpoint, students often are given the opportunity to co-author articles with faculty members and these experiences are extremely valuable. What may be missing is the opportunity to direct smaller research projects and write about them ourselves. I understand the dissertation process is meant to develop this ability, but writing a dissertation does not really prepare a person for the type of writing to be done in order to be published. One idea that addresses this issue is the notion of the dissertation as a series of articles. In many of the hard sciences, the dissertation is written as a series of publishable articles and then bound together into a larger document. If this approach had been a part of my program, I could have had some guided experience in doing what I am expected to do now-to conduct a research study and present the ideas in a series of shorter articles. As it stands I am challenged with taking a 220 page document and finding ways to break it into smaller pieces. This is an experience I will learn from, but a dissertation is not something I am likely to do again in my career.

## The Importance of New Faculty Induction

In writing this paper I thought about the things I felt I was lacking and realized that many of these experiences are usually addressed with the assistance of senior faculty at the hiring institution. New faculty members need certain supports in order to become acclimated, stabilized, and productive in their new careers. This process can be similar to the induction process of school teachers where attention is given to issues such as number of teaching preparations, the need for supportive teacher colleagues, and the opportunity to develop proficiency in teaching. These same ideas are germane to the induction of new faculty members.

Teaching is a large part of any new professor's responsibilities and it is one area in which new faculty members could use some assistance in order to be more successful. In school teacher induction, one would be concerned with number of preparations as well as the ability level of students a new teacher was assigned. We would also try not to assign new teachers to all of the least desirable classes. For new university faculty members our concerns are somewhat the same. Course matching and number of preparations are also germane to new faculty induction. Some new faculty are assigned courses that other, more experienced faculty members choose not to teach-regardless of whether or not the new faculty member's background is a fit for that particular course. For those new faculty members who do not have a strong background in teaching, these assignments can make their teaching load more arduous. Matching new faculty members' strengths with new teaching assignments is one way to support their success. Another way institutions support new faculty members in their teaching involves some type of course release within the first few years of their contract. Having a release from teaching a course can allow the faculty member extra time to devote to the establishment of their research program. One bit of helpful advice I was given was not to take a course release during the first semester of my job. I was cautioned not to do so because a course release should be used to further my scholarly work. In using release time in the first semester however, there is a concern that time I should be writing might be spent in the process of acclimating to the job and settling in to a new living situation. Plus, teaching a full load my first semester helped me to become more acclimated with the students and the program.

The importance of supportive colleagues and the opportunity to develop proficiency are also applicable to new faculty members, and not just as instructors. It is important that new faculty members are mentored in all three main branches of their jobs: teaching, research and service. While teaching, research and service form a working core, experienced faculty members can provide insight into the relative importance of the core elements as new faculty work toward promotion and tenure consideration. Depending on the type of institution, these core elements take on different levels of importance. For example, in research oriented institutions, service is typically given the lowest priority during the initial years in rank. Since young faculty need to keep the promotion and tenure goal on their radar screen, knowing the priority of these job expectations helps young faculty better allocate their time.

In order to develop fruitfully, a new career needs individual guidance from more experienced faculty members and the opportunity to participate within a strong intellectual community. Intellectual community was described by many of the participants of the conference as the key component of a successful doctoral program in mathematics education. I would argue that it is just as important to the development of young faculty as it is to the development of graduate students.

New faculty members need the opportunity to learn from and along side more experienced colleagues in choosing appropriate service activities, in their scholarly writing, and in their teaching. The problem in many cases however, including my own, is that many new faculty take positions at institutions with smaller programs and those supports are not always readily available. Many people may accept jobs in programs with only two or three faculty members. And if the other faculty members are also junior, where does the support come from? At times, new faculty may have to look outside of their content area for mentors. This is not as helpful as having someone in your field as a mentor. For although they can provide assistance on many issues, they may not be knowledgeable about our particular field and in some cases, what we need is specialized knowledge related to mathematics education.

Beyond the lack of mentors, the careers of new faculty members in small programs may also be hindered as they are not given the opportunity to develop at a slow and steady pace. In a perfect world responsibilities should gradually be brought on line after some experience with these tasks. Due to lack of senior faculty however, many new faculty members at smaller programs find themselves under prepared yet involved in activities such as program accreditation, preparing various institutional reports, chairing program or college committees, or serving as graduate coordinators.

I suppose I am not saying anything that many in our field are not aware of already. But as the leaders in our field move closer toward retirement, it is especially important that we address the needs of the up and coming members who will be expected one day take their places as the caretakers and directors of the field of mathematics education. Is has been well documented that there is a shortage of mathematics educators and the gap between the number of graduates and available jobs seems to be increasing each year (Reys, 2000, 2006). We need to find ways and commit to their enactment in order to ensure our junior faculty can be successful within their institutions and develop into the researchers, teachers and leaders who will continue to push the field forward.

*Andrew Tyminski*
*Purdue University*
*West Lafayette, IN 47907-2098*
*atyminsk@purdue.edu*

CBMS Issues in Mathematics Education
Volume **15**, 2008

# Mathematics Content for Elementary Mathematics Education Graduate Students: Overcoming the Prerequisites Hurdle

David Kirshner and Thomas Ricks

## The Problem

Mathematics education as a field of study is carved out of many fields, most importantly Mathematics and Education (Freudenthal, 1983). Expositions of mathematical understanding, even at the elementary level, frequently reference such abstractions as *function*, *partition*, and *field* derived from mathematical theories studied in upper level undergraduate or graduate level mathematics courses (e.g., Vergnaud, 1988).

For secondary mathematics educators entering a doctoral program in mathematics education, mathematical grounding generally is not a serious issue. In many state jurisdictions, secondary mathematics teachers are required to have nearly the equivalent of a bachelor's degree in mathematics. Based on a recent survey, Reys, Glasgow, Teuscher, & Nevels (2007) reported that 55% of mathematics education doctoral programs require candidates to have the mathematics degree prior to entry, and most prefer a master's degree. Fully 70% of programs include mathematical content courses within the education graduate degree.

But, what about elementary (and middle school) educators (grades K-8) interested in graduate level studies in mathematics education? The typical elementary education undergraduate program requires few, if any, mathematics courses at or beyond the level of calculus. Thus an elementary educator may need a sequence of 3 or more undergraduate level mathematics courses to become eligible to take senior/graduate level courses that could count as part of a graduate program. What sorts of accommodations, if any, should be made to enable elementary educators to pursue a doctorate in mathematics education?

Our interest in this problem is motivated by the fact that our program at Louisiana State University simply does not accommodate such students. Almost all of the elementary educators who make inquiries about graduate work in mathematics education end up selecting a different concentration for their graduate studies because of the mathematics prerequisites hurdle. In this respect, we match most institutions in regarding advanced mathematical content as inextricably connected with mathematics education as a field of study-even at the cost of shutting out scholars with specialized expertise in mathematics teaching that is vital to our field.

A look at the overall structure of mathematics teacher education provides perspective on the importance of this issue. We take our institution as a case in point. Preservice mathematics education course work serves two distinct populations—future elementary teachers and future secondary mathematics teachers. At LSU, we have two required mathematics education courses for each of these program areas. Yet in a typical year we graduate 200 elementary teachers and 20 secondary mathematics teachers. Our overwhelming need is for faculty with expertise in elementary mathematics education, yet we ourselves supply virtually none of the doctoral graduates who might fulfill this pressing need.

Clearly, the mathematics requirements that we—along with the majority of doctoral programs—place on elementary/middle school mathematics educators create an untenable situation for the field. In response, a sizeable minority of doctoral programs (40% of those surveyed by Reys, et al., 2007), have developed specializations for elementary/middle school educators that require mathematics preparation equivalent only to what a middle school teacher would take as an undergraduate. Of course, students in these doctoral specializations do not have the prerequisites to take senior/graduate level mathematics courses, nor are such courses required as part of the graduate program (Reys, et al., 2007). Such programs do not meet the content recommendations of Dossey & Lappan (2001) for middle school mathematics education doctoral programs: "a background in mathematics equivalent to that of an individual getting a strong undergraduate major in mathematics" (p. 70).

A broad policy perspective on mathematics education requires that we address and come to terms with contradictory imperatives of our field:

- the centrality of mathematics in conceptions of mathematics education, versus
- the need to serve the field of elementary education.

Our purpose in this brief paper is to stimulate and contribute to discussion related to this policy issue. As we consider opening up a graduate track for elementary mathematics educators at our institution we ask the pragmatic question:

- What kinds of mathematical experiences can we provide for elementary/middle school educators participating in a mathematics education graduate program who do not have the prerequisites to take senior/graduate level content courses in Mathematics?

## Possible Solutions

This paper reports on ideas and information garnered at an inverse poster session at the 2007 Kansas City Conference on Doctoral Programs in Mathematics Education. In an inverse poster session we, as presenters, had sketched out the problem on one side of the poster board, and respondents wrote up solution ideas on the other side. Eight respondents suggested solutions to the prerequisites problem—in many cases, those practiced at their institutions: H. S. Kepner, University of Wisconsin Milwaukee; D. Lambdin, Indiana University; G. Foley, Ohio University; E. Rutter, Wright State University; P. M. Taylor, University of Tennessee-Knoxville; M. Brenner, UC Santa Barbara; S. Sword, Educational Development Center; P. Wilson, University of Georgia. We report on two categories of mathematics course work gleaned from the poster data:

- Mathematics courses in Education that foster valued mathematics dispositions rather than the traditional mathematical content knowledge, and
- Graduate courses (in Mathematics or Education) that shadow undergraduate mathematics-for-elementary-school-teachers courses.

**Mathematics Education Courses to Foster Valued Mathematical Dispositions.** Several respondents argued that the crucial qualification for elementary mathematics educators is the ability to productively explore and extend elementary mathematical problems, rather than familiarity with particular content knowledge. Such forms of mathematical expertise can be fostered through education courses that enmesh elementary educators in rich mathematical problem solving, and involve them in critique and discussion of their collective mathematical efforts. Indeed, Sarah Sword, director of EDC's Center for the Scholarship of School Mathematics, and Dan Chazan at University of Maryland, have developed such a course for elementary education students, and provided training for mathematics education professors on how to implement the course (http://cssm.edc.org/index.html).

**Graduate Level Shadow Courses.** According to this second proposal, graduate students in mathematics education sit in on (or assist with) the undergraduate level mathematics courses for elementary education majors. These experiences form the basis for a concurrent graduate level course (either in Mathematics or Education) in which the undergraduate course content is probed more deeply in the context of analyzing its pedagogical applications in K-8 education.

These two models demonstrate that creative and proactive solutions to the mathematics prerequisites problem are being formulated by scholars in our field concerned about the mathematical preparation of elementary educators. From this foundation we feel more comfortable taking the next step in establishing an elementary mathematics education graduate concentration at Louisiana State University. But beyond the pragmatic issues of designing a new graduate concentration, the question of mathematics requirements for elementary mathematics educators raises a host of crucial policy questions we recommend for systematic attention:

- What is the relationship between content knowledge in mathematics and pedagogical content knowledge? To what extent, and in what ways, does the latter depend on the former? Are the two forms of knowledge acquired simultaneously in the context of explorations of elementary school mathematics?
- What benefits do students (secondary and elementary education majors) actually derive from senior level mathematics course work? Are many of them surviving these courses by gaining procedural skills but missing the concepts and dispositions intended by those courses? Are courses that target the specific needs of elementary mathematics education at the graduate level possibly more beneficial to elementary educators than the canonical senior level mathematics courses?
- Some elementary mathematics educators gain their doctoral credentials through educational psychology programs that may impose few mathematics requirements. We have little systematic knowledge about these programs, which are not part of the current data base on mathematics

education doctoral education. Are these educators seriously handicapped by the absence of senior level mathematics course work?

- As we develop alternative routes for elementary educators that avoid traditional mathematics content, are we creating a new problem when such faculty members are called upon to teach secondary methods courses?

These are knotty issues that probe the gap between our ideals and realities in preparation of mathematics education doctoral students. In part, we need more quantitative information about programs, requirements, qualifications, and teaching responsibilities. However, we also need hard qualitative analyses of the role that advanced mathematical training for mathematics education doctoral candidates actually plays in the design, delivery, and outcomes of their subsequent work in elementary teacher education.

*David Kirshner*
*Louisiana State University*
*Baton Rouge LA 70803-4728*
*dkirsh@lsu.edu*

*Thomas Ricks*
*Louisiana State University*
*Baton Rouge LA 70803-4728*
*tomricks@lsu.edu*

CBMS Issues in Mathematics Education
Volume **15**, 2008

# Intellectual Communities: Promoting Collaboration Within and Across Doctoral Programs in Mathematics Education

Dawn Teuscher, Anne Marie Marshall, Jill Newton, and Catherine Ulrich

This paper provides reflections from the diverse perspectives of four graduate students at different phases in our doctoral programs. We represent four institutions: University of Missouri-Columbia, University of Maryland, Michigan State University, and University of Georgia. We also represent three Centers for Learning and Teaching (CLTs) funded by the National Science Foundation: Center for Proficiency in Teaching Mathematics (CPTM), Center for the Study of Mathematics Curriculum (CSMC), and Mid-Atlantic Center of Mathematics Teaching and Learning (MAC-MTL). Our paper provides a voice from doctoral students at institutions that have established doctoral programs in mathematics education, and who will soon become faculty members in institutions of higher education.

In the opening session Robert Reys asked participants to reflect on the following questions throughout the conference:

- "Should there be a common core of courses for doctorates in mathematics education?"
- "In what ways can your doctoral program be improved?"

Following the opening session, Chris Golde introduced the idea of intellectual communities in mathematics education doctoral programs. She described an intellectual community as a condition that is built on five characteristics: *knowledge-centered, broadly inclusive, flexible and forgiving, respectful and generous,* and *deliberately tended* (Golde, this volume).

As we reflected on our experiences, we noted examples of intellectual communities being built within our own programs, but also outside of our institutions. We began to consider the many layers of intellectual communities that can be developed during a doctoral student's program of study and how these communities can improve doctoral programs in mathematics education.

## Within Programs

Representing an intellectual community at the finest grain size is the individual program to which we belong. Among the four of us, we reflected on our programs as well as specific components of programs as opportunities for building intellectual communities. Although each of our programs is unique, we share how the programmatic components of coursework, research projects, and apprenticeships helped establish intellectual communities for us.

**Courses.** The nature of coursework was a common topic discussed. It is a complex issue and raises many questions: How can a program serve students that have research experiences prior to entry into the program as well as those with no such experience? How much course time should be spent on content knowledge, conducting research, or consuming research? How important is course sequencing?

Coursework provides an opportunity for doctoral students to work within an intellectual community. Courses provide a natural place where the five tenants of intellectual communities are experienced by students in common ways. For example, the knowledge that students have gained through their own set of experiences can be shared for others to build upon. Questions can be asked and topics discussed in a safe environment where all members are respectful of others' thoughts. We share one episode to demonstrate how coursework can build intellectual communities both in and outside of the classroom.

> During my program, I took a mathematics curriculum course focused on a historical view of mathematics curriculum from the late 1890s to the present. All doctoral students were required to work with another student in the class learning and presenting information about national reports that influenced the development of mathematics curricula. Although this was done within my own program, we also worked with graduate students at another institution. Both groups of doctoral students were reading and presenting on the same reports; however, what was being done on the two campuses was slightly different. After presentations were made in class, the four doctoral students who had made the presentations in their respective classes worked together to produce a common paper and PowerPoint that could be used by someone else teaching this course. The discussions that happened among students and across institutions helped me develop a deeper understanding of how K-12 mathematics curricula have changed over time. I was able to listen to other students' perspectives and share my own understanding within a respectful environment.

In courses which embody an intellectual community, there is often a shared authority in what is studied and what knowledge is considered important. In addition, students' voice and experience are critical to the development of ideas and knowledge in classes establishing intellectual communities. In such courses, there is also a high level of interaction among students, between students and instructors, and between students and the content. This includes working collaboratively both in and outside of the classroom. The conversations during the doctoral conference confirmed how courses can provide doctoral students opportunities to be a part of an intellectual community.

**Research Projects.** The question of how to prepare researchers was discussed in several sessions. Participating in research projects is another intellectual community developed with graduate students and faculty members. It provides an avenue for doctoral students to become actively engaged in the research process. Students can be involved from the identification of research questions through conducting the research, analyzing the data, and disseminating the results. Students are able to contribute to the process with their own understanding, yet learn with hands-on experience working side-by-side with experienced researchers.

Each of us came into our programs with different research backgrounds; however, we gained knowledge and expertise as we participated in research projects. We share two episodes to demonstrate how these experiences influenced our participation in intellectual communities.

> I remember vividly my first meeting with my faculty advisor in which she gave me a CD-rom with data from state standards documents and asked me to begin an analysis of the algebra strand. I also vividly remember walking back into my office, closing the door, sitting down at my desk, putting my head down on my desk, and asking myself, "Does she really think that I know how to do that?" Two weeks later, I had analyzed some data, and three years later, I am just about as comfortable with state standards documents as I am with the morning newspaper.

> During my first year as a doctoral student I became involved with CPTM. I joined several graduate students doing research on creating professional learning communities or other topics related to in-service teacher education as we observed student teachers. The number of people involved with CPTM meant that their focus effected my conversations, articles I read, feedback I got from faculty members and ultimately, my focus.

Although these experiences are unique to the individuals, they underscore the importance of balancing a student's need to grow, yet providing enough guidance to help them move forward and shape their research interests.

Understanding how to conduct research is crucial for those who will seek a tenure-track faculty position at a research institution. Research projects may have unique differences in the types of data collected (e.g., qualitative vs. quantitative), research questions, and frameworks used to guide the research. However, each project develops new ideas and builds knowledge. Some of us also have had opportunities to disseminate findings through presentations at regional and national conferences as well as co-author journal articles. All of these research experiences help doctoral students assimilate into an intellectual community.

**Apprenticeship.** Golde (this volume) suggested a new 21st century apprenticeship model that includes the notion of "apprenticed *with*, not apprenticed *to*." An apprenticeship *with* means the learner is actively involved in the decision making process; whereas, an apprenticeship *to* means the learner is an outsider who watches and is not able to contribute to the situation. An example of an apprentice *to* model would be the standard teaching assistant who attends a class and watches the teacher teach, but is not involved in the decision making process with the teacher in or outside of the classroom. This model provided the teaching assistant observation time and little more. Here we share two episodes to demonstrate the apprentice *with* model.

> We have a large undergraduate certification program for secondary mathematics. Between professors and TAs, there can be as many as eight teacher educators involved in planning and implementing related courses. I took part in one of these groups. The instructors

of record for these courses collaborated quite a bit; as a teaching assistant I worked closely with one faculty member. In addition, I was able to observe some of the same students the following semester as they did their student teaching, and finally I helped plan and teach a seminar that helped them reflect on their student teaching experience. Both semesters the collaboration with faculty members allowed me to grow tremendously as a teacher educator and feel much more comfortable interacting with a different student population about a subject related to, but not the same as, mathematics. In addition, following the same students allowed me to hear (and see) in what areas they felt (and appeared) prepared and unprepared as future teachers.

Teaching elementary mathematics methods courses was an experience afforded to me as part of my doctoral student preparation. Prior to teaching the first course by myself, I was required to shadow a faculty member. This included planning together prior to the course, planning and debriefing throughout the semester, sharing teaching responsibilites, and collaborating on assessments and grading. The opportunity to work collaboratively with a faculty member was foundational in helping me to prepare for teaching independently. Not only did the experience provide me with strategies for teaching college students but it helped me further understand the important content decisions made while teaching a mathematics methods course. Finally, the relationship formed with the faculty member is one that remains today as we continue to share our experiences, course modifications, assignments and current resources even as we teach at different institutions.

Each of us experienced this apprenticeship *with* model in different parts of our programs. Opportunities to be apprenticed *with* have included shadowing experienced faculty, conducting research with faculty from other disciplines or school district personnel, being supported in our teaching, and having multiple opportunities to engage with others and *do* the work of a mathematics education community member.

The idea of conducting lesson studies of mathematics education classes was raised. This would allow graduate students the chance, either within or between institutions, to collaborate with other graduate students and with faculty to plan, enact and reflect on a particular lesson while teaching methods classes. The lesson study provides an opportunity for novice teacher educators to try out ideas and to see how expert teacher educators reflect on their practice.

Another aspect of the apprenticeship model is attending and participating in seminars. We have had opportunities to share and/or critique research in a flexible and forgiving environment as Golde (this volume) described. This is conveyed in the following situation:

I was in my doctoral program for a week when I received an invitation to two upcoming (and regularly scheduled) mathematics education events at the university. At my first meeting, I entered

feeling quite intimidated until I realized that virtually all of the participants were other graduate students, many of whom were also
new to the program. I was blown away by a third year graduate
student's research presentation and the discussion that followed
among the graduate students. I was fascinated by the research,
and it was at that moment when I realized that I was in the right
place. The feeling of belongingness was confirmed the following
week when I was captivated by the presentation of a visiting professor's research at the mathematics education colloquium.

Our experiences working in an apprenticeship *with* model has provided us a unique
chance to grow and learn from senior faculty members. We feel better able to enter
the profession with a solid foundation of knowledge in many areas.

Doctoral programs should consist of layers of intellectual communities including those developed by coursework, research projects, and apprenticeships. This
conference afforded us opportunities to engage in conversations that helped connect
our experiences in each of the communities to the range of roles that our career
path might demand from us.

## Across Programs

Each of our individual programs are a part of a broader intellectual community,
that of a CLT. As reported by doctoral students, being a CLT fellow allowed for
unique opportunities to learn from and with doctoral students and faculty from
other universities. First, professional friendships were developed across institutions
with both faculty and graduate students. Second, working within a larger group of
researchers (faculty and graduate students) provided a network of resources. Third,
this intellectual community provided learning and growth for all members. These
opportunities were critical in encouraging and fostering discourse and collaboration
as well as helping to build and support professional relationships. Several sessions
at the conference mentioned the importance of communication and collaboration
across institutions as a way to province rich experiences for doctoral students. We
share another episode to demonstrate how collaboration within and across institutions influenced our participation in a broader intellectual community.

Twenty-nine doctoral students from seven different institutions
participated in a doctoral seminar in May 2007 hosted by the
CSMC. Research associates and faculty attended as observers and
mentors. Doctoral students were at different points in their program, some just beginning the journey while others were moving on
to faculty positions. Several students presented their dissertation
ideas. This was followed by questions and comments from doctoral students and faculty. This experience provided another opportunity to work within an intellectual community learning from
graduate students and research associates who have expertise in
the research field. This collaboration opened new doors for future
research projects, but also helped create an environment where
students' ideas were respected, yet challenged.

It came to our attention, being from larger programs, that many other doctoral
programs struggle with how to provide teaching experiences for part-time students,
or struggle with how to provide courses for doctoral students if the number of

available faculty is not sufficient to offer graduate-level classes. The existence of distance learning courses provides an excellent resource to more efficiently utilize the faculty resources from across the country. Institutions are already pioneering this work such as the Appalachian Collaborative Center for Learning, Assessment and Instruction in Mathematics (ACCLAIM). Their expertise was shared during the online delivery of doctoral programs session. This session opened our eyes to the kinds of situations we may face and had never considered surrounding issues such as distance learning. Yet it also helped us realize that as we go into the profession we will need to rely on others who have expertise in areas not familiar to us. The network built through CLTs provides an on-going intellectual community that can help us as we move into faculty positions.

## Mathematics Education Community

Lastly, we considered our participation at professional conferences, such as the *Doctoral Programs in Mathematics Education: Progress in the Last Decade* conference, as being situated within an even larger intellectual community. We were provided a place to examine, discuss, and make recommendations for the future of doctoral programs in mathematics education.

Attending as doctoral students provided a unique opportunity to reflect on our own programs. It permitted us to hear voices of those in the field. These voices spoke with knowledge and experience. It also allowed us to hear the voices of doctoral students from other institutions. This was beneficial because it provided us the opportunity to take stock of our own experiences, comparing them to those offered in other programs. It was interesting to compare what our programs afforded us and to hear the similarities and differences of what other doctoral students were being afforded at their institutions. It was reassuring to hear both that we are all concerned about our preparedness in some area or another, but also that our preparation was indeed foundational for whom we are becoming, namely future stewards of our discipline of mathematics education.

In the end, our eyes were opened and we were infused with new ideas and possibilities for how doctoral programs can be structured and implemented. As we become faculty members entrusted with the education of doctoral students in mathematics education, our experiences at the conference have great promise for helping us be more deliberate in providing opportunities for our graduate students, to engage in and embody intellectual communities at our institutions, across institutions, and within the mathematics education community at large.

*Dawn Teuscher*
*Arizona State University Polytechnic Campus*
*Tempe, AZ 85287*
*dawn.teuscher@asu.edu*

*Anne Marie Marshall*
*University of Maryland*
*College Park, MD 20742*
*anne.m.marshall@gmail.com*

*Jill Newton*
*Purdue University*
*West Lafayette, IN 47907*
*janewton@purdue.edu*

*Catherine Ulrich*
*University of Georgia*
*Athens, GA 30602*
*culrich@uga.edu*

# Part 7

# Closing Commentary

CBMS Issues in Mathematics Education
Volume **15**, 2008

# Reflecting On the Conference and Looking Toward the Future

## James Hiebert, Diana Lambdin, and Steve Williams

Authors of summary chapters for conference proceedings sometimes provide a summary of the conference. We won't do that. At least we won't try to recapture the chronological flow and content of the conference. Instead, we will return to the doctoral improvement framework suggested in the summary chapter after the previous (1999) conference (Hiebert, Kilpatrick, and Lindquist, 2001), consider where we are now based on the 2007 conference discussions, and extend the framework by specifying a more concrete strategy for improvement than proposed by Hiebert et al. (2001). Our aim is to provide some continuity to the field's collective discussions about doctoral programs and to propose some additional and more detailed ideas for improvement, ideas that seemed to be coalescing during the 2007 conference discussions.

## Improving Complex Systems

Viewing the collection of U.S. doctoral programs in mathematics education as a "complex system," Hiebert et al. (2001) borrowed ideas from those who study such systems to propose a framework for improving the U.S. doctoral programs. The framework is aimed at improving the system of doctoral education as a whole, not just individual institutional programs. The framework consists of four steps, each requiring participation by members of the system. Each step is enacted in order and then cycled through continuously as the system gradually improves.

**Assess Current Conditions.** The first step is to assess where the system is now, to collect information on the status of individual programs as well as the full profile of all programs within the system. Without knowing where the system is now, it is impossible to plan specific strategies for moving the system forward.

**Clarify Goals.** Goals for the system are essential for improving the system. Goals tell the system participants in what directions to move, and they provide the standards against which changes are evaluated. Without goals, it is impossible to know whether changes in the system are improvements or just changes. If goals are to be achieved system-wide, they need to endorsed by all participants. Systems rarely improve without strong commitments by all participants to work together to achieve the goals.

**Develop Strategies for Moving from Current Conditions to Goals.**
Strategies for improving complex systems necessarily come in the form of hypotheses. The complexity of the system rules out the possibility of finding algorithms that ensure improvement. Consequently, defining a potentially useful strategy depends on proposing an idea with a clear rationale (i.e., proposing well-developed hypotheses), recruiting support for the strategy from participants of the system, and designing an evaluation process that assesses the effects of implementing the strategy.

**Document and Share Information About the Effects of Improvement Strategies.** Improving a complex system requires that the system learn from its experience. Effects of implementing improvement strategies must be assessed and the information must be fed back into the system, perhaps to refine the strategies and try again. This process depends on system participants sharing the same goals so that the information gathered at one site will be of interest at another site. Only if participants at all sites are working toward the same goals will there be a motivation to share the information and a demand for receiving it. When this happens, even small improvements will be valued because all sites can benefit from them and the system can improve, as a whole. When this does not happen, improvements will occur only locally and the system as a whole is unlikely to become more effective.

## Current Conditions

**Surveys of Doctoral Education in the United States.** A sketch of current conditions in mathematics education doctoral studies in the United States can be found in this volume (Reys, Glasgow, Teuscher, & Nevels, this volume; Teuscher, Nevels, & Ulrich, this volume). The number of institutions offering doctoral programs in mathematics education has remained stable over the past two decades (about 115) as has the number of graduates (about 850 per decade), yielding on average about 7.5 graduates per institution per decade or less than 1 graduate per institution per year, on average. With a few large programs (e.g., Teachers College, Columbia University) graduating 6-7 students per *year*, this means that most doctoral programs in mathematics education are quite small.

The nature of programs, student entry requirements, and students' later career choices all differ considerably within the system of doctoral education. Programs differ along a variety of dimensions, including the kinds of courses they offer, the nature of outside-of-course experiences and requirements, and the expectations for exams and dissertations. Students differ in qualifications and past experiences, including the number and kind of mathematics courses taken, the extent and level of teaching experience, and their motivation for enrolling in doctoral studies. These differences are compounded by the range of careers that graduates choose, from significant research activity at graduate universities to teaching activities in mathematics departments or schools of education to leadership roles in school districts and state departments of education.

This sketch of the U.S. doctoral education system focuses on two important features: (1) the relatively small size of many programs along with (2) the challenge of preparing students with different entry skills using different resources and program activities for a range of professional responsibilities. These features, apparent on similar surveys conducted for the 1999 conference (Reys, Glasgow, Ragan, &

TABLE 1. Estimated Percentage Reported by Conference Participants of Doctoral Students from their Institutions Accepting Positions in Each of Four Areas (Percentages Can Add to More Than
100).

| Area | Range | Median |
|---|---|---|
| Teacher Education | 10% - 100% | 60% |
| Teaching Mathematics | 0% - 100% | 40% |
| Research | 0% - 90% | 25% |
| School Leadership | 0% - 50% | 10% |

Simms, 2001), pose serious challenges for improving the system. These conditions
shape the nature of the proposals described below.

**Impressions from the Conference.** We used three data gathering techniques during the conference to get a sense of the major concerns, interests, and
goals of the conference participants with respect to building their own doctoral
programs. We distributed a survey to all participants (which was to be returned
at the end of the conference), we rotated through the breakout sessions during
the conference listening to the discussions and taking notes, and we attended all
plenary sessions. The three data sources converged toward two major impressions.

A first impression confirmed the national survey results: the diversity of students, faculty, programs, and career goals is nearly overwhelming. As an example,
many institutions educate graduates who pursue careers that require substantial
work in conducting research, educating teachers, and/or teaching university-level
mathematics-all quite different areas of expertise (see Table 1). A small portion of
graduates also take jobs as school leaders. The range in the percentages indicate
that institutions vary widely in what they must prepare students to do, and the
fact that many institutions see their graduates enter into varied kinds of careers
means that they must provide training in a wide range of competencies. In other
words, many programs apparently try to be all things to all students. They might
do this by preparing each student for a variety of career paths, or by providing a
number of specialized paths through a program. However it is done, attempting to
prepare doctoral students for the diverse career paths open to them presents real
problems for doctoral programs in mathematics education.

A second impression is that many conference participants were increasingly
attracted to the concept of "intellectual communities" as a critical context for educating doctoral students. Chris Golde (this volume) opened the conference by
reviewing the findings and recommendations of the Carnegie Initiative on the Doctorate. Central to the recommendations for improving doctoral programs in *all*
disciplines was the notion of an intellectual community formed around domains of
knowledge and consisting of active faculty participation and leadership along with
student apprenticeships. The idea of intellectual communities surfaced repeatedly
during the conference and found application in most core components and delivery
systems examined during the breakout sessions as well as the plenary talks (see
earlier chapters in this volume). Such communities of study also were highlighted

TABLE 2. Conference Participants' Identification of Issues About Which There Was Most Agreement

| Response | Number Responding |
|---|---|
| The importance of building community | 15 |
| The importance of examining and improving doctoral programs | 13 |
| The importance of building networks and sharing resources | 8 |
| Lack of resources (time, money) | 4 |
| The wide range of programs, students, and outcomes | 3 |

TABLE 3. Conference Participants' Identification of the Most Important Components of a Doctoral Program

| Response | Number Responding |
|---|---|
| Authentic engagement in a community of scholars | 28 |
| Research | 13 |
| Mentoring / Supervision | 5 |
| Dissertation | 5 |
| Integrating Teaching and Scholarship | 3 |
| Mathematics | 3 |

during the presentations of other countries' doctoral programs in mathematics education with particular emphasis in Brazil (D'Ambrosio, this volume).

Evidence of the appeal of intellectual communities to support doctoral education was found in the participants' ongoing conversations and their responses on the survey. When asked which issue garnered the most agreement during the conference, the most frequent response was "The importance of building community" or similar phrasing (see Table 2). When asked about the most important component of a doctoral program, the most popular response, by far, was some form of authentic engagement in a community of scholars (see Table 3). And when asked what should be the next step in improving the quality of doctoral programs nation-wide, a frequent response was to develop connections among institutions to amplify the capacity and resources of single institutions (see Table 4).

These two impressions, the diversity of the doctoral training system and the appeal of intellectual communities as a training context, resonate with a number of recent reports on doctoral education (Levine, 2007; Walker, Golde, Jones, Bueschel, & Hutchings, 2008). Diversity is viewed as a considerable challenge for doctoral programs in all disciplines, and intellectual communities are seen as a common standard that would help to address the challenge. Indeed, Levine (2007) cited the diversity or "confused character" of doctoral programs (the numerous and differing requirements and expectations across institutions and programs) as one of the most

TABLE 4. Conference Participants' Identification of Next Steps in Improving the Quality of Doctoral Programs

| Response | Number Responding |
|---|---|
| Hold regular conferences like this one; create information exchange venues at other conferences | 12 |
| Develop connections between multiple institutions to amplify resources (e.g., faculty expertise) | 12 |
| Adopt common standards or goals (or different sets of standards for different types of programs) to provide guidance and increase consistency | 11 |
| Create a website to share information about programs | 4 |

severe obstacles to improving the quality of doctoral programs in education. He proposed that improvement required the capacity to offer authentic apprenticeships as part of a community of scholars.

We will argue that, in mathematics education, the diversity of programs and the thin resources of many programs pose severe problems for improving the system of doctoral education. We will also argue that the concept of intellectual communities provides a strategy for moving forward, a mechanism for working together as a field to raise the quality of doctoral studies nation-wide.

**The Challenge of Diversity within and Among Programs.** We continue the discussion of diversity by considering directly the challenges that such diversity presents. First, we want to be clear that diversity, in some senses and in some contexts, can be useful and even essential for growth. In mathematics education doctoral studies, diversity can be useful if it generates innovative initiatives and fosters creativity. The system of doctoral education is in constant need of new ideas. But, if the diversity is of a kind that creates too many differences and if the differences present more difficulties than solutions, then diversity is a problem-both for individual programs and for the system of doctoral education as a whole.

Diversity is a challenge for individual programs because it results mostly from trying to prepare students with different entry competencies for all facets of mathematics education and to support research in any area of the student's choosing. Many programs try to be almost everything to almost everyone. Yet it is difficult to imagine any single program, especially a relatively small program, preparing students well in all areas of future work. The result is a system that does not serve students well, that can graduate students unprepared to take on the varied tasks of mathematics educators and unprepared to contribute to the profession. Although the intentions of the faculty often are commendable (e.g., providing doctoral education for students geographically trapped in the area), trying to do more than resources allow does not help the student or the profession.

Diversity is a challenge for the system of doctoral studies in mathematics education because it makes system-wide improvement difficult, if not impossible. Improving as a system requires that participants learn from others' experiences. No single program, no matter how high the quality, can help the system improve if other programs cannot learn from its experience. And the key to enabling learning from each other, as noted earlier, is a shared set of clearly defined goals. If program A is working toward the same goals as program B, then what is learned by the faculty in program A about how to achieve a goal more effectively is of great interest to faculty in program B. The demand for information sharing among sites is high. But with a wide range of differences in program goals-driven by different kinds of students, different faculty interests and areas of expertise, different career choices of graduates-there is little demand for learning from each other. What is learned at one site probably will not help solve the problems at another site. The system becomes stuck. Every program is on its own. Individual programs might improve but only in haphazard ways. The system as a whole has no way of moving forward.

In sum, the typical program of mathematics education doctoral studies in the United States includes a tireless faculty trying to stretch thin resources to offer at least some training in very different areas of expertise (e.g., research-in a variety of areas, teacher education, mathematics teaching) for students with different entry competencies and with different career goals. Such efforts, although heroic, do not necessarily serve students well. In addition, the variation this creates among programs undermines attempts to improve the system. What is learned at one site is not viewed as useful at another site because the conditions are too different. How can the field break out of this paralysis? The concept of an intellectual community provides a key for opening a way forward, a path we will soon explore. First, however, we consider the second step in the framework for improving complex systems.

### Clarifying Goals

After assessing current conditions to identify challenges as well as resources, the next step in moving a system forward is to develop a consensus about the primary goals of the system. In our case, this means developing a consensus about the primary competencies that doctoral students should possess. What competencies are most needed? What competencies can others expect of graduates?

Answering questions about essential competencies requires describing clearly the work of mathematics educators. It makes no sense to design doctoral programs that are not aligned with the kind of work graduates actually do.

It is well known by every mathematics educator that the list of work activities is long: conducting research, publishing articles and giving presentations, teaching courses in mathematics and in education for prospective teachers, conducting workshops for practicing teachers, consulting with school districts and state departments, working with teachers in local schools, serving on state and national committees, to name a few. Is it possible to develop expertise in all of these areas during a doctoral program? Surely not! A critical thesis of this chapter is that our field underestimates what it takes to develop expertise, or even competence, in complex domains. Helping students develop competencies needed to successfully engage in, and contribute to, mathematics education requires deeper understanding and more know-how than we usually admit.

To get a sense of the challenge faced by faculty mentors in doctoral programs, consider what James March (2002) had to say about teacher training in the foreword to Dana Cattani's book *A Classroom of Her Own: How New Teachers Develop Instructional, Professional, and Cultural Competence*:

> Training for a role inadequately captures the nature of the real
> thing. Performing as a physician is not well anticipated by train-
> ing as a medical student. Leading a platoon in battle is not well
> anticipated by training as a cadet. Being a teacher is not well
> anticipated by teacher training. . . . The generality of the phe-
> nomenon suggests that it is not simply a problem with training
> but also stems from some fundamental difficulties both in commu-
> nicating general knowledge and in integrating that knowledge with
> contextual knowledge (p. xiii).

Effectively communicating general knowledge and integrating it with contextual
knowledge is a daunting challenge for doctoral students and faculty. To manage
this challenge in an honest and realistic way, the mathematics education community must identify the few areas of competence that, taken together, address the
key aspects of the *community's* work. In what areas is competence most critical,
not only to do one's job well, but also to sustain the profession and move it forward? Table 1 provides a clue because it identifies the major work areas of recent
graduates. Using these results as well as our own experiences, we propose, for
purposes of illustration, three primary goals for mathematics education doctoral
programs: conducting and publishing research, engaging in teacher education and
its improvement, and teaching university-level mathematics in a self-reflective and
continually improving way. In our definition, competence in one of these specialties
means not only being able to function effectively in the specialty but understanding
it deeply enough to improve one's own practice and that of others (e.g., doctoral
students). That is, competence includes the ability and disposition to study one's
specialty-to become familiar with the research literature, to conduct at least local,
action research on one's practice and that of colleagues, and to use appropriate
data to improve one's own practice and suggest improvements to the profession.
As a reminder, our proposal for improving doctoral education does not depend on
adopting the three goals or specialties we identified, but it does depend on developing a consensus within the field about the several primary areas of competence
needed for successful work in mathematics education.

## Designing Strategies for Achieving Goals

**Assess the Resources and Expertise Available.** The goals just articulated are ambitious. They aim not just to familiarize students with the practices of
the mathematics education profession but to help students develop deep and rich
understandings of a particular specialty or practice so they can become full participants in that aspect of the profession, contributing to the profession's growth and
improvement over time.

Teaching a mathematics methods course or conducting a workshop for teachers
is not likely to prepare doctoral students for educating teachers or for studying and
improving the profession's practice of educating teachers. Similarly, taking courses
in research design and statistics and conducting a research study for a dissertation
are not likely to prepare doctoral students to do high-quality research and to study
the research process itself in order to advance the research quality of the field.
More authentic and sustained experiences are needed (Golde, this volume; Lester
& Carpenter, 2001; Levine, 2007; Schoenfeld, 1999; Walker et al., 2008). As a
field, we need to be honest about what resources and expertise are required to help

students develop competence in each of the primary areas of work. Otherwise, the field risks doing a disservice to students and to its own long-term health.

What does it take for students to develop competence, even in one specialty area? What kinds of resources and expertise are needed?

**Create Intellectual Communities.** As we noted earlier, the concept of intellectual communities around shared problems of practice emerged during the conference as an ideal environment for educating doctoral students. We endorse this idea, but we propose it as necessary, not just as an ideal. In other words, we propose the following short answer to the question of what resources and expertise are needed to effectively educate a doctoral student in each of the primary specialties: an intellectual community around that practice. Others have proposed similar requirements for doctoral training but most of them focus on research competence (Eisenhart & DeHaan, 2005; Levine, 2007; National Research Council, 2005). We propose that the same standards should apply to each of the primary specialties in mathematics education. That is, an active intellectual community around teacher education must be available to offer sufficient training for a doctoral student intending to work primarily in teacher education. The same is true for conducting research and for teaching university-level mathematics. We see these competencies as different enough that one does not automatically transfer to another.

We define an intellectual community as a collaborative group focused on the exploration and critical examination of ideas (cf. Golde, this volume). In our opinion, an intellectual community consists of at least two faculty members who are expert practitioners in the area plus some number of doctoral students who serve as apprentices. By expert practitioners, we mean faculty who are actively engaged in the practice itself (conducting research, educating teachers, or teaching university-level mathematics) and also studying the practice and working to improve it — their own practice and that of the profession. In addition, expert practitioners are developing pedagogies of practice that continually improve the way in which the essential knowledge and skills are passed along to the apprentices (see J. March's challenge in the earlier quote). Expert practitioners actively study the practice itself and search for increasingly effective ways to help the student apprentices learn similar skills. Clearly, we are proposing high standards. Expert practitioners are highly skilled practitioners *and* thoughtful scholars. It is useful to recognize here that this should be the overarching goal for doctoral programs—to graduate apprentices who, over time, become expert practitioners in at least one specialty.

If the field wants to educate expert practitioners, then we believe the field must take seriously the fact that the training required is considerably deeper and more extensive than most programs now offer. In particular, the training for a particular specialty requires that a program be located within the context of an intellectual community working together to improve practices in the specialty—their own practices and those of the profession.

A first corollary of this proposal is that evaluations of program quality should focus more on the richness of the intellectual community than the specific components of the program. The logic is that if a sufficiently rich and active intellectual community exists, say, around teaching university-level mathematics, then the expert practitioner faculty members will design program experiences to train well their apprentices. In fact, the under-specification of components in our proposal implies that communities *should* experiment with innovative experiences and pedagogical approaches, document their effects, and share them with other like communities. For example, depending on the specialty, a traditional dissertation might be replaced by a terminal project more aligned with the central work of the area. Leaving the components of programs unspecified is a different approach than that outlined in the Task Force of the Association of Mathematics Teacher Educators (2003) and in other proposals (e.g., Dossey & Lappan, 2001; Lambdin & Wilson, 2001). Our proposal assumes that the intellectual communities would facilitate appropriate experiences and that the innovations tried at local sites and shared with other sites offering a degree in the same specialty would provide the new ideas and innovations needed to keep programs improving rather than stagnating.

A second corollary of our proposal is that beginning students who have little background in mathematics teaching and learning might be able to complete a degree only in one specialty in the normal 4-5 year program, even though the university might offer programs in more than one specialty. As Labaree (2003) noted, students often enter education doctoral programs with the orientation of a classroom teacher rather than a scholar (an expert practitioner in our language). Shifting orientations requires more time and conscious effort than we often acknowledge. A consequence of the increased specialization we are recommending is that post-doctoral positions could now serve a very useful and distinctive purpose. Students who graduate with a degree in one specialty can pursue other specialties through post-doctoral work.

Two questions need to be addressed: (1) What consequences does our proposal have for individual institutions that do not have active intellectual communities centered around a specialty? and (2) What consequences does this approach have for the common degree structure (e.g., should different degree labels be assigned to degrees in different specialties)? With regard to the first question, our proposal says that doctoral degrees should be offered only in the specialty areas for which intellectual communities exist. In our opinion, this requires at least two faculty members who are actively engaged in practicing, studying, and improving the relevant specialty: research, teacher education, or teaching university-level mathematics. It is likely that many institutions could offer degrees only in one, or perhaps two, areas and some institutions, by themselves, could offer no degrees.

There are strategies for developing intellectual communities across sites that would allow smaller institutions to join forces around a particular specialty. Several tested ideas for collaborating across sites with some making innovative uses of current technologies (Burke & Long, this volume). Many of these ideas were created through the collaborative work of institutions bound together as a National Science Foundation Center for Teaching and Learning. Regardless of the configuration, the ultimate question is whether an authentic intellectual community exists in which an apprentice can acquire the knowledge, skills, and dispositions to become an expert practitioner in the area.

The second question concerns the appropriate degree and label (Ph.D., Ed.D., other?) assigned to graduates with particular specialties. We do not have an immediate answer to this question, and we realize that resolving the question can be met with institutional constraints. We also are not sure how best to recognize students who complete degrees in more than one specialty. But, we hope that the institutional challenge of implementing these ideas does not drive the discussion of them. Rather, we hope that the field first debates the merits of the ideas and then worries about how to implement them.

**Summary.** In spite of the lengthy prose, the points we wish to make are quite simple. The U.S. system of mathematics education doctoral studies severely underestimates the depth of training required to do the work of a mathematics educator. If the system is to improve, it must acknowledge the extent of the problem and generate realistic approaches to address it. For us, this means to adopt strategies for improvement that identify the major work areas or specialties for mathematics educators and then provide authentic and extensive preparation in just these areas. Given the qualitative differences among these specialties, it is likely that somewhat different programs must be designed for each one. In our view, adequate programs in a particular specialty can exist only within the context of an intellectual community formed around the ideas and problems of that specialty. If such a community exists, sufficiently rich training can be provided and doctoral degrees (of whatever designation) can be offered in the relevant specialty.

### Documenting and Sharing What Is Learned

The final step in the cycle of improving complex systems is collecting information from attempts to achieve the immediate and long-term goals, and feeding the information back into the system to guide revisions that will work a little better. This requires that the system learn from its experiences. Said another way, this requires that participants learn from each other's experiences. And a prerequisite for wanting to learn from others' experiences is that everyone shares the same goals. Then what is learned at one site is relevant for, and even eagerly anticipated by, all the others.

Developing a consensus about the specialties, or major areas of competence, needed to sustain and advance the field of mathematics education would be a start to solving the problem of shared goals. Suppose the specialties are those identified earlier—conducting research, educating teachers, and teaching university-level mathematics. Programs, or intellectual communities, offering degrees in the same specialty would find more agreement on the goals for their programs than currently exists. This opens the door to documenting what works at one site and sharing across sites. To the extent that sites share goals, especially subgoals about the desired elements or features of beginning expertise in a particular specialty, there will be an increasing demand for shared information. This would be a significant step forward because sharing local successes and testing them at other sites is a central mechanism for improving complex systems.

One issue begging further attention and potentially benefiting from sharing ideas and experiences across sites with the same specialty is an elaborated definition of "expert practitioner." Earlier we defined expert practitioner as one who both practices a specialty (e.g., conducting research, educating teachers, teaching university-level mathematics) and studies and improves the relevant practices. That is, an expert practitioner is one who is both a practitioner and a scholar. Beyond the general descriptors of studying and improving practice, what exactly is a scholar of research, a scholar of teacher education, or a scholar of university-level mathematics teaching? Golde (2007) highlighted "working *with* the literature" as a key aspect of scholarship and proposed some pedagogical approaches for inducting students into this practice. March (2002) provided one way of elaborating the mentoring aspect of scholarly expertise by pointing to the importance of developing pedagogies of expert practice that continually improve the way in which the essential knowledge and skills of a specialty are passed along to the apprentices. Still further elaboration is needed, however, and could emerge from exchanges among sites that offer doctoral study in the same specialty. Such an exchange would, at the same time, clarify learning subgoals that could be shared across sites.

## Some Final Considerations

The outcome of our recommendation would be a quite different system of doctoral programs, a system that chooses quality over convenience. Many traditional conveniences would end. Aspiring doctoral students would not be able to go to their local university and, as their professional interests developed, expect a custom designed Ph.D. program. They would need to reflect beforehand on their own professional interests, match these against the specialties identified by the profession as warranting doctoral preparation, and then seek out a university that offered a degree in the preferred specialty. This might require a geographic move. Faculty also would be inconvenienced. At some institutions, faculty would need to expend time and energy working out genuine collaborations with others, sometimes at distant sites, to create an intellectual community around a specialty. Building and sustaining an authentic intellectual community around any of the specialties will be a considerable challenge.

The benefits of dealing with this inconvenience would be substantial. Enacting the concept of an intellectual community would increase the quality of most doctoral programs. The preparation of individual students would become more specialized and more aligned with the degree goal (and the student's future career). Future employers could search for those candidates specially trained in the area of primary work of the advertised position. Graduates would feel more prepared to take on their primary responsibilities and would feel capable of improving their practice over time. The profession would benefit from graduates trained sufficiently well to contribute to the profession's knowledge and practice in each primary specialty.

The advantages of this proposal are also evident when seen from a distance, when viewing the nation's collection of mathematics education doctoral programs. Improving the *system*, as we've outlined in this chapter, requires looking at the quality of the national portfolio of doctoral programs (Ferrini-Mundy, this volume) rather than the excellence of a few programs. We believe the distinction among a few primary specialties determined by primary work responsibilities, along with the formation of intellectual communities as "homes" for doctoral programs in particular areas, will yield a national portfolio of programs that is stronger than the portfolio we have now. That is, given the appropriate choices of specialties, each graduating student will enter the profession better prepared for their primary work *and*, together, the cohort of students nation-wide will be better prepared to advance the field as a whole. Perhaps most important, however, we believe that such a portfolio, with increasingly clear learning goals developed for each specialty, will create the opportunity for faculty who work in similar specialties at different sites to share what they learn and thereby enable our system, as a whole, to learn from its experience and improve steadily over time.

*James Hiebert*
*School of Education*
*University of Delaware*
*Newark, DE 19716*
*hiebert@udel.edu*

*Diana V. Lambdin*
*School of Education*
*Indiana University*
*Bloomington, IN 47405*
*lambdin@indiana.edu*

*Steve Williams*
*Department of Mathematics*
*Brigham Young University*
*Provo, UT 84602*
*williams@mathed.byu.edu*

# Appendices

# Appendix A. List of Conference Participants

| Name | Institution | Email |
|------|-------------|-------|
| Adams, Thomasenia | University of Florida | tla@coe.ufl.edu |
| Allison, Dean | University of Northern Colorado | dean.allison@unco.edu |
| Alspach, Dale | Oklahoma State University | alspach@math.okstate.edu |
| Arbaugh, Fran | University of Missouri | ArbaughE@missouri.edu |
| Barger, Rita* | University of Missouri - Kansas City | bargerr@umkc.edu |
| Bartell, Tonya | University of Delaware | tbartell@udel.edu |
| Bass, Hyman | University of Michigan | hybass@umich.edu |
| Bay-Williams, Jenny* | University of Louisville | j.baywilliams@louisville.edu |
| Becker, Jerry* | Southern Illinois University Carbondale | jbecker@siu.edu |
| Berk, Dawn | University of Delaware | berk@udel.edu |
| Berkaliev, Zaur | Illinois Institute of Technology | berkaliev@iit.edu |
| Blanton, Maria | University of Massachusetts - Dartmouth | mblanton@umassd.edu |
| Boyd, Brian | Wright State University | brian.boyd@wright.edu |
| Brenner, Mary | University of California, Santa Barbara | betsy@education.ucsb.edu |
| Burke, Maurice | Montana State University | burke@math.montana.edu |
| Bush, William | University of Louisville | bill.bush@louisville.edu |
| Capraro, Mary Margaret | Texas A & M University | mmcapraro@coe.tamu.edu |
| Capraro, Robert | Texas A & M University | rcapraro@coe.tamu.edu |
| Chamberlin, Michelle | University of Wyoming | michelle.chamberlin@unco.edu |
| Chapin, Suzanne | Boston University | schapin@bu.edu |
| Chappell, Michaele | Middle Tennessee State University | chappell@mtsu.edu |
| Chavez, Oscar* | University of Missouri | ChavezO@missouri.edu |
| Chazan, Dan | University of Maryland | dchazan@umd.edu |
| Cicmanec, Karen | Morgan State University | kbcicmanec@earthlink.net |
| Clark, Kathleen | Florida State University | kclark@coe.fsu.edu |
| Confrey, Jere* | North Carolina StateUniversity | jere_confrey@ncsu.edu |
| Cooper, Sandi | Baylor University | sandra_cooper@baylor.edu |
| Cramer, Kathleen | University of Minnesota | crame013@umn.edu |
| Cuevas, Gilbert | Texas State University | gc24@txstate.edu |
| DAmbrosio, Beatriz | Miami University | dambrobs@muohio.edu |
| Dickey, Ed | University of South Carolina | edickey@gwm.sc.edu |
| Dingman, Shannon | University of Arkansas | sdingman@uark.edu |
| Dixon, Juli | University of Central Florida | jkdixon@mail.ucf.edu |

*Continued on next page*

The * denotes participants that attended the 1999 National Conference on Doctoral Programs in Mathematics Education.

| Name | Institution | Email |
|---|---|---|
| Donoghue, Eileen* | City University of New York | donoghue@mail.csi.cuny.edu |
| Dougherty, Barbara | University of Mississippi | bdougher@olemiss.edu |
| Ellis, Amy | University of Wisconsin | aellis1@education.wisc.edu |
| Engle, Randi | University of California - Berkeley | raengle@berkeley.edu |
| Fennell, Francis (Skip)* | McDaniel College | ffennell@mcdaniel.edu |
| Ferrini-Mundy, Joan | National Science Foundation | jferrini@msu.edu |
| Fi, Cos | University of Iowa | cos-fi@uiowa.edu |
| Foley, Greg | Ohio University | foleyg@ohio.edu |
| Franke, Megan | UCLA | mfranke@ucla.edu |
| Galindo, Enrique | Indiana University | egalindo@indiana.edu |
| Gay, Susan* | University of Kansas | sgay@ku.edu |
| George, Melvin | University of Missouri | GeorgeMD@missouri.edu |
| Glasgow, Bob* | Southwest Baptist University | bglasgow@sbuniv.edu |
| Golde, Chris | Stanford University | golde@stanford.edu |
| Goldin, Jerry | Rutgers University | geraldgoldin@dimacs.rutgers.edu |
| Grevholm, Barbro | Agder University College | Barbro.Grevholm@hia.no |
| Hauk, Shandy | University of Northern Colorado | hauk@unco.edu |
| Heid, Kathy* | Pennsylvania State University | mkh2@email.psu.edu |
| Herbel-Eisenmann, Beth | Iowa State University | bhe@iastate.edu |
| Hiebert, James* | University of Delaware | hiebert@UDel.edu |
| Hirsch, Chris | Western Michigan University | christian.hirsch@wmich.edu |
| Horak, Virginia | University of Arizona | horak@math.arizona.edu |
| Hutchison, Linda | University of Wyoming | lhutch@uwyo.edu |
| Jacobbe, Tim | University of Kentucky | jacobbe@coe.uky.edu |
| Jakubowski, Elizabeth | Florida State University | ejakubow@coe.fsu.edu |
| Jansen, Amanda | University of Delaware | jansen@udel.edu |
| Jones, Dustin | Sam Houston State University | dljones@shsu.edu |
| Kent, Laura | University of Arkansas | lkent@uark.edu |
| Kepner, Henry | University of Wisconsin - Milwaukee | kepner@uwm.edu |
| Kersaint, Gladis | University of South Florida | kersaint@tempest.coedu.usf.edu |
| Kilpatrick, Jeremy* | University of Georgia | jkilpat@uga.edu |
| King, Karen | New York University | karen.d.king@nyu.edu |
| Kirshner, David | Louisiana State University | dkirsh@lsu.edu |
| Kitchen, Rick | University of New Mexico | kitchen@unm.edu |
| Klerlein, Jake | Middle Tennessee State University | klerlein@mtsu.edu |
| Klespis, Mark | Sam Houston State University | klespis@shsu.edu |
| Knight, Genevieve | Coppin State University | gmk01@juno.com |
| Knott, Libby | The University of Montana | knott@mso.umt.edu |
| Knuth, Eric | University of Wisconsin | knuth@education.wisc.edu |
| Koyama, Masataka | Hiroshima University | mkoyama@hiroshima-u.ac.jp |
| Lambdin, Diana* | Indiana University | lambdin@indiana.edu |
| Langrall, Cynthia | Illinois State University | langrall@ilstu.edu |
| Lappan, Glenda* | Michigan State University | glappan@math.msu.edu |
| Lee, Carl | University of Kentucky | lee@ms.uky.edu |
| Lewis, W. James* | University of Nebraska - Lincoln | jlewis@math.unl.edu |
| Lim, Kien | University of Texas at El Paso | kienlim@utep.edu |
| Lloyd, Gwen | Virginia Tech | lloyd@vt.edu |
| Long, Vena* | University of Tennessee | vlong@utk.edu |
| Lubienski, Sarah | University of Illinois at Urbana-Champaign | stl@uiuc.eduv |

*Continued on next page*

| Name | Institution | Email |
|---|---|---|
| Magid, Andy | University of Oklahoma | amagid@math.ou.edu |
| Marrongelle, Karen | Portland State University | karenmar@pdx.edu |
| Marshall, Anne Marie | University of Maryland - College Park | anne.m.marshall@gmail.com |
| Masingila, Joanna | Syracuse University | jomasing@syr.edu |
| Mathews, Susann | Wright State University | susann.mathews@wright.edu |
| Mayes, Robert | University of Wyoming | rmayes2@uwyo.edu |
| McCallum, William | University of Arizona | wmc@math.arizona.edu |
| McGraw, Rebecca | University of Arizona | rmcgraw@email.arizona.edu |
| Mewborn, Denise | University of Georgia | dmewborn@uga.edu |
| Middleton, Jim | Arizona State University | james.middleton@asu.edu |
| Mikusa, Michael | Kent State University | mmikusa@kent.edu |
| Miller, Diane | Middle Tennessee State University | dmiller@mtsu.edu |
| Mohr, Margaret | University of Kentucky | m.mohr@uky.edu |
| Morris, Anne | University of Delaware | abmorris@udel.edu |
| Moyer-Packenham, Patricia | George Mason University | pmoyer@gmu.edu |
| Nevels, Nevels | University of Missouri | nnnc4f@mizzou.edu |
| Newton, Jill | Michigan State University | newtonji@msu.edu |
| Newton, Kristie | Temple University | kknewton@temple.edu |
| Owens, Doug* | The Ohio State University | owens.93@osu.edu |
| Pape, Stephen | University of Florida | spape@ufl.edu |
| Papick, Ira | University of Missouri | papicki@missouri.edu |
| Powers, Robert | University of Northern Colorado | robert.powers@unco.edu |
| Prime, Glenda | Morgan State University | glprime@moac.morgan.edu |
| Rachlin, Sid | East Carolina University | rachlins@mail.ecu.edu |
| Reeder, Stacy | University of Oklahoma | reeder@ou.edu |
| Remillard, Janine | University of Pennsylvania | janiner@gse.upenn.edu |
| Reys, Barbara* | University of Missouri | reysb@missouri.edu |
| Reys, Robert* | University of Missouri | reysr@missouri.edu |
| Ricks, Thomas | Louisiana State University | tomricks@lsu.edu |
| Rico Romero, Luis | Universidad de Granada | lrico@ugr.es |
| Royster, David | University of North Carolina at Charlotte | droyster@uncc.edu |
| Rutter, Edgar | Wright State University | edgar.rutter@wright.edu |
| Sheffield, Linda | University of Kentucky | wsheffield@insightbb.com |
| Shih, Jeff | University of Nevada Las Vegas | jshih@unlv.nevada.edu |
| Shimizu, Katsuhiko | Tokyo University of Science | shimizu@ma.kagu.tus.ac.jp |
| Silver, Edward | University of Michigan | easilver@umich.edu |
| Smith, Ken | Central Michigan University | ken.w.smith@cmich.edu |
| Speer, William | University of Nevada-Las Vegas | william.speer@unlv.edu |
| Stallings, Lynn | Kennesaw State University | lstalling@kennesaw.edu |
| Star, Jon | Harvard University | jonstar@msu.edu |
| Stohl Lee, Hollylynne | North Carolina State University | hollylynne@ncsu.edu |
| Strutchens, Marilyn | Auburn University | strutme@auburn.edu |
| Stylianides, Gabriel | University of Pittsburgh | gstylian@pitt.edu |
| Sword, Sarah | Education Development Center | ssword@edc.org |
| Tarr, James | University of Missouri | TarrJ@missouri.edu |
| Taylor, Edd | University of Wisconsin | evtaylor@wisc.edu |
| Taylor, P. Mark * | University of Tennessee - Knoxville | pmark@utk.edu |
| Teuscher, Dawn | University of Missouri | dty78@mizzou.edu |
| Thomas, Christine | Georgia State University | cthomas11@gsu.edu |

*Continued on next page*

| Name | Institution | Email |
|------|-------------|-------|
| Thompson, Denisse | University of South Florida | thompson@tempest.coedu.usf.edu |
| Thompson, Tony | University of Alabama | anthony.thompson@ua.edu |
| Tyminski, Andrew | Purdue University | atyminsk@purdue.edu |
| Ulrich, Katy | University of Georgia | culrich@uga.edu |
| Walker, Erica | Teachers College Columbia University | ewalker@exchange.tc.columbia.edu |
| Weber, Keith | Rutgers University | khweber@rci.rutgers.edu |
| Wilkerson, Trena | Baylor University | Trena_Wilkerson@baylor.edu |
| Williams, Steve | Brigham Young University | williams@mathed.byu.edu |
| Wilson, James* | University of Georgia | jwilson@uga.edu |
| Wilson, Pat | University of Georgia | pswilson@uga.edu |
| Winsor, Matthew | University of Texas at El Paso | mwinsor@utep.edu |
| Wolff, Kenneth* | Montclair State University | wolffk@montclair.edu |
| Zbiek, Rose Mary | Pennsylvania State University | rmz101@psu.edu |
| Ziebarth, Steven | Western Michigan University | steven.ziebarth@wmich.edu |

# Appendix B: Conference Agenda

Sunday, September 23

| 4:00 pm | Registration | Foyer |
|---|---|---|
| 5:00-6:15 | Opening Session:<br>*Doctoral Programs in Mathematics Education: A Look at What's Happening*<br>    Bob Reys, University of Missouri | Ballroom |
| 6:15-7:00 | Dinner | |
| 7:00-8:00 | Keynote Session:<br>*Creating a broader vision of doctoral education: Lessons from the Carnegie Initiative on the Doctorate*<br>    Chris Golde, Carnegie Foundation/Stanford University<br>Session Presider:<br>    Sid Rachlin, East Carolina University | |

Monday, September 24 (Theme - Core Knowledge of Mathematics Education)

| 8:30-9:30 | Keynote Session:<br>*What core knowledge do doctoral students in mathematics education need to know?*<br>    Joan Ferrini-Mundy, Michigan State University/NSF<br>Session Presider:<br>    Barbara Reys, University of Missouri | Ballroom |
|---|---|---|
| 9:30-10:00 | Break | |
| 10:00-11:30 | Breakout Sessions (Topics and Facilitators):<br><br>*Mathematics*<br>    Dan Chazan, University of Maryland<br>    Jim Lewis, University of Nebraska<br>*Curriculum*<br>    Chris Hirsch, Western Michigan University<br>    Rose Zbiek, Penn State University<br>*Policy*<br>    Ed Silver, University of Michigan<br>    Erica Walker, Teachers College, Columbia University<br>*Teaching*<br>    Megan Franke, University of California-Los Angeles<br>    Pat Wilson, University of Georgia<br>*Diversity*<br>    Rick Kitchen, University of New Mexico<br>    Edd Taylor, University of Wisconsin<br>*Technology*<br>    Kathy Heid, Penn State University<br>    Hollylynne Stohl Lee, North Carolina State University | Salon F-G<br><br>Seville II<br><br>Seville I<br><br>Westport<br><br>Plaza<br><br>Millcreek<br>(3rd Floor) |
| 11:30-1:00 | Lunch | Ballroom |
| 1:00-2:30 | Breakout Sessions (repeat of earlier sessions) | (as above) |
| 2:30-3:00 | Break | |
| 3:00-4:30 | Panel: *Preparing Doctorates in Mathematics Education: An International Perspective*<br>    Moderator:<br>        Jeremy Kilpatrick, University of Georgia<br>    Panelists:<br>        Bea DAmbrosio, Miami University, USA<br>        Barbro Grevholm, Agder University College,<br>            Norway and Director of Nordic Center<br>        Masataka Koyama, Hiroshima University, Japan<br>        Luis Rico Romero, University of Granada, Spain | Ballroom |

Supported by a grant from the National Science Foundation (Award # 0333879)

## Tuesday, September 25 (Theme - Program Delivery: Issues and Strategies)

| | | |
|---|---|---|
| 8:30-9:30 | Keynote Session:<br>    *Program Delivery Issues, Challenges and Opportunities*<br>        Denise Mewborn, University of Georgia<br>Session Presider:<br>    Jim Wilson, University of Georgia | Ballroom |
| 9:30-10:00 | Break | |
| 10:00-11:30 | Breakout Sessions (Topics and Facilitators):<br><br>*Preparation of Researchers*<br>    Barbara Dougherty, University of Mississippi<br>    Jim Middleton, Arizona State University<br>*Doctoral Program Components*<br>    Bill Bush, University of Louisville<br>    Enrique Galindo, Indiana University<br>*Online Delivery of Doctoral Courses*<br>    Maurice Burke, Montana State University<br>    Vena Long, University of Tennessee<br>*Doctoral Program Elements for Part-Time Students*<br>    Jerry Goldin, Rutgers University<br>    Gladis Kersaint, University of South Florida<br>*Induction of Doctoral Graduates into the Profession*<br>    Gwen Lloyd, Virginia Tech University<br>    Barbara Reys, University of Missouri | Salon F-G<br><br><br>Seville II<br><br><br>Seville I<br><br><br>Westport<br><br><br>Plaza |
| 11:30-1:00 | Lunch | Ballroom |
| 1:00-2:30 | Breakout Sessions (repeat of earlier sessions) | (as above) |
| 2:30-3:00 | Break | |
| 3:00-4:30 | Reception and Poster Session:<br>    *Ideas from the Field* | Foyer |

## Wednesday, September 26

| | | |
|---|---|---|
| 8:30-9:30 | Panel: *Accreditation of Doctoral Programs in Mathematics Education*<br>    Moderator:<br>        Glenda Lappan, Michigan State University<br>    Panelists:<br>        Jenny Bay-Williams, University of Louisville<br>        Jere Confrey, North Carolina State University<br>        Skip Fennell, McDaniel College<br>        Mark Klespis, Sam Houston State University | Ballroom |
| 9:30-10:00 | Break | |
| 10:00-11:00 | *Reflections on conference discussions*<br>    Jim Hiebert, University of Delaware<br>    Diana Lambdin, Indiana University<br>    Steve Williams, Brigham Young University | Ballroom |
| 11:00-11:30 | *Closing Session, next steps*<br>    Jim Hiebert, University of Delaware<br>    Bob Reys, University of Missouri | Ballroom |

# References

American Statistical Association. (2007). *Using statistics effectively in mathematics education research.* Washington, DC: Author.

Apple, M. (1992). Do the standards go far enough? Power, policy, and practice in mathematics education. *Journal for Research in Mathematics Education, 23*(5), 412-431.

Association of Mathematics Teacher Educators. (2003). *Principles to guide the design and implementation of doctoral programs in mathematics education.* San Diego, CA: Author.

Ball, D. L. (2003, February). *What mathematical knowledge is needed for teaching mathematics.* Paper presented at the U.S. Department of Education Secretary's Mathematics Summit, Washington, DC.

Ball, D. L. & Forzani, F. M. (2007). What makes education research "educational"? *Educational Researcher, 36*(9), 529-540.

Ball, D. L., Hill, H., & Bass, H. (Fall, 2005). Knowing mathematics for teaching: Who knows mathematics well enough to teach third grade, and how can we decide? *American Educator*, 14-22, 43-46.

Banks, J. A., Cochran-Smith, M., Moll, L., Richert, A., Zeichner, K., & LePage, P. (2005). Teaching diverse learners. In L. Darling-Hammond & J. D. Bransford (Eds.), *Preparing teachers for a changing world* (pp. 232-275). San Francisco: John Wiley & Sons.

Bass, H. (2006). Developing scholars and professionals: The case of mathematics. In C. M. Golde & G. E. Walker (Eds.), *Envisioning the future of doctoral education: Preparing stewards of the discipline. Carnegie essays on the doctorate* (pp. 101-119). San Francisco, CA: Jossey-Bass.

Berliner, D. C. (2006). Toward a future as rich as our past. In C. M. Golde & G. E. Walker (Eds.), *Envisioning the future of doctoral education: Preparing stewards of the discipline. Carnegie essays on the doctorate* (pp. 268-289). San Francisco, CA: Jossey-Bass.

Bishop, A. (2001). Doctoral programs in mathematics education: Features, options and challenges. In R. Reys & J. Kilpatrick (Eds.), *One field, many paths: U. S. doctoral programs in mathematics education* (pp. 55-62). Providence, RI: American Mathematical Society.

Blume, G. (2001). Beyond course experiences: The role of non-course experiences in mathematics education doctoral programs. In R. Reys & J. Kilpatrick, (Eds.), *One field, many paths: U. S. doctoral programs in mathematics education* (pp. 87-94). Providence, RI: American Mathematical Society.

Blume, G. W., & Heid, M. K. (Eds.). (In press). *Research on technology in the learning and teaching of mathematics: Syntheses and perspectives. Vol. II.* Charlotte, NC: Information Age Publishing, Inc.

Boaler, J. (2002). Learning from teaching: Exploring the relationship between reform curriculum and equity. *Journal for Research in Mathematics Education, 33*(4), 239-258.

Boaler, J. (2006). Promoting respectful learning. *Educational Leadership, 63*(5), 74-78.

Board on Mathematical Sciences. (1997). *Preserving strength while meeting challenges: Summary report of a workshop on actions for the mathematical sciences.* Washington DC: National Academy Press.

Bottge, B. A. (1999). Effects of contextualized math instruction on problem solving of average and below-average achieving students. *Journal of Special Education, 33*(2), 81-92.

Bransford, J. D., Brown, A. L., & Cocking, R. R. (Eds.). (2000). *How people learn: Brain, mind, experience, and school.* Washington DC: National Academy Press.

CAPES (Coordenação de Aperfeiçoamento de Pessoal de Nível Superior - *Agency for the Improvement of Human Resources in Higher Education*). Brasilia, Brazil: Ministry of Education. Information on specific aspects of programs is available at:
Recommended programs–http://www.capes.gov.br/avaliacao/recomendados.html
Program evaluation criteria–
    http://www.capes.gov.br/avaliacao/criterios/avaliacao_trienal_2007.html
In country scholarships–http://www.capes.gov.br/bolsas/nopais/
Study abroad scholarships–http://www.capes.gov.br/bolsas/noexterior/

Centers for Learning and Teaching Network (CLTNet). (2006). *Centers for learning and teaching: Building the nation's leadership in science, technology, engineering, and mathematics education.* Arlington, VA: SRI International.

Chan, T. F. (2006). A time for change? The mathematics doctorate. In C. M. Golde & G. E. Walker (Eds.), *Envisioning the future of doctoral education: Preparing stewards of the discipline. Carnegie essays on the doctorate* (pp. 120-134). San Francisco, CA: Jossey-Bass.

Chazan, D., Sword, S., Badertscher, E., Conklin, M., Graybeal, C., Hutchison, P., Marshall, A. M., & Smith, T. (2007). Learning to Learn Mathematics: Voices of Doctoral Students in Mathematics Education. In M. Strutchens & W. Gary Martin (Eds.) *The Learning of Mathematics.* 69th Yearbook of the National Council of Teachers of Mathematics (pp. 367-379). Reston, VA: NCTM.

Civil, M. & Andrade, R. (2002). Transitions between home and school mathematics: Rays of hope amidst the passing clouds. In G. de Abreu, A. J. Bishop, & N. C. Presmeg (Eds.), *Transitions between contexts of mathematical practices* (pp. 149-169). Boston, MA: Kluwer.

CNPQ (Conselho Nacional de Desenvolvimento Científico e Tecnológico - *National Council of Scientific and Technological Development*). Brasilia, Brazil: Ministry of Science of

Technology. Information available at: http://www.cnpq.br/cnpq/index.htm

Council of Graduate Schools. (2007). *Mission statement of the Council of Graduate Schools.* Washington, DC: Author. Available at: http://www.cgsnet.org/

Cuoco, A., Goldenberg, E., & Mark, J. (1996). Habits of mind: An organizing principle for mathematics curricula. *Journal of Mathematical Behavior, 15*, 375-402.

Dossey, J., & Lappan, G. (2001). The mathematics education of mathematics educators in doctoral programs in mathematics education. In R. Reys & J. Kilpatrick (Eds.), *One field, many paths: U. S. doctoral programs in mathematics education* (pp. 67-72). Providence, RI: American Mathematical Society.

Duke, N. K., & Beck, S. W. (1999). Education should consider alternative formats for the dissertation. *Educational Researcher, 28*(3), 31-36.

Eisenhart, M., & DeHaan, R. L. (2005). Doctoral preparation of scientifically based education researchers. *Educational Researcher, 34*(4), 3-13.

European University Association. (2005). *Doctoral programs for the European knowledge society. Results of EUA doctoral programs project.* Brussels, Belgium: Author. Available at: http://www.eua.be/fileadmin/user_upload/files/EUA1_documents/
Doctoral Programs_Project_Report.1129278878120.pdf

Even, R. (1993). Subject-matter knowledge and pedagogical content knowledge: Prospective secondary teachers and the function concept. *Journal for Research in Mathematics Education, 24*(2), 94-116.

Ewing, J. (Ed.). (1999). *Towards excellence: Leading a doctoral mathematics department in the 21st century.* Providence, RI: American Mathematical Society.

Ferrini-Mundy, J., & Floden, R. E. (2007). Educational policy research and mathematics education. In F. K. Lester (Ed.) *Second handbook of research on mathematics teaching and learning* (pp. 1247-1279). Charlotte, NC: Information Age Publishing.

Ferguson, R. F. (1998). Teachers' perceptions and expectations and the Black-White test score gap. In C. Jencks & M. Phillips (Eds.), *The Black-White test score gap*, (pp. 273-317). Washington, DC: The Brookings Institution.

Fernádez-Cano, A., Torralbo, M., and Vallejo, M. (2007). Análisis longitudinal de las tesis doctorales españolas en pedagogía (1976-2006). In F. Etxeberría (Ed.). *Actas del XIII° Congreso Nacional de Modelos de Investigación Educativa* (pp. 829-832). San Sebastián: Associatión Interuniversitaria de Investigación Pedagógica (AIDIPE).

Fey, J. T. (2001). Doctoral programs in mathematics education: Features, options, and challenges. In R. E. Reys & J. Kilpatrick, *One field, many paths: U. S. doctoral programs in mathematics education* (pp. 55-62). Providence, RI: American Mathematics Society.

Freudenthal, H. (1983). *Didactical phenomenology of mathematical structures.* Dordrecht, The Netherlands: D. Reidel Publishing Company.

Fry, R. (2007). *The changing racial and ethnic composition of U.S. public schools.* Washington, DC: Pew Hispanic Center.

Glasgow, R. (2000). *An investigation of recent graduates of doctoral programs in mathematics education,* Unpublished doctoral dissertation, University of Missouri-Columbia, Columbia, Missouri.

Goldberger, M., Maher, B., & Flattau, P. (1995). *Research-doctorate programs in the United States: Continuity and change.* Washington, DC: National Academy Press.

Golde, C. M. (2006). Preparing stewards of the discipline. In C. M. Golde & G. E. Walker (Eds.), *Envisioning the future of doctoral education: preparing stewards of the discipline. Carnegie essays on the doctorate* (pp. 3-20). San Francisco, CA: Jossey-Bass.

Golde, C. M. (2007). Signature pedagogies in doctoral education: Are they adaptable for the preparation of education researchers? *Educational Researcher, 36*(6), 344-351.

Golde, C. M., Bueschel, A. C., Jones, L., & Walker, G. E. (in press). Apprenticeship and intellectual community: Lessons from the Carnegie initiative on the doctorate. In R. Ehrenberg & C. Kuh (Eds.), *Doctoral education and the faculty of the future.* Ithaca, NY: Cornell University Press.

Golde, C. M. & Walker, G. E. (2006). *Envisioning the future of doctoral education: Preparing stewards of the discipline.* San Francisco, CA: Jossey-Bass.

Grant, C. A. (1989). Equity, equality, teachers and classroom life. In W. G. Secada (Ed.), *Equity in education* (pp. 89-102). London: Falmer Press.

Gravemeijer, K. (1994). *Developing realistic mathematics education.* Utrecht, The Netherlands: Vakroep Onderzoek Wiskundeonderwijs en Onderwijscomputer-centrum, Rijksuniversiteit.

Graybeal, C. D. (2007). Whole number multiplication: There's more to it than might be expected! *Mathematics Teacher, 101*(4), 312-316.

Green, J., Camilli, G., & Elmore, P. (Eds.). (2006). *Handbook of complementary perspectives for education research.* Washington, DC: AERA

Grevholm, B. (2004a). A Nordic Graduate School in mathematics education starts in 2004. *Nordic Studies in Mathematics Education, 9*(1), 75-76.

Grevholm, B. (2004b). What are the needs for doctoral students in mathematics education? *Nordic Studies in Mathematics Education, 9*(3), 67-69.

Grevholm, B. (2004c). New courses in mathematics education for doctoral students. *Nordic Studies in Mathematics Education, 9*(4), 65-67.

Grevholm, B. (2005a). Activities in the Nordic Graduate School of mathematics education during 2005. *Nomad, 10*(1), 57-59.

Grevholm, B. (2005b).The third year of activities in the Nordic Graduate School in mathematics education. *Nomad, 10*(3-4), 101-104.

Grevholm, B. (2006a). The Nordic Graduate School in mathematics education. Summer school of 2006. *Nordic Studies in Mathematics Education, 11*(2), 71-74.

Grevholm, B. (2006b). Continued activities for the Nordic Graduate School. *Nordic Studies in Mathematics Education, 11*(3), 85-88.

Grevholm, B. (2006c). New dissertations in mathematics education by doctoral students in the Nordic Graduate School. *Nordic Studies in Mathematics Education, 11*(1), 75-78.

Grevholm, B., Persson, L. E., & Wall, P. (2005). A dynamic model for education of doctoral students and guidance of supervisors in research groups. *Educational Studies in Mathematics, 60*(2), 173-197.

Grouws, D. A. (Ed.) (1992). *Handbook of research on mathematics teaching and learning.* New York: Macmillan.

Guin, D., Ruthven, K., & Trouche, L. (Eds.). (2005). *The didactical challenge of symbolic calculators: Turning a computational device into a mathematical instrument.* New York, NY: Springer.

Gutstein, E. (2005). *Reading and writing the world with mathematics: Toward pedagogy for social justice.* New York, NY: Routledge Falmer.

Gutiérrez, K. D., Baquedano-López, P., & Tejada, C. (2000). Rethinking diversity: Hybridity and hybrid language practices in the third space. *Mind, Culture, and Activity, 6*(4), 286-303.

Hartnett, R. T. (1976). Environments for advanced learning. In J. Katz & R. T. Hartnett (Eds.), *Scholars in the making: The development of graduate and professional students* (pp. 49-84). Cambridge, UK: Ballinger Publishing.

Hiebert, J., Kilpatrick, J., & Lindquist, M. M. (2001). Improving U. S. doctoral programs in mathematics education. In R. E. Reys & J. Kilpatrick (Eds.), *One field, many paths: U. S. doctoral programs in mathematics education* (pp. 153-159). Providence, RI: American Mathematical Society.

Heid, M. K., & Blume, G. W. (Eds.). (In press) *Research on technology in the learning and teaching of mathematics: Syntheses and perspectives, Vol. I.* Charlotte, NC: Information Age Publishing, Inc.

Heid, M. K. & Zembat, I. (2007, April). *Representational and Object Understanding of Mathematical Entities: The Case of Function.* Paper presented at the annual meeting of the American Educational Research Association, Chicago, IL.

Hiroshima University. (2007). *Handbook of Graduate School of Education.* (In Japanese). Hiroshima, Japan. Available at: http://www.hiroshima-u.ac.jp/ed/daigakuin/

Hollebrands, K., & Zbiek, R. (2004). Teaching mathematics with technology: An evidence-based road map for the journey. In R. Rubenstein & G. Bright (Eds.), *Perspectives on the Teaching of Mathematics* (pp.259-270). Reston, VA: National Council of Teachers of Mathematics.

Hoyles, C., & Noss, R. (2003). What can digital technologies take from and bring to research in mathematics education. In A. J. Bishop, K. Clements, C. Keitel, J. Kilpatrick, & F. K. S. Leung (Eds.), *Second international handbook of mathematics education, Part One* (pp. 323-349). Dordrecht, The Netherlands: Kluwer.

Hyogo University of Teacher Education. (2007). *Handbook of Joint Graduate School (Ph. D. program) in Sciences of School Education.* (In Japanese). Hyogo, Japan: Author. Available at: http://www.office.hyogo-u.ac.jp/jgs/

Ingersoll, R. M. (2007). Teaching science in the 21st Century. The science and mathematics teacher shortage: Fact and myth. *NSTA News Digest.* Available at http://www.nsta.org/publications/news/story.aspx?id=538

Jones, L., Lindzey, G., & Coggeshall, P. E. (1982). *An assessment of research-doctorate programs in the United States.* Washington, DC: American Council on Education.

Kaput, J. (1992). Technology and mathematics education. In D. Grouws (Ed.), *Handbook of research on mathematics teaching and learning* (pp. 515-556). New York, NY: MacMillan.

Kieran, C., & Yerushalmy, M. (2004). Research on the role of technological environments in algebra learning and teaching. In K. Stacey, H. Chick, M. Kendal (Eds.), *The future of the teaching and learning of algebra* (pp. 99-152). Boston, MA: Kluwer.

Kilpatrick, J., Rico, L., & Sierra, M. (1994). *Educación matemática e investigación.* Madrid, Spain: Editorial Síntesis.

Knapp, M. S., & Woolverton, S. (1995). Social class and schooling. In J. Banks & C. Banks (Eds.), *Handbook of research on multicultural education* (pp. 548-569). New York: Macmillan.

Knuth, E. J. (2002). Secondary school mathematics teachers' conceptions of proof. *Journal for Research in Mathematics Education, 33*(5), 379-405.

Koehler, M. J., & Mishra, P. (2005). What happens when teachers design educational technology? The development of technological pedagogical content knowledge. *Journal of Educational Computing Research, 32*(2), 131-152.

Krathwohl, D. (1994). A slice of advice. *Educational Researcher, 23*(1), 29-32, 42.

Labaree, D. F. (2003). The peculiar problems of preparing educational researchers. *Educational Researcher, 32*(4), 13-22.

Ladson-Billings, G. (1997). It doesn't add up: African American students' mathematics achievement. *Journal for Research in Mathematics Education, 28*(6), 697-708.

Ladson-Billings, G. (2001). *Crossing over to Canaan: The journey of new teachers in diverse classrooms.* San Francisco: Jossey-Bass Publishers.

Lambdin, D. V., & Wilson, J. W. (2001). The teaching preparation of mathematics educators in doctoral programs in mathematics education. In R. E. Reys & J. Kilpatrick (Eds.), *One field, many paths: U. S. doctoral programs in mathematics education* (pp.

77-83). Providence, RI: American Mathematical Society.

Lave, J. (1996). Teaching, as learning, in practice. *Mind, Culture, and Activity, 3,* 149-164.

Lave, J., & Wenger, E. (1991). *Situated learning: Legitimate peripheral participation.* Cambridge, UK: Cambridge University Press.

Leder, G. C., Brandell, G., & Grevholm, B. (2004). The Swedish graduate school in mathematics education: Conception, birth and development of a new doctoral programme. *Nordic Studies in Mathematics Education, 9*(2), 165-182.

Lee, H. S. (2005). Facilitating students' problem solving: Prospective teachers' learning trajectory in a technological context. *Journal of Mathematics Teacher Education, 8*(3), 223-254.

Lesh, R., Crider, J. A., & Gummer, E. (2001). Emerging possibilities for collaborating doctoral programs. In R. E. Reys and J. Kilpatrick, *One field, many paths: U. S. doctoral programs in mathematics education* (pp. 113-128). Providence, RI: American Mathematics Society.

Lester, F. K. (Ed.). (2007). *Second handbook of research on mathematics teaching and learning.* Charlotte, NC: Information Age Publishing.

Lester, F. K. & Carpenter, T. P. (2001). Research preparation of doctoral students in mathematics education. In R. E. Reys & J. Kilpatrick (Eds.), *One field, many paths: U.S. doctoral programs in mathematics education* (pp. 63-66). Providence, RI: American Mathematics Society.

Lester, F. K., & Lambdin, D. (2003). The ship of Theseus and other metaphors for thinking about what we value in mathematics education research. In J. Kilpatrick & A. Sierpinska (Eds.), *Mathematics education as a research domain: A search for identity* (pp. 415-425). Dordrecht, The Netherlands: Kluwer.

Levine, A. (2007). *Educating researchers.* Report #2. Education Schools Project. Princeton, NJ: Woodrow Wilson Foundation. Available at: http://www.edschools.org/

Lipka, J. (2005). Math in a cultural context: Two case studies of a successful culturally based math project. *Anthropology & Education Quarterly, 36*(4), 367-385.

March, J. (2002). Foreward. In D. Cattani (Ed.), *A classroom of her own: How new teachers develop instructional, professional, and cultural competence* (pp. xi-xiv). Thousand Oaks, CA: Corwin Press.

Marshall, A. M. (2008). *Opportunities to practice what we preach: Mathematical experiences of mathematics education doctoral students.* Unpublished doctoral dissertation. University of Maryland, College Park, MD.

Ministerio de Educación y Ciencia (2006). *Propuesta: La organización de la enseñanza universitaria en España.* Madrid, Spain: Author. Available at: http://www.mec.es/educa/ccuniv/html/documentos/Propuesta.pdf

Moschkovich, J. N. (1999). Supporting the participation of English language learners in mathematical discussions. *For the Learning of Mathematics, 19*, 11-19.

Moschkovich, J. N. (2002). A Situate and sociocultural perspective on Bilingual mathematics learners. *Mathematical Thinking and Learning, 4*(2&3), 189-212.

Moses, R., & Cobb Jr., C. (2001). *Radical equations: Math literacy and civil rights.* Boston: Beacon Press.

Murray, J., & Male, T., (2005). Becoming a teacher educator: Evidence from the field. *Teaching and Teacher Education, 21*, 125-142.

National Center for Education Information (2005). *Profile of teachers in the U.S.* Washington, DC: Author.

National Commission on Excellence in Education. *A Nation At Risk.* Washington, D.C.: U.S. Department of Education, 1983.

National Council of Teachers of Mathematics. (1980). *An agenda for action.* Reston, VA: Author.

National Council of Teachers of Mathematics. (1989). *Curriculum and evaluation standards for school mathematics.* Reston, VA: Author.

National Council of Teachers of Mathematics (2000). *Principles and standards for school mathematics.* Reston, VA: Author.

National Council of Teachers of Mathematics. (2006). *Curriculum Focal Points for Prekindergarten through Grade 8 Mathematics.*, VA: Author.

National Education Association. (1894). *Report of the Committee of Ten on secondary school studies with the reports of the conferences arranged by the committee.* New York: American Book Company.

National Mathematics Advisory Panel. (2008). *Foundations for Success: The Final Report of the National Mathematics Advisory Panel.* Washington, DC: United States Department of Education. As of March 2008, available at: www.ed.gov/about/bdscomm/list/mathpanel/index.html

National Opinion Research Center (NORC). (2006). *Summary reports: Doctoral recipients from United States universities-1960-2005.* Chicago, IL: Author.

National Research Council. (1989). *Everybody Counts: A report to the nation on the future of mathematics education.* Washington DC: National Academy Press.

National Research Council. (2005). *Advancing scientific research in education.* Washington, DC: National Academies Press.

National Science Foundation. (2007). *Integrative Graduate Education and Research Traineeship Program (IGERT). Program Solicitation 07-540.* Available at: http://www.nsf.gov/pubs/2007/nsf07540/nsf07540.htm

National Science Foundation, Division of Science Resources Statistics. (2006). *U.S. doctorates in the 20th century.* NSF 06-319. Arlington, VA: NSF.

Neiss, M. L. (2005). Preparing teachers to teach science and mathematics with technology: Developing a technology pedagogical content knowledge. *Teaching and Teacher Education, 21,* 509-523.

Niss, M. (1999). Aspects of the nature and state of research in mathematics education. *Educational Studies in Mathematics, 40,* 1-24.

Oakes, J. (1990). *Multiplying inequalities: The effects of race, social class, and tracking on opportunities to learn mathematics and science.* Santa Monica, CA: RAND.

Oakes, J., Franke, M., Quartz, K. H., & Rogers, J. (2002). Research for high-quality urban teaching: Defining it, developing it, assessing it. *Journal of Teacher Education, 53,* 228-234.

Presmeg, N. C., & Wagner, S. (2001). Preparation in mathematics education: Is there a basic core for everyone? In R. E. Reys and J. Kilpatrick, *One field, many paths: U. S. doctoral programs in mathematics education* (pp. 73-76). Providence, RI: American Mathematics Society.

Public Agenda. (2007). *Important, but not for me: Parents and students in Kansas and Missouri talk about math, science, and technology education.* New York, NY: Public Agenda.

PUC-SP (Catholic University at São Paulo). Sao Paulo, Brazil: Author. Available at: http://www.pucsp.br/pos/edmat/

Reys, B. (Ed.). (2006). *The Intended Mathematics Curriculum as Represented in State-Level Curriculum Standards: Consensus or Confusion,* Charlotte, NC: Information Age Publishing.

Reys, R. E. (2000). Doctorates in mathematics education: An acute shortage. *Notices of the American Mathematical Society, 47*(10), 1267-1270.

Reys, R. E. (2002). Mathematics education positions in higher education and their applicants: A many to one correspondence. *Notices of the American Mathematical Society, 49*(2), 202-207.

Reys, R. E. (2006). A report on jobs for doctorates in mathematics education in institutions of higher education. *Journal for Research in Mathematics Education, 37*(4), 262-269.

Reys, R. E., Glasgow, B., Ragan, G.A., & Simms, K. W. (2001). Doctoral programs in mathematics education in the United States: A status report. In R. E. Reys & J. Kilpatrick (Eds.), *One Field, Many Paths: U. S. Doctoral Programs in Mathematics Education* (pp. 19-40). Providence, RI: American Mathematical Society.

Reys, R., Glasgow, R., Teuscher, D., & Nevels, N. (2007). Doctoral programs in mathematics education in the United States: 2007 status report. *Notices of the American Mathematical Society, 54*(11), 1283-1293.

Reys, R., & Kilpatrick, J. (Eds.). (2001). *One field, many paths: U.S. doctoral programs in mathematics education.* Providence, RI: American Mathematical Society.

Richardson, V. (2006). Stewards of a field, stewards of an enterprise: The doctorate in education. In C. M. Golde & G. E. Walker (Eds.), *Envisioning the future of doctoral education: Preparing stewards of the discipline. Carnegie essays on the doctorate* (pp. 251-267). San Francisco, CA: Jossey-Bass.

Rodriguez, A. J. & Kitchen, R. S. (Eds.) (2005). *Preparing mathematics and science teachers for diverse classrooms: Promising strategies for transformative pedagogy.* Mahwah, NJ: Lawrence Erlbaum Associates.

Schifter, D. (1998). Learning mathematics for teaching: From a teachers' seminar to the classroom. *Journal of Mathematics Teacher Education, 1*(1), 55-87.

Schoenfeld, A. H. (1988). When good teaching leads to bad results: The disasters of "well-taught" mathematics courses. *Educational Psychologist, 23*(2), 145-166.

Schoenfeld. A. H. (1999). The core, the cannon, and the development of research skills: Issues in the preparation of education researchers. In E. Lagemann & L. Shulman (Eds.), *Issues in education research: Problems and possibilities* (pp. 166-202). New York, NY: Jossey-Bass.

Sfard, A., & Linchevski, L. (1994). The gains and the pitfalls of reification–the case of algebra. *Educational Studies in Mathematics, 26*, 191-228.

Sierpinska, A. (2003). Research in mathematics education through a keyhole. In E. Simmt & B. Davis (Eds.), Canadian Mathematics Education Study Group: Proceedings 2003 (pp. 13-35). Edmonton, Alberta, Canada: CMESG. Available at: http://publish.edu.uwo.ca/cmesg/

Society for Research on Educational Effectiveness. *Mission statement.* Ithaca, NY: Author. Available at: http://www.educationaleffectiveness.org/

Stiff, L. V. (2001). Discussions on different forms of doctoral dissertations. In R. E. Reys & J. Kilpatrick, *One field, many paths: U. S. doctoral programs in mathematics education* (pp. 85-86). Providence, RI: American Mathematical Society.

Tate, W. F. & Rousseau, C. (2007). Engineering change in mathematics education: Research, policy, and practice. In F. K. Lester (Ed.). *Second Handbook of Research on Mathematics Teaching and Learning* (pp. 1209-1246). Charlotte, NC: Information Age Publishing.

Tokyo Gakugei University. (2007). *Handbook of United Graduate School* [Ph. D. program) in Sciences of School Education, Document in Japanese.]. Tokyo, Japan: Author. Available at: http://www.u-gakugei.ac.jp/09daigakuin/07rengo.html

UNESP- Rio Claro (State University of São Paulo in Rio Claro). Rio Claro, Brazil: Author. Available at: http://www.rc.unesp.br/igce/matematica/pedu/apres_matematica.html

UNICAMP (State University of Campinas - State of São Paulo). Campinas, Brazil: Author. Available at: http://www.posgrad.fae.unicamp.br/inf_gerais_frame.html

USP (University of São Paulo). Sao Paulo, Brazil: Author.
Available at: http://www3.fe.usp.br/pgrad/

University of Tsukuba. (2007). *Handbook of Graduate School of Comprehensive Human Sciences.* [In Japanese]. Tsukuba, Japan: Author.
Available at: http://www.tsukuba.ac.jp/organization/doctoral.html

Vergnaud, G. (1988). Multiplicative structures. In J. Hiebert & M. Behr (Eds.), *Number concepts and operations in the middle grades* (pp. 141-161). Reston, VA: National Council of Teachers of Mathematics. Hillsdale, NJ: Lawrence Erlbaum Associates.

Walbesser, H. H. & Eisenberg, T. (1971), What research competencies for the mathematics educator? *American Mathematics Monthly, 58*, 667-73.

Walker, G. E., Golde, C. M., Jones, L., Bueschel, A. C., & Hutchings, P. (2008). *The formation of scholars: Rethinking doctoral education for the 21st Century.* San Francisco, CA: Jossey-Bass.

Wenger, E. (1998). *Communities of practice: Learning, meaning and identity.* Cambridge, MA: Cambridge University Press.

Wiggins, G., & McTighe, J. (1998). *Understanding by design.* Alexandria, VA: Prentice Hall.

Wilson, J. (2003). Mathematics education: A personal perspective. In G. Stanic & J. Kilpatrick (Eds.), *A history of school mathematics* (Vol. 2, pp. 1779-1807). Reston, VA: National Council of Teachers of Mathematics.

Wilson, P., Bismarck, S., & DuCloux, K. (2006, April). Relationships that foster learning within a student teaching experience. Paper presented at the annual meeting of the American Educational Association, San Francisco, CA.

Wittrock, M. C. (Ed.). (1986). *Handbook of research on teaching.* New York: MacMillan

Zaslavsky, O., & Leikin, R. (2004). Professional development of mathematics teacher educators: Growth through practice. *Journal of Mathematics Teacher Education, 7*, 5-32.

Zbiek, R. M., Heid, M. K., Blume, G. W., & Dick, T. P. (2007). Research on technology in mathematics education: The perspective of constructs. In F. Lester (Ed.), *Second handbook of research on mathematics teaching and learning* (pp. 1169-1207). Greenwich, Connecticut: Information Age Publishing, Inc.

Zbiek, R., & Hollebrands, K. (in press). A research-informed view of the process of incorporating mathematics technology into classroom practice by inservice and prospective teachers. In M. K. Heid & G. Blume (Eds.) *Research on technology in the learning and teaching of mathematics: Syntheses and perspectives. Vol. I.* Charlotte, NC: Information Age Publishing, Inc.

Zeichner, K. M. (1996). Educating teachers to close the achievement gap: Issues of pedagogy, knowledge, and teacher preparation. In B. Williams (Ed.), *Closing the achievement gap: A vision for changing beliefs and practices* (pp. 56-76). Alexandria, VA: Association for Supervision and Curriculum and Development.